"Funny and illuminating."

—*The Economist* (a best book of 2024)

"A fascinating and necessary project . . . Funny but not snarky, inventive but not obnoxious, learned but not pedantic, this book will make readers think about the nation's founding document more deeply than ever."

—*Booklist*

"This book, written with a light heart and a gentle touch but a very big brain and a deep soul, might be just what's needed to help turn the fateful tide we confront. It's a journey that's at once hilarious and educational. Everyone should read it."

—Laurence Tribe, author of *The Invisible Constitution* and University Professor of Constitutional Law Emeritus at Harvard University

"Both hilarious and illuminating."

—*New York Post*

"A marvelously witty and wise consideration of the Constitution's legacy."

—*Kirkus Reviews*

"I don't know how I learned so much while laughing so hard. This book is more fun than a cruise on a superyacht with a Supreme Court justice, and considerably less expensive."

—Andy Borowitz, *New York Times* bestselling author of *Profiles in Ignorance*

"Hilarious . . . fascinating."

—*Entertainment Weekly*

"Jacobs's well-researched romp carefully reckons with the Constitution's ethical blind spots while staying consistently entertaining. U.S. history buffs will have fun with this one."

—*Publishers Weekly*

"I'll be honest: this is a really funny book . . . And—dare I say it—the book actually offers better ideas about how to improve modern constitutional democracy than most legal scholarship."

—Kermit Roosevelt III, professor at the University of Pennsylvania Carey Law School and author of *The Nation That Never Was*

"A much-needed primer on civics."

—Pittsburgh Post-Gazette

"We the People of the United States, in Order to form a more perfect Union, should make The Year of Living Constitutionally Mandatory Reading. Jacobs reveals both the majesty and absurdity in America's founding document by applying it literally (and hilariously) to his daily life. Adventures which start out as whimsical exercises—including his quixotic attempt to amend the Constitution—often end up with profound, even provocative results. In approaching the document as a series of Odyssean tasks, Jacobs underscores the conflicts and confusions which hold it together. And, in a sense, hold us together, as a country."

—Greg Young, cohost of The Bowery Boys history podcast

"A phenomenal book."

—Dahlia Lithwick, Slate writer and host of the podcast Amicus with Dahlia Lithwick

"At a time when a majority on the Supreme Court favors . . . originalism (at least when convenient), and is actively attacking freedoms such as reproductive rights and the power of federal agencies to protect the environment, it's vital to question the philosophical underpinnings of their approach. Jacobs seems to me essentially correct in calling the Constitution 'a national Rorschach test.' We see what we want to see; the idea of a definitive interpretation should be treated with suspicion."

—The Washington Post

"In the distinctively irreverent manner that has endeared him to readers, A.J. Jacobs takes a deep, entertaining dive into the U.S. Constitution. . . . Readers will appreciate Jacobs's animated overview of constitutional history, in part a celebration of the cherished freedoms enshrined in the 237-year-old text, and his wise observation that Americans would benefit from balancing their emphasis on individual rights with equal attention to the common good."

—Shelf Awareness

"The book is marvelous. It's such a unique, thoughtful, clarifying and fun attempt to resurrect what it was like to live at the time of the founding and what it can tell us about the Constitution today."

—Jeffrey Rosen, CEO of the National Constitution Center

THE YEAR OF LIVING CONSTITUTIONALLY

BY A.J. JACOBS

The Know-It-All
The Year of Living Biblically
My Life as an Experiment
Drop Dead Healthy
It's All Relative
Thanks a Thousand
The Puzzler

THE YEAR OF LIVING
Constitutionally

**ONE MAN'S HUMBLE QUEST TO FOLLOW
THE CONSTITUTION'S ORIGINAL MEANING**

A.J. JACOBS

CROWN
NEW YORK

To the people who contribute the most to my domestic
tranquility: Julie, Jasper, Zane, and Lucas

CROWN
An imprint of the Crown Publishing Group
A division of Penguin Random House LLC
1745 Broadway
New York, NY 10019
crownpublishing.com
penguinrandomhouse.com

2025 Crown Trade Paperback Edition

Originally published in hardcover in the United States by Crown, an
imprint of the Crown Publishing Group, a division of Penguin Random
House LLC, in 2024.

Library of Congress Cataloging-in-Publication Data
Names: Jacobs, A.J., 1968- author.
Title: The year of living constitutionally : one man's humble quest to follow the
Constitution's original meaning / A.J. Jacobs. New York : Crown Publishing, 2024. |
Includes bibliographical references. Identifiers: LCCN 2023057911 (print) |
LCCN 2023057912 (ebook) | ISBN 9780593136744 (hardcover) |
ISBN 9780593136751 (ebook)
Subjects: LCSH: Constitutional law—United States. | United States. Supreme Court. |
Constitutional amendments—United States. | Constitutional conventions—United States.
Classification: LCC KF4550 J325 2024 (print) | LCC KF4550 (ebook) |
DDC 342.73—dc23/eng/20240117
LC record available at https://lccn.loc.gov/2023057911
LC ebook record available at https://lccn.loc.gov/2023057912

Hardback ISBN 978-0-593-13674-4
Paperback ISBN 978-0-593-13676-8
Ebook ISBN 978-0-593-13675-1

Manufactured in the United States of America

2 4 6 8 9 7 5 3 1

The authorized representative in the EU for product safety and
compliance is Penguin Random House Ireland, Morrison Chambers, 32
Nassau Street, Dublin D02 YH68, Ireland, https://eu-contact.penguin.ie.

CONTENTS

viii | *Contents*

PREAMBLE

I recently discovered that if you walk around New York City while carrying an eighteenth-century musket, you get a lot of questions.

"You gonna shoot some redcoats?"

"Can you please leave?"

"What the hell, man?"

Questions aside, a musket can come in handy. When I arrived at my local coffee shop at the same time as another customer, he told me, "You go first. I'm not arguing with someone holding that thing."

Why was I carrying around a ten-pound firearm from the 1790s? Well, it's because I'm deep into my year of living constitutionally. For reasons I'll explain shortly, I've pledged to try to express my constitutional rights using the tools and mindset of when they were written in 1787. My plan is to be the original originalist.

I will bear arms, but only those arms available when the Second Amendment was written. Hence the musket and its accompanying bayonet.

I will exercise my First Amendment right to free speech—but I'll do it the old-fashioned way: by scratching out pamphlets with a quill pen and handing them out on the street.

My right to assemble? I will assemble at coffeehouses and taverns, not over Zoom or Discord.

If I'm to be punished, I will insist my punishment not be cruel and unusual, at least not cruel and unusual by eighteenth-century standards (when, unfortunately, Americans considered it acceptable to have your head stuck in a pillory and get pelted by mud and rotten vegetables).

Thanks to the Third Amendment, I may choose to quarter soldiers in my apartment—but I will kick them onto the street if they misbehave.

My goal is to understand the Constitution by expressing my rights as they were interpreted back in the era of Washington and Madison (or, in the case of the later amendments, how those amendments were interpreted when they were ratified). I want, as much as possible, to get inside the minds of the Founding Fathers. And by doing so, I want to figure out how we should live today. What do we need to update? What should we ignore? Is there wisdom from the eighteenth century that is worth reviving? And how should we view this most influential and perplexing of American texts?

I undertook this quest because reading the news over this past year led me to three important revelations.

The first revelation was just how much our lives are affected by this 4,543-word document inscribed on calfskin during that long-ago Philadelphia summer. The Supreme Court's recent controversial decisions on a multitude of issues—including women's rights, gun rights, environmental regulations, and religion—all claim to stem from the Constitution.

The second revelation was just how shockingly little I knew about the Constitution. I'd never even read it—not the whole thing, anyway. Thanks to *Schoolhouse Rock!*, I was familiar with the "We the People" preamble. And I could recall a handful of other famous passages, most notably the First Amendment, which is beloved by me and my fellow writers (as well as by my kids, who cite it whenever I ask them not to curse at me). But as for the entire document, from start to finish? Never read it.

And third, I realized just how much the Constitution is a national Rorschach test. Everyone, including me, sees what they want. Does the Constitution support laissez-faire gun rights, or does it support strict gun regulation? Does it prohibit school prayer or not? Depends on whom you ask.

And it's not just the issues we're divided on—it's the Constitution itself. Is the Constitution a document of liberation, as I was taught in high school? Or is it, as some critics argue, a document of oppression? Should we venerate this brilliant road map that has arguably guided American prosperity and expanded freedom for 230-plus years? Or should we be skeptical of this set of rules written by wealthy racists who thought tobacco-smoke enemas were cutting-edge medicine?*

It reminds me of a William Blake quote I once read about the Bible:

> [We] both read the Bible day and night
> But thou read'st black where I read white.

And, as with the Bible, whether you see black or white in the Constitution depends largely on one crucial question: What is your method for interpreting this text?

Should we try to discover the original meaning from when the text was written? Or does the meaning of the text evolve with the times?

In fact, the Bible-Constitution parallels helped give birth to this book. I decided to steal an idea from myself. Several years ago, I wrote a

---

* Tobacco-smoke enemas were a mainstream medical treatment for all sorts of ills. They involved hoses, smoke, and hand-powered bellows. It is quite possibly the origin of the phrase "blowing smoke up your ass."

book called *The Year of Living Biblically*, in which I explored the ways we interpret the Bible. I did this by following the rules in the Good Book as literally as possible. I followed the Ten Commandments, but I also followed the hundreds of more obscure rules. I grew some alarmingly sprawling facial hair (Leviticus says you should not shave the corners of your beard) and tossed out my poly-cotton sweaters (Leviticus says you cannot wear clothes made of two kinds of fabric). I became the ultimate fundamentalist.

The project was absurd at times but also enlightening and inspiring. I found that some aspects of living biblically changed my life for the better (the emphasis on gratitude, for instance). I also learned the dangers of taking the Bible too literally (I don't recommend stoning an adulterer in Central Park, even if those stones are pebble-sized, as mine were). And I learned how challenging it is to figure out what we should replace literalism with.

I'm not the first to notice that we treat the Constitution and the Bible in similar ways. Scholars have long described the Constitution as the sacred text of our civic religion. Jefferson called the delegates "demigods." And as with the Bible, there is an ongoing debate between those who say we should hew to the original meaning and those who say the meaning evolves. It's the originalists versus the living constitutionalists. The two camps have been around for decades, but in the past five years, the originalists have gained surprising power. Five of the six conservative justices on the Supreme Court are originalists of some sort (John Roberts is the exception), a position that has affected their rulings on abortion, gun rights, and many other topics. I felt it was time. I began prepping for a year of living constitutionally.

Before I started my adventure, I figured I'd better sit down and actually read the Constitution.

So on a random Thursday night, I set the mood. I lit a beeswax candle, settled into our most Spartan wooden chair, and unrolled my U.S.

Constitution. It's a four-page khaki-colored replica I bought on Amazon. Each crinkly page is the size of a poster. I'm accustomed to reading on small glowing screens, so it was an awkward feeling. My wife, Julie, would be better at this—she still reads the print version of *The New York Times*, which I find charmingly archaic. ("So what's President Eisenhower up to today?" I'll ask. To which she'll respond, "Oh, because I'm reading it like they did in the 1950s. I get it. Good one.")

I soldiered on and read the first sentence:

> We the People of the United States, in Order to form a
> more perfect Union, establish Justice, insure domestic
> Tranquility, provide for the common defence, promote
> the general Welfare, and secure the Blessings of Liberty to
> ourselves and our Posterity, do ordain and establish this
> Constitution for the United States of America.

Now that's an inspiring fifty-two words! I love how it builds tension, comma by comma by comma, till we get to the majestic and self-referential phrase "this Constitution." I also like the mention of the "general Welfare." We could all use more attention to "general Welfare" nowadays as a balance to America's focus on individual rights. I'm also a fan of the mention of "Posterity"—that's us they're talking about. We're the posterity. I'm a part of this American experiment.

I even like the promiscuous use of capital letters. Over the years, several copyeditors have told me that I'm an Overcapitalizer. Ben Franklin wanted to reform American spelling so that all Nouns were capitalized. Sadly, this didn't happen, but his Advice had an Impact on our founding Document and this Book you are reading.

After that gorgeous preamble, I got to Article I. Frankly, it was kind of a letdown. It's a list of rules for setting up Congress, and the prose switches from grand and soaring to technical and lawyerly.

Article I reads more like the instructions to a complicated board game—like Settlers of Catan, but the players are the branches of government. *When it's Congress's turn, it can do any of the following: impose duties, raise an army, etc. After Congress's turn is over, pass the dice to the president.*

The mix of emotions continued as I read on. I bounced between highs and lows, awe and confusion, things I loved and things I found baffling, disappointing, even offensive. In fact, I made two lists—stuff I like and stuff I don't. Here's a sample:

STUFF I LIKE

THE PHRASE "WE THE PEOPLE"

We're lucky to have that phrase. The Constitution's original draft was different. It said "We the People of the States of New-Hampshire, Massachusetts"—and went on to list all thirteen states. But Gouverneur Morris, a Founding Father often described as "colorful" (which seems to be a euphemism for the fact that he had a lot of extramarital sex), deleted the state names. He wanted it to simply say "We the People." And that was a huge shift. Whether Morris meant it to or not (there's some debate), the new version altered the meaning of our country. America went from a collection of states to a collection of people.

THEY HATED AUTHORITARIANS

I never really appreciated the checks-and-balances idea until reading the Constitution. It often seems more a cause of gridlock than of progress. But after reading the Constitution, I see what they were doing and why it was brilliant. I see how checks and balances can be a feature, not a bug.

It's such an intricate system, with so many safeguards against the power-hungry. The Founders even split up the powers of war. Congress declares war, and the president executes it. I like this division. It seems wise. Sadly, it seems to have gone out of style, as over the decades, the president has gained more and more war powers. Maybe this is one place America could be more originalist?

THE PENMANSHIP

As someone who spent weeks of elementary school learning cursive, I appreciate the curls and slopes and spirals. It makes me nostalgic for when letters were little works of art. From a purely aesthetic point of view, we probably have the most beautiful constitution in the world. (Though the Bhutanese constitution was written with a pen dipped in gold ink, so that one's a contender too.)

STUFF I FIND BAFFLING, DISAPPOINTING, OR WORSE

THE SPELLING

I'll start with the nitpicks, then get to the bigger issues. So, spelling. Granted, spelling was different then, so I won't complain about words such as *chusing*. But how do you explain away the fact that there are two spellings of the Keystone State: Pennsylvania and Pensylvania? How did the state somehow lose an N in its journey from the first page to the fourth page? It's anoying.

Plus, there is an extraneous apostrophe in one of the "it's"es in Article II. It should be "its," no apostrophe. That's a classic mistake that would have gotten a thousand snarky social media comments if Ben Franklin had invented social media.

That's not to mention grammar. I decided to run the entire text of the Constitution through the Grammarly software. Grammarly was not impressed. It found 663 problems. It complained, for instance, that the Second Amendment has an "incorrect form of the verb 'being'" and said, "Consider changing it."* I know that eighteenth-century grammar

---

* Grammarly also did not like the phrase "more perfect," telling me that "the adjective *perfect* is nongradable and may not require a qualifier. Consider removing the qualifier *more*."

was different from modern grammar, but even by the standards of early America, some phrases were needlessly confusing.

On the upside, I do think the flubs in spelling and grammar point to an important truth we shouldn't forget: The Constitution is an imperfect document written by humans, not dictated by an infallible deity.

THE LAUGHABLY ARCHAIC PARTS

The Constitution is a 237-year-old document, so it's no shock that some sections are dated. But parts are practically written in another language. In Article I, Congress is given the power to "grant Letters of Marque and Reprisal." I'd never heard of such a thing. I googled the phrase, and it turns out it is basically government-sanctioned piracy. The preferred term is *privateering*. If you got a letter of marque from Congress, it meant that as a private citizen, you could use your fishing vessel to intercept enemy ships and seize their goods.

The permits were actually hugely important at the time. Congress granted hundreds of such letters during the Revolutionary War, and we probably would not have a country without them. Privateers captured nearly two thousand British ships, seizing everything from cannons to barrels of sherry.

Congress hasn't granted any letters of marque since 1815, but the rule is still on the books. I made a mental note: Borrow my friend Paul's waterskiing boat and ask Congress for a letter of marque.

THE TRULY OFFENSIVE PARTS

Archaic is one thing, but the Constitution also contains jarring and disturbing parts—most notably about slavery. There are several mentions of slavery, including the rule that fugitive enslaved people are not free even if they escape to a free state. It doesn't actually say the word *slave* or *slavery*. The text uses euphemisms such as "Person held to Service or Labour." The Founding Fathers—at least some of them—knew enough to be ashamed, but they still failed to abolish it.

The Thirteenth Amendment, passed in 1865, abolished slavery. (For my project, I am following this and all other amendments, not just the original 1787 text.) But the words of the Thirteenth Amendment are tacked on at the end of the Constitution, as are the other amendments. Which means the original offensive passages about slavery are still right there in the Constitution. James Madison didn't like that format. He wanted the amendments to be woven into the document. He wanted the Constitution to be like a Google Doc that we'd revise with every amendment. He was overruled, and the ugly text remains for all to see.

I'm not sure whether it's good or bad that these noxious words are still in the Constitution. Akhil Reed Amar, a Yale Law School professor, argues that as painful as those passages are to read, they serve as a reminder of how much progress we've made as a country. He argues it's good they have stayed. They remind us that "We the People" once meant "We the white, male People" and that much of constitutional history has been the ongoing struggle to expand the word "People" to include other races and genders.

After reading the Constitution, I felt a mix of emotions: pride, awe, confusion, shame, and excitement.

I came away with lots of ideas on which rights I would attempt to exercise. I would petition the government (on what, I wasn't sure yet). I would freely exercise my religion in an appropriately eighteenth-century way.

But I also felt another emotion: I was overwhelmed.

Even though it's just four pages, the Constitution seems almost infinitely complex. I could go broke buying books about the Constitution. There are hundreds of them covering every angle, every phrase, every amendment. There are three entire books on the Third Amendment, for crying out loud—that obscure amendment about how you don't have to quarter soldiers in your home without your consent.

And perhaps most crucial of all, the Constitution never gives any instructions on how to interpret itself. It has no user's manual, no glossary.

I realized I couldn't do this project alone. I needed a Board of Constitutional Advisers. Over the next few weeks, I assembled a group of generous legal scholars whom I could call and email with questions. They hold beliefs from all over the political spectrum. One of my advisers is so originalist, he refuses to capitalize the word *supreme* in Supreme Court, because it's not capitalized in the Constitution. Others are practically postmodern, saying that there's no intrinsic meaning in the Constitution at all and that it's completely up to the interpreter. It is textual Play-Doh for us to mold as we wish.

I asked my advisers to explain the theories behind the two main types of interpretation: living constitutionalism and originalism. Before we embark on my year, it might be helpful to have a quick and vastly oversimplified summary (I'll go into more detail and nuances later in the book, since both theories come in many flavors).

Living constitutionalism argues that we need to adapt the meaning of the words to fit with changing moral standards. For instance, the Fourteenth Amendment promises "equal protection" and "liberty" for all. The ratifiers of the Fourteenth Amendment in 1868 almost certainly did not mean for these protections to apply to gay marriage. But living constitutionalism says they do. We need to adapt.

The biggest criticism of living constitutionalism is this: If you're not anchored to the original meaning, then what stops you from changing the Constitution's meaning to whatever you want? The slope is slippery.

Originalism came to the fore in the 1980s as a way to stop what the conservatives saw as the liberal Supreme Court's overreach. They worried that the Supreme Court—which had ruled in favor of affirmative action and a right to abortion—was untethered and was willy-nilly making rulings that aligned with liberal politics. The liberals were "legislating from the bench."

And that's where originalism comes in. It says you need to go back to the original meaning of the text when it was ratified. Originalists like to argue that the Constitution is not a poem or a metaphor. It's more like a recipe for, say, chicken salad. And just because it was written over 230 years ago, you still need to follow the recipe if you want to make chicken salad. Originalism is mostly linked to conservatism (though there are progressive originalists as well as conservative living constitutionalists).

So, for instance, hard-core originalist Clarence Thomas says that the Constitution's references to "equal protection" and "liberty" do not apply to gay marriage. The phrases appear in the Fourteenth Amendment, which was ratified in 1868, an era when the average American would never have conceived of gay marriage.

Originalists are not completely frozen in time. A thoughtful originalist takes the centuries-old principles of the Constitution and applies them to current technology and situations, using history and tradition as a guide. So the prohibition against unreasonable searches and seizures, originally meant to stop the constable banging on your door, now applies to government snooping through the contents of your smartphone.

But critics say originalists are too stingy when it comes to updating the meanings to adapt to current morals, especially if they involve women's rights, gay rights, or environmental regulations.

Another charge against originalists: Judges apply the theory inconsistently. Sometimes, a certain constitutional right is interpreted as narrowly as possible—as with Thomas's view of gay marriage. Other times, a right can be stretched to the breaking point. Most originalists say the "right to bear arms" covers flintlock muskets as well as AR-15s, even though these two objects are arguably vastly different.

So that helped inspire my mission: What if I try to be 100 percent consistent? What if I always apply the narrowest interpretation of what was written in 1787 (or, in the case of the amendments, whenever they were written)? I pledged to avoid the hubris of assuming we know what the founding generation would have thought about modern innovations. I would go back to the basics.

When I told my wife that I planned to live for a year constitutionally—muskets, quill pens, and all—her reaction was not "Huzzah!" She was no fan of my year of living biblically. For starters, she hated the beard. She didn't kiss me for seven months. She also didn't love that I couldn't touch her when she was menstruating.

"I'm not going to churn butter," she said.

"You won't have to," I said. "That's not part of it. Unless the soldiers who quarter in our house really want it."

But the butter-churning comment raises an interesting question: Just how much should I commit to an eighteenth-century lifestyle? The Constitution does not say "All citizens shall wear a tricorne hat and drink rum punch," just as the Bible didn't say "Thou shalt bake bread from scratch and wear a robe." But I baked the bread and wore the robe because I believed it might help me get into the mindset of my ancestors.

And I think it did. In fact, my attempt to look and act like my biblical forefathers was one of my favorite parts of that project. It was a lesson in how much the outer affects the inner, how much behavior affects our thoughts. Even my flowing garments affected my outlook. There's truth in the saying "Clothes make the man."

So I want to do the same thing with the constitutional era. I want to walk the walk and talk the talk and eat the mutton and read the Cicero. I believe it will help me see the world differently.

This is a distinct but related part of my year of living constitutionally. One goal of my journey is to follow the text strictly, but another goal is to learn if there is any wisdom to be gleaned from eighteenth-century life. So much of the Constitution springs from the Founders' beliefs about virtue and duty, beliefs that molded their actions. I want to replicate those actions when I can.

Naturally, there is plenty of horrible stuff that I want to avoid—it was an insular, racist, sexist, homophobic, and smelly time. But maybe there are some parts that we should revive. Did writing long letters by hand instead of responding with a thumb-typed acronym make people more thoughtful? Did their emphasis on public service make them better citizens? Are there advantages to stoicism as opposed to letting all emotions gush freely? I'd like to find out.

Several of my advisers told me they appreciated the goal but that getting into an eighteenth-century mindset is a tough task. "They thought about life in a completely different way back then," one historian said to me. "The past is another country. It's like trying to get inside the mind of a mollusk—it's just so foreign to us."

I take his point. But I still want to try. I went online and, for starters, bought an American flag—one of the first versions with just thirteen stars arranged in a circle. I hung it on our bedroom wall hoping it would get me into an eighteenth-century mentality.

It reminded me that I used to have patriotic art in my room. When I graduated from high school, my grandfather gave me a poster of the Statue of Liberty by the artist Peter Max. It hung in my apartment throughout college and in my home after I graduated. I loved that this was the same statue my great-great-grandparents saw when arriving at Ellis Island after fleeing Russia in 1904. I loved what it stood for. It made me feel patriotic. For most of my life, I've been a fan of the American experiment despite its flaws. But lately I've been having profound doubts about our country. Can America survive this cultural divide? Am I being alarmist, or are we really in some sort of national existential crisis?

I feel myself losing my optimism—and that depresses me, because optimism is one of my favorite American characteristics. In fact, I just read that Ben Franklin presented an ode to optimism at the end of the Constitutional Convention.

During the convention, Franklin had been looking at the wood carving on the back of George Washington's chair. (Washington was president of the convention and sat at the front of the room in a special chair, which you can still see at Philadelphia's Independence Hall.)

The carving portrays half a sun. You can see the top half of the sun, but the horizon cuts off the bottom half. Franklin said that during the long debates, he'd wonder whether the image was of a rising sun or a setting sun. But as the convention was ending, and the delegates had actually forged a constitution, Franklin said, "Now I know that it is a rising sun." I relate more to Franklin in the middle of the convention. I don't know whether the sun is rising or setting on the American experiment. I'm hoping this year will convince me it's dawn, not dusk.

Voting, Eighteenth-Century Style

SECTION 1.

One thing is clear right at the start—this is going to be a noisy book to write.

I'm writing these words with a goose quill I ordered online. (I know the online part isn't so eighteenth century, but at least I'm using my laptop by candlelight.) I'm writing in the kitchen because I've been banished from my usual spot in the living room. Julie can't stand the scratch, scratch, scratch of the quill as it makes its way across the cotton rag paper, which is what the Founders used for everyday writing.

"Worse than nails on the chalkboard," she said. There's no doubt it's a tingle-inducing sound. In fact, you can find several ASMR videos on YouTube featuring people writing with quills and whispering, in case you crave that feeling. Julie does not.

On the other hand, I like the squeaky sound. It makes me feel like I'm accomplishing something. I like the ritual of dipping my quill in ink every few words. I like that writing with a quill helps me focus my thoughts. It's so peaceful, no dings or chimes or pop-ups to distract me. I like the occasional Jackson Pollock splatter that makes the page look beautifully imperfect. This quill business lends itself to a less impulsive, slower style of writing. I can't bang something out and immediately press send, then regret it. The quill provides a sort of waiting period for your thoughts.

If the world returned to quills, would we see a decline in trolls and rage writing? Maybe. Or what if the Founding Fathers had written the Constitution on a shared cloud document? Would they have ever come to an agreement? I'll have to think about that in a slow and considered way.

In any case, I'll be writing much of my book with a quill. What's more, I'm already so steeped in the Constitution, I can't help but organize my book into Articles and Sections. It feels too appropriate. Which brings us to Article I, Section 2, of my book.

SECTION 2.

I'm writing my noisy words on the evening of November 8. That's the day I decided to start my project: Election Day. It seemed like the most appropriate day to embark on the year of living constitutionally since democracy is at the heart of our founding document. Or at least that's what its boosters contend.

In some ways, starting on November 8 is not true to the founding era, since the rule about holding elections on the first Tuesday in November wasn't passed until 1845. Before that, Election Day ranged all over the calendar. Still, the symbolism of beginning on Election Day was too tempting for me.

I kicked the day off by making myself a large glass of rum punch from Martha Washington's recipe (orange juice, lemon juice, cloves, cinnamon, etc.). I did this because, for one thing, day drinking was the norm in the 1790s. Booze was especially common during election season. Voting was much more festive then—at least for the privileged few who were allowed to vote. When George Washington ran for the Virginia legislature in 1758, he provided voters with 28 gallons of rum, 50 gallons of rum punch, 34 gallons of wine, 46 gallons of beer, and 2 gallons of hard cider. He won the election with more than 300 well-lubricated votes.

But mostly, I did it because I needed the liquid courage. I was about to embarrass myself publicly. At 11 A.M., I strode into our local polling station—the high school cafeteria near our home—wearing a black tricorne hat from an Alexander Hamilton costume. I approached a poll worker sitting at a table just past the entrance. She had on a gray sweater and wire-rimmed glasses.

"Hello," I said, projecting my voice as best I could. "For governor, I would like to vote for Kathy Hochul. And for senator, I would like—"

"Oh, don't tell me!" she said, cutting me off.

"But I'd like to vote out loud, by voice, like our Founding Fathers did," I explained.

"No, no, no. You can't say it in here. You can say it outside, but not in here."

"But I want everyone to know my vote," I said. "That's the way they used to vote in the late seventeen hundreds."

"Well, times are changing," the poll worker said.

I glanced at Julie, who was behind me in line. She was looking down, her hands shielding her eyes.

The woman sent me to another table, where I reluctantly voted the newfangled way—secretly, silently, at a well-shielded desk. (Though perhaps not as newfangled as one would expect in this smartphone-driven world—I filled out the paper form with a ballpoint pen.)

My goal had been to express my constitutional right to vote in the most 1790s way I could.

The Constitution says that "the People" get to vote. Of course, it was notoriously vague on who counts as "the People." In the beginning, it was mostly white male people, and much of American history was—and remains—the struggle to make "the People" more inclusive.

So "the People" can vote, yet the Constitution doesn't say *how* the people vote. There's no constitutional right to a secret ballot. In fact, the idea of a secret ballot barely existed in early America.

Instead, the Constitution lets the *states* choose the "times, places and manner" of holding elections, with some oversight from Congress. This setup still has an impact today, as states differ on how easy or hard voting should be. From the 1700s until the mid-1800s, many states had their voters announce their preferred candidate out loud for all to hear. Viva voce, it was called—voting by voice. So that's what I was trying to do. I wanted to experience originalist voting by voice.

And how did it feel? Humiliating, for sure. But also liberating. I felt like I was smashing the taboo of secrecy. Let the truth come out! Own my opinions. I don't need to keep my vote private like it's a case of hemorrhoids.

The loud-and-proud voting method had other advantages, at least from the eighteenth-century point of view. First, it made elections harder to rig. Second, as University of Virginia historian Don DeBats writes, "In those times political choices were understood to be communal, not private, matters. Voting to advance private individual interests calls for secrecy—but public voting made perfect sense when politics was understood to be about group or communal interests."

I'm not sure voting by voice made you more communal minded. It could have just made you more pressured and intimidated to vote in accordance with your eavesdropping boss. I did find it liberating, but maybe I'd feel differently if my book editor had been in line behind me. In the end, I still prefer the secret ballot, an idea we imported from Australia in the late 1800s, one of that continent's great contributions along with Cate Blanchett and boxed wine.

SECTION 3.

Voting by voice isn't the only difference between today's Election Day and the founding era's. In fact, if a Founding Father were transported to my polling station, he'd think someone had slipped something into his rum punch.

He would be confused by the sight of Julie, as women didn't get the national right to vote until the Nineteenth Amendment in 1920. (Though there is an interesting early exception—New Jersey briefly allowed women to vote in 1790 before rescinding the right in 1807. They buckled to media mockery that they were setting up a "petticoat" government. When I told Julie, a Jersey girl, about this, she said, "Well, at least they tried, which is better than New York.") It wasn't just women. At the founding, Black people could not vote in most states, whether they were free or enslaved. And Indigenous people could not vote in any state.

The Founding Fathers had profoundly mixed feelings about democracy. In fact, there's still an ongoing debate about how democratic the Constitution is.

On the one hand, the author and Yale professor Akhil Reed Amar says that, for its time, the Constitution was startlingly democratic. "It was the Big Bang of democracy," he likes to tell his students. "It was the most democratic deed in the history of planet Earth."

An elected government—that was an astoundingly bold idea. It hadn't been tried in earnest since ancient Greek times, and even then it was restricted to just a few influential citizens. The Constitution said that people could directly elect Congress. And not just landowning people. The Constitution had no requirement that voters own property, even though land ownership was a feature found in several colonies' constitutions.

On the other hand, many scholars argue that the Constitution wasn't democratic at all, even for its time. For instance, I read a book with the title *How Democratic Is the American Constitution?* The answer to the title's question is not "Pretty darn democratic!"

In a nutshell, the book's answer is "Not so much." The author and like-minded scholars argue that the Founding Fathers were terrified of democracy. They did not like the idea that everyone, whether poor or rich, educated or uneducated, was entitled to an equal vote. And indeed, it's not hard to find antidemocratic quotes from the Founding Fathers about the tyranny of the mob. Hamilton, for one, wrote in a letter just before he died that "Democracy" is the "real disease."

Instead, most of these men wanted democracy filtered through and tempered by an educated elite. This is why we have the Electoral College: to make sure there's a method to stop a demagogue. It's why we have a Senate that was initially chosen by state legislatures, not the people. It's why the vote was mostly restricted to white men.

The Founders preferred a *republic*—where elected representatives make the decisions—over a pure democracy, where people vote on issues directly. In this view, the Founders were alarmed by the excesses of democracy in several state constitutions, such as that of Pennsylvania, which had a popularly elected legislature with few checks or balances. The U.S. Constitution was designed to counteract that.

SECTION 4.

We can clearly see the centuries-long battle to expand the vote in the Constitution itself. Or more precisely, in the amendments.

The Fifteenth Amendment, ratified in 1870, gave suffrage to Black men.

The Nineteenth Amendment in 1920 gave the vote to women.

The Twenty-Fourth in 1964 banned poll taxes, which required people to pay a fee before being allowed to vote. The poll taxes had been used as a way to deny impoverished voters, especially impoverished Black voters, their right to vote.

The Twenty-Sixth Amendment in 1971 lowered the voting age from twenty-one years to eighteen. (Fun fact: Jerry Springer, best known for such thoughtful TV topics as "I Married a Horse," testified before Congress as a young man in favor of the Twenty-Sixth Amendment.)

I'm abiding by the amendments as well as the original text, so, happily, I don't have to ask Julie to stay home on Election Day.

Regardless, the expansion of voting rights has not been a straight line of progress. There have been—and continue to be—setbacks and struggles. There's gerrymandering, which makes some votes practically worthless. There are counties that slash the number of polling stations in districts with low-income or Black people. There's voter intimidation.

From the 1890s right up to the 1960s, some states gave literacy tests or character tests designed to make it harder for Black people to vote.

Often, white voters would be exempted from the tests, which could be ridiculously hard.

Consider the civic literacy test from Sumter County, Georgia, in 1963. You can find it online. There are twenty-eight questions, some incredibly arcane. Here is question 22:

> "What does the Constitution of the United States provide regarding the suspension of the privilege of the writ of Habeas Corpus?"

Or number 24:

> "What are the names of the persons who occupy the following offices in your county? 1) Clerk of the Superior Court. 2) Ordinary. 3) Sheriff."

I revised the test to make it fit current-day New York and gave it to Julie, myself, and several of our friends. No one passed. Not even a friend of ours who works in city government. The Supreme Court ruled that literacy tests were unconstitutional in 1949. But even today, there are still many troubling ways that votes are being suppressed, including lack of voting booths in low-income districts.

SECTION 5.

Plenty of things about early-American voting deserve to be left behind—the blatant racism, the sexism, the voting by voice. But I've decided that one thing was worth resurrecting: Elections were much more festive, at least for those who could participate.

There were parades, music, and farmers markets. Voting in early America "was an engaging social experience, as voters at the polls talked with friends, threw down shots of free whiskey, listened to lively entertainment, and generally had a good time," wrote a group of political scientists in the journal *Political Science & Politics* in a 2007 paper titled "Putting the Party Back into Politics." For their experiment, the researchers set up little festivals with music and food at various voting stations around the country. The result? The festivities boosted turnout by almost 7 percent. Which is not nothing.

The researchers think we should bring back the good times. And I couldn't agree more. I want to party like it's 1799. My plan was to reintroduce an early-American treat: the election cake. Americans would bake cakes and hand them out at the polls. The first known printed recipe for election cake was in a 1796 edition of a cookbook called *American Cookery*. I found the recipe online. In addition to the usual cake dough, an election cake is filled with figs, cinnamon, cloves, raisins, and nutmeg.

My niece has a side hustle of baking cakes, and she said the recipe sounded inedible. I was not deterred. Right after I voted, I went to the grocery store with my son Zane to pick up the ingredients. (Julie and I have three teenage sons: Jasper, Lucas, and Zane, who is the most culinarily inclined.) We came home, chopped the figs, baked the cake, topped it with red-white-and-blue icing, and tried a piece. Not bad! Tastes like participatory democracy! Actually, the spices make it taste vaguely like Worcestershire sauce.

We carried the cake to the polling station near our apartment and set up a table with forks and napkins and paper plates on the corner by the poll entrance (one hundred feet away, as required by current New York law).

"What's this?" asked a curly-haired woman. She was on the corner by our table, handing out pamphlets for something called "the Medical Freedom Party," an antivaccine group.

"I'm trying to revive the eighteenth-century tradition of election cakes," I said. "I'm trying to make voting more festive."

"Is it gluten-free?" she asked.

.   .   .

Zane, Julie, and I stood on the corner, offering cake to New Yorkers exiting and entering the polls. We received plenty of rejections—but friendly ones.

"That's nice, but no thanks" was a frequent comment from passersby.

But we also got a surprising number of people who accepted unwrapped food on the street from strangers. Having Julie there probably helped. She radiates friendliness. She counterbalanced the perplexing sight of a guy in a tricorne hat.

No one spat the cake out, and one person even asked for the recipe.

"I'll have a piece," said a man wearing a suit and red tie. He was a Republican running for Congress—quite the long shot on the liberal Upper West Side—and he was greeting voters as they entered. This would not have happened in early America. It was considered unseemly to campaign like that. You didn't run for office. You stood for office.

"You want something to drink with that?" I asked. "A little of Martha Washington's rum punch?"

"I better wait till nine P.M.," he said.

In addition to the cake, I'd made a pitcher of rum punch to bring to the polls. Again, not terrible tasting at all. The candidate turned it down, but plenty of other voters did take the rum. Over the afternoon, we handed out about twenty-five cups of rum punch to exiting citizens.

At one point, a woman came over and asked for a cup. I recognized her from the high school cafeteria. She was a poll worker, a volunteer.

"I'm on my break," she said. "And I could use a drink. Some of these people are so mean. Such complainers!"

I got nervous. Was I allowed to give booze to an election worker? What if she got wasted and miscounted a vote? On the other hand, she was an adult and could always go to the deli and get a six-pack.

So I poured her a small cup.

"Thanks. I have five hours left to go and I need this," she said, taking a gulp.

I figured there were greater threats to democracy right now than a slightly buzzed poll worker.

I considered the election cake experiment a victory. In fact, I decided to go bigger for next year's election. What if we blanket the country in 2023 with festive cakes to celebrate suffrage? Maybe come up with a catchphrase like "Democracy is sweet"? Part of my goal for this project is to figure out not just what is outdated from the founding era but also what might be worth reclaiming.

Election cakes are a great candidate. To be safe, I'll skip the rum punch.

SECTION 6.

It's been two days since my attempt to vote by voice. Ben Franklin— America's original self-help author—advised frequent self-examination and reflection. So let me pause here to examine my first seventy-two hours. I have split my observations into those things that are helping my pursuit of happiness, which I'm calling "Huzzahs," because I'm a fan of the word, and those things that are impeding my pursuit of happiness, which I'm calling "Grievances," because it's a good constitutional term that appears in my beloved First Amendment.

Huzzahs

THE CANDLELIGHT.

As I mentioned, I have twin goals in this project: First, to express my constitutional rights using the original meaning and technology. And second, to try to understand the Founders' mindset by trying to adopt their lifestyle as much as possible. That second goal is why I'm trying to live by candlelight. At night, when I walk around the apartment, I carry a little brass candlestick with a handle. Julie hated the first type of candle I used. It was beef tallow. I'd bought it on Etsy, and Julie complained it made the apartment smell like unrefrigerated meat loaf. So I've switched to beeswax. (George Washington favored candles made from whale spermaceti, but I'm opting against that for several reasons, legal and otherwise.)

I carry my beeswax candle around the apartment. I flick off the electric lights whenever I come into a room—after which my wife and kids flick the lights back on, and then I flick them off, and so on. I like having the soft glow of the dancing flame in my life. Overall, my nights are darker—and I think it's affected my schedule. I'm going to sleep earlier and waking up earlier. Not five in the morning, like Ben Franklin suggests on his daily schedule, but before seven o'clock. I think it might be better for me. One lesson from the lack of electric light: The Founders were much more at the mercy of natural rhythms, such as the sunset and sunrise at the heart of Franklin's allegory.

While I'm on the topic, a word about online purchases, such as the candles. I had this same quandary when I lived biblically. I bought my robes and frankincense with my laptop. I figured there's no biblical law that says, "Thou shalt not use computers." I'm employing the same strategy here: I'll use eighteenth-century objects whenever possible, but I won't completely forgo modern technology if it helps my quest. I'll also be taking antibiotics if necessary, since I don't want to die. I do pledge to use Etsy whenever possible, since artisans are much more in line with early America than Walmart or Amazon.

WATCHING PERIOD DRAMAS.

I'm trying to wean myself off all streaming. But when I do break down and open Netflix, at least I'm confining myself to shows and movies set in the eighteenth century. Which allows me the petty thrill of spotting all the inaccuracies. (*That quill pen should have most of the feathery stuff stripped off! The feathers just got in the way!*) Years of experience have trained me not to share every such observation with Julie.

Grievances

THE MENTAL DISCOMFORT.

By "discomfort," I mean the constant uncertainty about my previous assumptions. I'm reading with Madisonian fervor. (Madison had a personal library of about four thousand books, many of which he read in preparation for the Constitutional Convention; I don't think I'll beat his record, but it's a good goal.) And the more I read, the more I see the ethical subtleties. I'm reading *The Federalist Papers,* the pro-Constitution series of essays written by Madison, Hamilton, and John Jay. But I'm also reading Anti-Federalist writers and their argument that the Constitution is the work of corrupt power mongers. I'm reading books by those who argue America was the cradle of liberty and those who call it the brainchild of elitists. I just listened to a podcast by two British historians who were brazenly dismissive of the American Revolutionaries. They called the colonists "whiny" and "paranoid" and argued that the colonists actually paid much less in taxes than the average Brit. I found myself simultaneously amused and infuriated.

My opinions are being tugged in all directions. Weird directions as well. What if the Bill of Rights was actually a bad idea? James Madison, at first, believed that it might be. He worried that if the Founders etched certain rights in stone, people might assume that other rights didn't exist. Or what about this radical idea: What if they had gotten rid of states? Some of the Founding Fathers, including, at one point, Hamilton, wanted to all but do away with states. People can't be loyal to two different governments, they argued.

All this flux is unsettling, but I'm trying to reframe it more positively. I should embrace uncertainty. As the great philosopher Bertrand Russell said, "The whole problem with the world is that fools and fanatics are always so certain of themselves, and wiser people so full of doubts."

The Founding Fathers, at their best, encouraged uncertainty and flexible thinking. At the Constitutional Convention, the individual votes of the delegates were counted but were not recorded by name. The Founders didn't want the delegates to feel locked into a position. They wanted them to be able to change their minds in the future with ease. As opposed to now, when those who change their minds are derided as flip-floppers.

At the end of the convention, Ben Franklin gave an address that was a wonderful paean to epistemic humility. He said, "I have experienced many instances of being obliged, by better information or fuller consideration, to change opinions even on important subjects, which I once thought right, but found to be otherwise. It is therefore that the older I grow the more apt I am to doubt my own judgment."

Not to mention my favorite fact about James Madison: His last utterance on planet Earth was that he had changed his mind. While Madison was on his deathbed, his niece noticed an odd expression on his face and asked if he was okay. He replied, "Nothing more than a change of mind, my dear." And then died. At least that's the legend. What did he allegedly change his mind about? We'll never know.

Flexible thinking is at the heart of my constitutional year. I want to embrace it. I believe that most Americans—and that includes me—are confined to mental ruts. We need to return to some of the fluidity of early America. Or so goes my hypothesis. Maybe I'll discover that flexible thinking is terrible and I'll change my mind.

PIPE SMOKING.

I ordered some historically accurate tobacco, and one of those white clay pipes from Pipeshoppe.com. Historians say the Founding Fathers smoked pipes nonstop, even while writing the Constitution in Independence Hall, a habit that couldn't have been healthy—especially since the hall's windows were shut tight for fear of eavesdroppers. I'm trying to puff away for a few minutes a day without getting too dizzy, but I'm not good at it. Somehow, I accidentally got the tobacco flakes in my mouth, after which I spent a minute gargling the bitter taste away.

Historians say the Founding Fathers at the Constitutional Convention smoked "tavern pipes," which are bigger pipes meant to be communal. Anyone could pick one up and start puffing. It points to a theme I'm noticing: It was a much more communal time. If a man went to a hotel, he often shared a room with other men—and also a bed. Perhaps that's linked to the era's greater concern for the common good (with the big caveat that only some humans were deemed worthy of the common good). But as a moderate germophobe, I won't be embracing communal pipes or beds.

Meet the Forefathers

SECTION 1.

Less than a fortnight after Election Day, Julie, our sons, and I rented a car to drive to New Jersey. (It's hard to find a place that rents horses for interstate travel, so a car it is.)

We drove past Washington Heights and across the George Washington Bridge on our way to our destination: to watch George Washington's troops in action. Today is a big day—the reenactment of a 1776 battle at Fort Lee, New Jersey.

I'm aware the Revolutionary War occurred several years before the Constitutional Convention of 1787. But frankly, it's hard to find reenactments of the convention. Americans prefer their reenactments with muskets and loud bangs, not compromises and points of order.

I figure the Revolution is better than nothing. I want to see what I can learn from these reenactor folks about how to eat, dress, talk, and think like an eighteenth-century American.

As Julie drove, I used my iPhone (a violation, I know) to look up the Battle of Fort Lee. America lost the battle. Actually, we didn't even truly lose. We fled the fort before there could even be a battle.

"Why are we celebrating it if they ran away?" Julie asked.

"Apparently, it was a very important running away," I said.

The "battle" has the gloriously paradoxical nickname of Retreat to Victory. A few days before, Washington's troops had lost a battle in Manhattan, so they fled to Fort Lee, after which they hightailed it from Fort Lee as well. If they hadn't run away, the Brits might have wiped out the Patriots right at the start of the war. There's even a nearby bridge called the Bridge That Saved a Nation. It's a bridge the Brits neglected to destroy, and it served as a crucial escape valve for Washington's beleaguered troops.

We were going to the site of a resounding defeat! To me, this fact is bursting with good life lessons: Choose your battles. Be patient. Sometimes, you've got to fail before you succeed. There's no shame in a strategic retreat.

I really, really wanted to share these lessons with my sons. But I resisted my paternal compulsion. I knew it was a victory just to have my sons join us for the day, so I stayed silent. I reminded myself: Choose your wisdom-dispensing moments.

SECTION 2.

We arrived in the parking lot in time to see a redcoat pulling his musket out of his supply carriage, aka his Nissan pickup truck. When we walked to the main field, we saw more reenactors. There were red coats but also a surprising array of other colored coats—green coats (which were worn by Loyalist soldiers), blue coats (Continental Army soldiers), even yellow coats (the foppish fife players in the New Hampshire Regiment). There were dozens of reenactors—more reenactors than spectators, in fact. They were marching to fifes and drums, tending to campfires, and eating beef stew out of tin cups.

"Is the stew for sale?" Julie asked a blue-coated man in a tricorne hat.

"It's for the troops only," he said.

We were cold and Julie wanted a snack, so we headed to the park's Revolutionary War–themed museum. It was packed with reenactors thawing out, schmoozing, and selling their wares.

One man had a table piled high with Revolutionary War–themed books. Two of his reenactor customers were chatting with each other. They were not happy about the recent New York State gun law that banned firearms—including muskets—from certain public areas. Muskets should be an exception, they believed.

"It's absolutely absurd," said one customer.

"Ridiculous," replied the other man. "You can't rob a store with a musket. 'Hey, let me rob you. Just hang on a minute while I pour out some gunpowder, ram down a lead ball, and . . . '"

Several feet away, we saw two friendly-looking women in bonnets and floral dresses. We approached them. They introduced themselves—Dakota and her aunt Mary. They were with the Third New Jersey Regiment.

I expected them to be in character, to address us as "Good sirs and madam," and maybe to say something about "God save George Washington from that pigheaded tyrant King George." But they were speaking in regular old twenty-first-century English.

"What was it like being a woman in the war back then?" Julie asked.

"There's a reputation that the women in the camp were all prostitutes, but that's not true," said Dakota, her blond hair peeking out from under her bonnet. Most of the women in the camps were wives of the soldiers. "You had to get permission from George Washington to be at the camp."

The women's camp was usually about two miles behind the soldiers' camp. It wasn't an easy life. The women did laundry, mended clothes—and they got half rations, said Mary.

"Half rations?" Julie said.

"I know," said Mary. "Different times."

Dakota and Mary told us they were both history teachers in New Jersey public schools. Mary's husband was one of the regiment's leaders, the adjutant.

"I'm wondering, if I want to join up, how would that work?" I asked. For the past couple of weeks, I'd been thinking of giving reenacting a go. It might be helpful to one of my goals: get inside the heads of eighteenth-century Americans.

Dakota broke down how to enter. If I want to join "the hobby" (as insiders call it), I must first decide if I want to be a Patriot or a redcoat.

"A Patriot, of course," I said.

"Good decision," Mary said.

I learned later that some reenactors aren't totally faking their hostility to the other side. There's some actual resentment.

One American soldier told me that the redcoats "kind of have a chip on their shoulder. They like the pomp, the pageantry. They're drawn in by the fancier uniforms." Another told me dismissively, "It takes a special kind of person to choose to be a redcoat."

I'd also have to procure the supplies. At first, the regiment could lend me clothes, but eventually I'd want my own. Ideally, I would sew the coat and breeches myself. But if I was strapped for time, I could buy them. Though only from authorized shops that used the right wool, stitching, and patterns.

"You don't want to be Captain Farb," said Mary's husband, Chris, who had joined us and was wearing specially crafted wire-rimmed spectacles.

A farb, I learned, is a term for lazy reenactors who wear inaccurate outfits or carry phony muskets. Some reenactors say that the word *farb* is a shortened form of Far Be It From Authentic, though no one's certain.

The point is, you need to take the hobby seriously. It's bad form to buy an Alexander Hamilton costume off Amazon. I suspected as much, which is why I didn't wear the tricorne hat from an Alexander Hamilton costume I bought off Amazon.

Some reenactors are super hard-core, fiercely devoted to authenticity. They're called *stitch counters*. The name comes from the practice of counting the stitches on other people's uniforms. A good reenactor should have stitches that are equal in number to the stitches in a 1776 uniform.

Dakota and Mary talked about one of their fully committed reenactor friends. He's exceedingly strict. During reenactment weekends, he won't use any modern conveniences. No phone, no electric razor, nothing.

A few winters ago, he tromped through the snow at Valley Forge—and he did it barefoot because that's what Washington's shoeless soldiers had to do.

"He lost a toe," Dakota said.

"He lost a toe?" said Mary. "I thought he just got frostbite."

"No, he lost a toe. I saw it. His pinkie toe," Dakota said, adding, "I love reenacting, but I also like to wear high heels. I am not going to sacrifice a toe."

My favorite detail about their hard-core friend: When he's at home and has to resort to sending an email, he uses an AOL address because he feels an old-timey AOL account is closer to 1770s technology. (Of course, we all know the Founding Fathers used Hotmail, but you have to admire the dedication.)

Dakota, on the other hand, has a Gmail account. She's less of a stitch counter, more of what is called a *hotelier*. "Come nine o'clock," she said, "I have to get out of my stays,* take a shower, and climb into a hotel bed. I know it can seem like a silly way to spend a weekend. But I love this way of teaching history—and I've grown to love the community."

SECTION 3.

It may be a little silly, but it's certainly no sillier than dozens of other rituals where people try to re-create the past—Christmas nativity plays, 1980s-themed parties, the ancient Greek festival at my kids' school where the kids wore sandals and bedsheets.

Throughout the day, I met other members of the Third New Jersey Regiment. I heard their stories, and I began to understand why they find this ritual meaningful.

I met Scott, the regiment's commander. He joined up twenty years ago after reading an obscure book called *Private Yankee Doodle: Being a Narrative of Some of the Adventures, Dangers, and Sufferings of a Revolutionary Soldier*. It was the diary of a Connecticut soldier, and when Scott read the book, he was blown away by this man's sacrifice.

"He wrote about how they had no food during certain times of the

---

* Stays are similar to corsets.

war," Scott told me. "They ate their shoes. They ate the camp dog. They ate the bark off trees. And I said to myself, 'What can I do to pay homage to these people who made these sacrifices?'"

I met Mark, who had been reenacting since the bicentennial, in 1976. He had a hearing aid, which I was told was thanks to decades of musket explosions. "I love the hobby," he said. "When you go to a regular party, what do you talk about? Work? The ball game? Here, we talk about history and philosophy."

I asked Mark how reenacting itself has changed since 1976. He said regiments have gotten a lot more diverse. There are Black soldiers, Asian soldiers, Latino soldiers, and gay soldiers. Some women choose to portray male soldiers fighting on the front. That said, judging by the crowd at this event, it's still a pretty white hobby.

Later in the day, I met a man named Mike who told me he joined up to honor his great-great-great-great-grandfather—who happened to be a Loyalist. He said Loyalists are often seen as traitors, but he wants to dispel that myth. "Loyalists got the shaft," he told me. His ancestor was a farmer who just wanted to keep farming and to stay neutral, but the Patriots would not tolerate it. They confiscated his farm and threw him in jail. "There wasn't a constitution yet, so they could do whatever they wanted. There was no oversight." The Loyalists busted his ancestor out of jail, and he joined their cause.

In fact, this desire to pay tribute to our ancestors is a theme that keeps popping up. It plays a part in the constitutional debate as well. I've been reading a book that lays out a case for originalism. It's called *A Debt Against the Living* by Ilan Wurman, and he argues that we owe it to the Founders to be faithful to the Constitution. When we live in this country, we are making a contract with them. This is a theme I want to explore more this year.

SECTION 4.

At three o'clock, it was time to watch the battle—even though, as I mentioned, there was not an actual battle on these grounds, because the Patriots fled. But the spectators wanted a battle, and a battle they would get.

We watched from behind a ribbon of yellow tape that marked off the spectator section. The British forces were on the left, the Patriots on the right. The two sides took turns shooting at each other, never letting the affair descend into unpleasant chaos.

A line of about thirty redcoats lifted their muskets—which they had loaded with gunpowder but no lead balls—aimed, and fired. There was a pop-pop-pop that sounded like very loud microwave popcorn. The muskets belched out smoke that lingered over the battlefield.

Half a minute later, the Patriots put their muskets to their shoulders and shot. Then the Brits shot. Then the Patriots. And so on. Julie looked at me and tapped her wrist. The rental car was due back soon. We needed to escape, but the yellow tape was blocking our exit.

We walked around the yellow tape, but that was a mistake. We'd gotten too close to the battle. "Get away from here!" a redcoat barked at us. So we took a back route and climbed through some prickly bushes to make our brave retreat to the parking lot.

SECTION 5.

When I got home, I filled out the online application for the Third New Jersey Regiment and paid the thirty-dollar membership fee. I also signed up Julie. Despite initial skepticism, she'd decided it would be fun to try it—plus, she liked the convenient eighteenth-century fanny packs that women tied around their waists. I was thrilled that she was enlisting.

A day later, I got an email from the commander: I was officially a private in the Continental Army. Or almost.

The commander wrote that he had "just a couple of questions" he must ask. . . .

"Do you have any physical limitations we need to know about? . . .

"Are you affiliated with any political para-military faction or group that may be deemed a threat to our Government?"

No and no.

The email went on to say:

> We have a couple of rules. We don't discuss modern politics or religion. . . . If you want to speak about the issues between Jefferson, Adams or Madison have at it. But we do not discuss modern politics or religion. We are not a political group nor are we affiliated with any political parties. The only party we are affiliated with is the Whig party.

I understand the desire to rise above politics. But I imagine that's gotten harder and harder. Many would say that the mere act of getting together and celebrating the Revolution is a political gesture. You are making choices in which parts you reenact. For one thing, you are ignoring wide swaths of America at the time, perhaps most notably enslaved Black people.

It raises some key questions: What is the role of the founding story in America today? Can it provide a glue that binds all citizens together? Or does it just serve to drive us further from one another?

I've been reading a thought-provoking book called *The Great Experiment: Why Diverse Democracies Fall Apart and How They Can Endure* by political scientist Yascha Mounk. His thesis is that every country needs some sort of glue to unite its citizens. This can come in one of three forms:

> First, the residents of a country can be bound by a shared ethnicity and ancestry.

Second, they can be bound by a shared culture.

Third, they can be bound by a respect for the nation's founding
myths, ideals, and documents.

Mounk argues, correctly, I think, that shared ethnicity is a terrible
option. It has resulted in World War II, hate crimes, ethnic cleansing,
and on and on. America doesn't have a shared ethnicity, a situation I
consider a feature of our country, not a bug.

In lieu of a common ethnicity, Mounk believes the best glue is a
shared culture. "Cultural patriotism," he calls it: being proud of American customs, food, buildings, and rituals. I agree that a shared culture
might help bond us, but it's not without its complications. I mean, America, especially now, has many cultures. Hip-hop is American culture,
and so is country music, and I wouldn't say the fans of one frequently
cozy up to fans of the other (notwithstanding happy exceptions such as
Lil Nas X).

The third possible glue Mounk identifies is "civic patriotism": a
shared respect for the founding myth, founding ideals, and founding
documents. This type of patriotism has become more problematic in
recent times. Some see the founding documents not as the birth of
democracy but as the continuation of a slavocracy. In this view, the Constitution is the very worst of America, an instrument of oppression that
continues to this day.

Can civic patriotism in America be saved? And should it? I don't
know, but I have read some interesting proposals on how to resurrect
such a feeling.

First, we can make the founding story more inclusive. We can high-
light the contributions of Black Patriots such as the Forten family of
Philadelphia, who were successful sailmakers, or women such as Esther
de Berdt Reed, also of Philadelphia, who helped raise seven thousand
dollars (about three hundred thousand in today's money) for the troops
by going door-to-door.

Another option: Change our view of who America's Founders are. I spoke to University of Pennsylvania law professor Kermit Roosevelt, who wrote a fascinating book called *The Nation That Never Was: Reconstructing America's Story*. He argues the true American heroes were not the 1780s Founders but instead the authors of the Fourteenth Amendment. Antislavery politicians wrote the Fourteenth Amendment after the Civil War, and they promised "equal protection" and guaranteed life, liberty, and property. The Fourteenth Amendment, he says, fundamentally changed the country. It was the second founding. Its writers are the ones we should be glorifying.

Yet another option is an old one, a route endorsed by Frederick Douglass. Before the Civil War, many abolitionists, including William Lloyd Garrison, condemned the Constitution as an "agreement with Hell." Garrison burned a copy of the Constitution in front of a crowd. He saw it as the work of a corrupt slavocracy.

Douglass, a former enslaved man who became the age's greatest orator, eventually split with Garrison. He took a different approach. He did not deny the sins of the 1780s Founders, but he said the document they created is actually better than the way some of them acted. It's aspirational. The Constitution contains the seeds of freedom. It is, as Martin Luther King Jr. would later say, a promissory note. And America needs to live up to that note. It owes justice to all groups. In fact, some argue Douglass and King should be considered Founders as well. The founding was not a static moment; it's a continuing process.

Can America embrace Douglass's view of the Constitution? Again, I'm not sure. But there is something to be said for focusing on the Constitution's promise of freedom and equality instead of its ugliest sections. The term *cherry-picking* has a negative connotation. But cherry-picking can be great if you pick the sweet cherries about equality, liberty, and the general welfare while leaving the bitter cherries to rot on the tree.

Freedom of Speech

SECTION 1.

Soon after the "battle," I decided it was time to delve into one of my favorite constitutional rights: freedom of speech. As a writer, I have many reasons to say "Thank you, First Amendment!" Well, to be precise, "Thank you, middle section of the First Amendment!" The First Amendment is overstuffed, a grab bag of six separate rights:

Freedom to exercise your own religion
Freedom to live in a country where the government cannot establish a religion
Freedom of speech
Freedom of the press
Freedom to peaceably assemble
Freedom to petition the government[*]

If I were the Constitution's copyeditor, I would have suggested splitting them up or at least bullet-pointing them. Give them a little room to breathe. Regardless, I'm a fan of all six rights (the freedom to petition coming in a distant last; no offense, petitions). But as a writer, I hold closest to my heart the rights of freedom of speech and the press.

I agree with the late civil rights pioneer and congressman John Lewis, who credits freedom of speech and press for America's progress. Without them, he said, "the civil rights movement would've been a bird without wings."

Sometimes I forget how amazing it is that we can say and write almost anything we want without fear that our government will throw

---

[*] Here is the full, nonbulleted text of the First Amendment: "Congress shall make no law respecting an establishment of religion, or prohibiting the free exercise thereof; or abridging the freedom of speech, or of the press; or the right of the people peaceably to assemble, and to petition the Government for a redress of grievances."

us in jail. But I'm reminded of this freedom every time I read about imprisoned journalists in Russia or Saudi Arabia. Or that a Chinese comedian faces three years in prison for making an irreverent pun about the army.

These days, both the left and the right in America believe that the other side is eroding the right to free speech, and I think there's some truth to both claims, which I plan to explore later. But still, free speech in America is more robust than in the vast majority of countries on earth.

When I started researching the history of American free speech, I learned something surprising: The free speech we know is mostly a modern phenomenon. The Founding Fathers meant something vastly different when they talked about free speech. Speech was far more restricted back then. Early America wasn't quite Afghanistan under the Taliban or the Soviet Union under Lenin. But modern Americans would be shocked if we time-traveled to the eighteenth century.

The government "routinely and uncontroversially restricted plenty of speech that did not directly violate the rights of others . . . Examples include profane swearing bans, blasphemy laws, restrictions on advertising, restrictions on theater performances, and rules against making certain agreements on Sundays."

This quotation is from a 2017 *Yale Law Journal* article by Stanford law professor Jud Campbell. The article was a blockbuster, at least by legal academia standards, and widely praised. With deep research and impressive evidence, Professor Campbell showed that "what we're doing today with First Amendment doctrine bears almost no resemblance at all to the way the Founders thought about the First Amendment. . . . It's important to realize the past was an utterly different place."

The Founding Fathers did not see free speech or free press as absolute rights, he contends. They believed humans are born with natural rights, including the right to free speech. But when humans live together, they enter into a social contract. And that social contract balances their natural rights against the common good. And the common good often wins.

According to Campbell and other scholars, when the framers talked about a free press, they meant it was free from *prior restraint,* meaning the government could not require a printer to get permission from the government before printing a pamphlet. This idea was to protect Americans from anything similar to a much-hated seventeenth-century English law that forced printers to get licenses from the king before they could print a pamphlet or any other text. I would have needed approval from the king to print this book.

However, once the pamphlet was printed, the Founders believed the government had the ability to punish the writer and printer for what they said. Swearing, for instance, "was thought to be harmful to society, and was thus subject to government regulation," Campbell wrote. "Some states even banned theater performances because of their morally corrupting influence."

If we actually returned to the original meaning of the First Amendment, we'd have to dismantle "a huge swath of modern free speech law," argues Professor Campbell.

Neither the left nor the right would be happy with a true 1790s view of speech. For instance, truly originalist free speech would not cover political donations or spending. This would nix some Supreme Court rulings beloved by modern-day conservatives. For instance, *Citizens United.* In 2010, SCOTUS ruled that the First Amendment prohibits the government from limiting corporations from making expenditures in support of candidates. This, and other rulings, have allowed for a flood of big business money to sway elections.

When I spoke to Professor Campbell, he told me, "There's no evidence that the Founders' limited idea of free speech would cover corporations giving money to political candidates. In fact, many of them were deeply concerned about the corrupting influence of money on politics."

On the other hand, the left would be appalled by the 1790s' restrictive view of what you were allowed to say and write about religion and the government, not to mention the curbs on cussing.

SECTION 2.

It wasn't just the content of free speech that was different. It was the method of communicating. So I decided my first free speech project would be switching to 1790s methods. At the time of our country's founding, free speech meant books, letters, pamphlets, newspapers, and chats at the local tavern. It did not mean viral tweets or doxing or ratioing.

Twitter would have been James Madison's "nightmare," said Jeffrey Rosen, president of the nonpartisan National Constitution Center, on his podcast *We the People*. The idea of people tweeting at politicians would appall him. Madison thought "the people definitely should be listened to, but their views have to be filtered through thoughtful deliberation. So you have to slow things down." The framers wanted speed bumps. Speech should be refined by literate and educated people, such as newspaper editors.

So I've decided to express my First Amendment rights in a slower, more eighteenth-century way. I got out my trusty goose quill. I opened my bottle of black ink (the ink is made from the nests of wasp larvae, by the way). I took several sheets of my bumpy cotton paper, which I'm using instead of the more expensive calfskin parchment the Constitution is written on (geese, wasps, cows—it took a barnyard to produce the Constitution, so I took a moment to appreciate the animals who sacrificed for our freedom).*

I wrote some thoughts on separate pieces of paper. After which, I headed to Midtown Manhattan to hand out these mini-pamphlets on the

---

* There's some debate over whether the Constitution's parchment is made of calfskin or sheepskin. But the head historian at the National Archives said she is confident it is calfskin, so I am going with her.

sidewalk. It was harder than I thought. Most people skillfully avoided my gaze, looking at the pavement, the skyline, anywhere but my face.

Finally, I approached a woman waiting for the light to turn green and read her my analog tweet out loud: "I find it egotistical that we capitalize the word 'I' but not 'he' or 'she' or 'they.'"

"Yeah," she said. "I guess that's interesting."

"Do you want to take my pamphlet?" I asked.

"No, I do not."

Next, I decided I should try some political speech. I spotted two men walking slowly, arm in arm. I ran up to them and read my tweet: "I rank ranked-choice voting as number one among voting systems."

I offered them the wheat-colored paper with my quill writing on it. "We do not speak English so much, but thank you," one said in a Brazilian accent as he took the paper.

A twentysomething guy also took my mini-pamphlet on ranked-choice voting. "I haven't heard of this, but I'm going to google it when I get home." Victory!

As mixed as the reaction was, it felt better than the social media cesspool. Just seeing people face-to-face has a healthy effect.

What would the Founding Fathers have done with social media? Would they have regulated it more than we do? Or imposed more fines or prison sentences for noxious disinformation? Of course, it's impossible to say for sure. And it depends on the Founding Father—these men had a wide range of beliefs.

But it brings up a huge question that I'm wrestling with this year: At what point, if ever, does the technology become so different from the Founding Fathers' time that a certain right no longer applies in the same way?

Liberals would argue that this phenomenon has happened a lot. For instance, guns. They contend that muskets and AR-15s are so fundamentally different, the Second Amendment should not apply to them in the same way. It's an "etymological coincidence" that muskets and AR-15s are referred to by the same word, says Peter Shamshiri, cohost of *5-4*, a podcast about the Supreme Court. Liberals argue it's like taking a law written for bicycles and applying it to an eighteen-wheel truck. Both are vehicles, but they are radically different. (More on muskets later.)

Or consider photography. In 1890, the legendary Justice Louis Brandeis cowrote a famous *Harvard Law Review* article that argued that the new technology of photography was so different from sketching a picture—and such an intrusion on privacy—it required a rethinking of our First Amendment rights. He wrote about a famous scandal of the day—a Broadway actress was photographed while onstage wearing tights, which were considered risqué at the time. Both the actress and Brandeis considered the photo a violation of privacy. Brandeis said photography required new laws.

SECTION 3.

After tackling my method of speech, it was time to eighteenth-centurize the *content* of my speech. I needed to clean it up. Many states in early America had laws prohibiting blasphemy and cursing.

When I first heard this, I was baffled. Blasphemy? Really? I associate blasphemy laws with tyrannical theocratic states, not early America. But, indeed, it's true.

I spent an afternoon reading the entire list of New York State laws from 1801. And there it was, in a section covering moral behavior: It is illegal for anyone to "profanely swear or curse." The punishment? A fine of "thirty seven and a half cents" for each offense (about ten dollars in today's money). And if you couldn't pay, then each offense earned an hour with your arms and head locked in the stocks.

What in God's name was going on? What happened to the separation of church and state? I called Professor Campbell, who explained to me that it was more about maintaining social order, not about the Founders' belief in God.

In his book *1776,* the late historian David McCullough writes that American soldiers were given twenty lashes for striking an officer but thirty lashes for damning an officer. That's right. Damning was worse than punching.

There's evidence that states and towns didn't strictly enforce anti-blasphemy and cursing laws in the late 1700s. It was more like jay-walking nowadays. It wasn't until the 1830s, during a religious revival, that states became stricter and started vigorously prosecuting naughty speech.

But enforced or not, these laws were on the state books at the founding. Since I want to express my First Amendment rights in the most 1790s way possible, I decided to follow the New York speech laws as strictly as I could. I pledged to refrain from blasphemy and cursing. And just to double-check what counts as cursing, I asked Campbell about the f-word. Is it just "damn" or "Jesus" that is forbidden, or would I be banned from saying "Fuck you"?

The f-word is definitely out, Professor Campbell responded. It would disturb public morality. "The justification for the founders is very much a public morality–based justification, not an offense-against-God justification."

In a way, this is great news. I've been growing increasingly alarmed by the speech of my three teenage sons. They pack enough curse words into their conversation to rival a Safdie brothers movie. At dinner the next night, I announced that from now on, "no taking the Lord's name in vain. No 'Jesus.' No 'damn.' No curse words."

I pulled out a mason jar I'd labeled with the New York law.

"If you curse, you have to put thirty-seven and a half cents into this jar," I told them.

The very next afternoon, Zane was trying to connect to the Wi-Fi, but it was on the fritz. "Goddamnit!" he said.

"That's thirty-seven and a half cents in the jar," I said.

"I don't have a half cent," he said.

Understandable since halfpennies were phased out in 1857.

"I'll take thirty-seven cents," I said. "You can owe me the half."

"Why don't we just wait till I curse again, and then I'll pay seventy-five cents?" said Zane.

A couple of hours later, I heard Zane curse again.

"Okay, now put seventy-five cents in the jar," I said.

"Dammit!" he said. Then smiled. "Oops, I just cursed again, so now it's up to a hundred and twelve and a half cents. Let's wait till it's a whole number."

Impudent little shit.

I told him he's lucky we're not in Virginia, where the penalty was eighty-three cents per curse.

I applied the no-cursing rule to myself as well. And though I slipped up, I was somewhat successful at tidying up my language.

I had actually experienced this G-rated speech while working on my Bible book. And weirdly, it had some benefits. I brought my old replacement curse words out of retirement: *fudge, sugar,* and *shoot.* I'd open a jar of salsa, and it would splatter onto my shirt, and I'd start to say the f-word. Then I'd remember to censor myself. So I'd turn it into *fudge* at the last second. When I heard myself say *fudge* out loud, it sounded so folksy, so Jimmy Stewart–ish and dorky, that I couldn't help but smile. My anger receded. Behavior shapes emotions.

As she did during my Bible year, Julie enjoyed mocking me. When I said *fudge,* Julie usually responded with something like, "Hey, Opie! You going fishin' this morning?"

Coincidentally, the other week, I got an email from a reader. He said he was deeply disappointed by my use of curse words in my first book, *The Know-It-All*. "Please do not allow your children to read it—I think their feelings toward their dad could well be diminished. I hope, in your maturity, you will tone down the 'bad' language in future texts."

I emailed him to say I was trying to eliminate curse words because I'm following early-American laws. He wrote back that he was proud of me.

SECTION 4.

When Julie cursed about losing her AirPods, I asked her to drop the thirty-seven and a half cents into the jar, as per early New York State law.

"Wait," she asked, "if your project is about the Constitution, why do I have to follow state laws?"

It's a good question, and one I've been thinking about a lot lately. I believe I have an answer for her. But first, I need to take a quick detour into the tricky relationship between the states and the federal government. It's not a harmonious marriage. I'd call them frenemies, at best.

After winning the Revolution, the states were still seen almost as separate countries. Your average citizen would likely identify more as a Virginian or a Rhode Islander than as an American. Which was part of the problem—the United States were barely united. They were a dysfunctional mess.

Hence the Constitutional Convention. In the face of this chaos, the Founders decided they needed to create a strong national government that could levy taxes, negotiate treaties, and declare war. A real country, in other words. But to get the states to join hands, the Founders needed to assure the states that they would retain a lot of power.

The resulting system is called *federalism*. Not everyone liked this compromise beast. Hamilton worried that it would be impossible for people to "serve two masters." At one point, he advocated all but abolishing the states. And granted, in some ways, it's an odd system—why should morality change depending on our latitude and longitude?

Early on, the states had a ton of power. In fact, the constitutional protections we know and love—freedom of speech, freedom of religion—simply did not apply to states. The Bill of Rights says *Congress* shall make no law abridging rights. The constitutional amendments were designed to rein in the federal government, not the state governments. State lawmakers could—and did—infringe on all sorts of rights.

You know the idea that America cannot have an established religion? The original meaning was that the *country* could not have an official religion. But states? No problem. For many years after the Constitution was ratified, several states continued to have established religions. For instance, Connecticut and New Hampshire were Congregational. New Jersey's established religion was Protestantism in general. Bizarre, right? How did that affect life for early Americans in those states? It depended on the state, but it could mean state taxes were used to support the official church or that there were religious tests to vote, run for office, or serve on a jury.

Ever since the founding, the states and the federal government have been engaged in a wrestling match. Neither is a clear winner. Since the *Dobbs* decision, states have gained power with the overturning of *Roe v. Wade*, which means that states can enact their own laws about abortion. But in the long term, the federal government has accrued more power than the states have. And one huge power shift occurred in the decades following 1868, when the Fourteenth Amendment was ratified.

The Fourteenth Amendment has many parts. But one important section broadened the Bill of Rights to cover both federal and state laws. At least that's what the Supreme Court later ruled this section meant. The fancy term is the *incorporation doctrine*. After the Fourteenth Amendment, if Kentucky tried to establish a state religion, it would be violating the First Amendment. And if Kentucky didn't back down, the president, Congress, or the Supreme Court could make it do so.

Which brings me back to Julie's question: What laws should I be following? State? Federal? And do I really need to stop cursing? After much pondering, I spent an afternoon writing up some rules, a Constitution of the Year of Living Constitutionally:

RULE 1. I shall express my constitutional rights using the technology and mindset of the era when those rights were ratified.

Examples: Handing out pamphlets instead of posting on social media, or bearing a musket, or voting by voice.

RULE 2. I shall follow all federal laws—both past and present—that might be allowed under an ultra-originalist interpretation of the Constitution.

Example: The Sedition Act of 1798. As I will explore in the next section, Congress in John Adams's time passed a national law banning citizens from criticizing the government. It was quite strict. From our modern perspective, and for its opponents, the law violates free speech and the First Amendment. But many of the founding generation considered it perfectly constitutional. To be safe, I will refrain from what Adams and his supporters considered seditious speech.

RULE 3. I shall follow all *state* laws—both past and present—that might be allowed under an ultra-originalist Constitution.

And here's where cursing comes in. If Professor Campbell is right, state anti-cursing laws didn't violate the founding generation's ideas of free speech. So the ultra-originalist First Amendment would allow for anti-cursing laws, whether those laws were made by the federal government or a state government. Many Founding Fathers would approve of state anti-cursing laws. If we return to an ultra-originalist world, these laws could be resurrected. I want to be ready if they are.

RULE 4. I shall only engage in activities that would be possible in an ultra-originalist America. If something has been tainted by a potentially unconstitutional agency or object, I should steer clear.

This self-imposed rule is the one that scares me the most. It could really mess with my life. For instance, some hard-core originalists argue that federal agencies such as the Food and Drug Administration are violating the Constitution. They contend that the Constitution only allows Congress, not regulatory agencies, to make laws. If this argument is true, then I'll need to avoid anything tainted by unconstitutional rules, such as those by the FDA. Which means what? Maybe that I can't eat food unless I grow it myself in the box of soil on my windowsill? I'm going to have to work up to it.

RULE 5. In case people find it helpful, I shall alert others when they do something that would not be protected under an ultra-originalist interpretation of the Constitution.

This is why I sent off a note to a crossword puzzle editor at *The New York Times*. I told the editor that they should not have used *damn* as an answer. This rule promises to make me a lot of friends.

There's my road map. When I clarified it to myself, I felt more settled. But also more terrified. This project is more daunting than I thought.

SECTION 5.

Back to my First Amendment freedoms and lack thereof. Cursing is off the table. What about political speech? In a 1964 decision, Supreme Court justice William Brennan said "the central meaning" of the First Amendment is to protect Americans who criticize the government.

But many scholars say that wasn't true at the founding. The idea was much more complicated. Partly, as always, it depended on which Founding Father you asked. This is one of the huge challenges with determining original meaning. As with today, different Founders, and different sectors of the public, had wildly different views.

There was an enormous split between, on the one hand, the Federalists (the party of John Adams and the followers of George Washington) and, on the other hand, the Democratic-Republicans (the party of Thomas Jefferson and James Madison). Both parties were made up of Founding Fathers and their peers, but they disagreed on many topics.

"Leading Federalists thought that it was impossible to attack members of the government without attacking the very foundation of government itself," writes Peter McNamara in *The First Amendment Encyclopedia*. The infant nation was too fragile. It needed to be protected from antigovernment speech. Which is why John Adams and Congress passed the 1798 Sedition Act, a law they undoubtedly considered perfectly constitutional. The Sedition Act said that Americans could be punished for "false, scandalous, and malicious" statements against the government. And it resulted in dozens of prosecutions.

A Vermont congressman named Matthew Lyon wrote a newspaper editorial saying that Adams had "an unbounded thirst for ridiculous pomp, foolish adulation and selfish avarice." Those words earned Lyon four months in prison—after which he returned to Congress.

Another man, Luther Baldwin, made an illegal ass joke. Or technically an illegal arse joke. In 1798, Adams's presidential boat landed in Newark and was greeted with a lavish ceremony, complete with bell ringing and cannon firing. Outside a tavern, Baldwin cracked, "I wish one of the [cannonballs] would pass through his arse." He was fined $150 and thrown in jail for two months until he paid. Can you imagine if this law were around today? Prisons would be overflowing with talk radio hosts and late-night comedians.

On the other hand, Jefferson's party was more amenable to political free speech—up to a point. When Jefferson defeated Adams in the 1800 election, it was partly because the public thought Adams was using the Sedition Act to punish political enemies.

Jefferson allowed the act to expire. You can find plenty of quotations from Jefferson endorsing freer speech, such as his contention that "speech limited is speech lost." But as is often the case with Jefferson, he didn't always practice what he preached. And his complaint was mainly with federal speech laws, not state laws. As historian Richard Brookhiser wrote in his book *What Would the Founders Do?*, when Jefferson was elected president, "he conducted his own backdoor war on press critics whom he considered liars, under the guise of concern for journalistic standards." States had their own laws against seditious libel, and Jefferson wrote to friendly governors, suggesting that they initiate "a few prosecutions of the most prominent offenders." He argued that clamping down "would have a wholesome effect in restoring the integrity of the presses (Jefferson would muzzle the press to save it)."

So what is *originalist* political speech? It depends on which founding-era interpretation you choose. To be totally safe, I decided I should be super strict about antigovernment speech. And as a service, I should alert my fellow citizens.

I chose to do it via social media (hypocritically enough). I went on Twitter, as it was called when I started writing this book, and opened an account under the name @OriginalDude89.

I replied to people calling President Biden or Republican senator Lindsey Graham traitors. "You realize your seditious comments are not protected by the First Amendment, at least as it was conceived of by some of the Founders, right? You could be prosecuted if this were the 1790s. Please remove."

One responded, "Lmao! Whatever dude!"

SECTION 6.

There are plenty of other differences between free speech then and now. Some states had laws banning plays since they might corrupt American minds. And other entertainment was taboo as well. One 1802 New Jersey law forbade folks from performing "tricks, juggling, sleight of hand, or feats of uncommon dexterity and agility of body."

I made a note to reprimand jugglers, magicians, and gymnasts later in my year. But in the meantime, I would use this fact to control my sons' morally dubious TV viewing. I told Lucas that the First Amendment does not necessarily protect his right to watch *Love Is Blind*. Lucas ignored me.

How did we end up with this much more powerful version of free speech we enjoy today? Weirdly, we can thank, in part, Jehovah's Witnesses. In the 1930s and 1940s, the group filed more than twenty suits that made it to the Supreme Court. The cases were all about the First Amendment: the religious sect's right to proselytize controversial beliefs, for example, and their right to avoid saying the Pledge of Allegiance in schools. They won many of the cases and expanded our First Amendment rights.

In sum, thank goodness for the modern conception of free speech. We have limits today, including fraud, perjury, and threatening the president—or vice president—of the United States. But we have fewer limits than we did at the country's origin. I can blaspheme and curse and make fun of politicians without fear of breaking the law. And I believe that makes for a better, happier, if saltier, society.

At the same time, we've seen a regression of free speech. Suzanne Nossel, the CEO of the writers' organization PEN America, says our modern conception of free speech is being impinged from both political sides. "The left is too quick to want to silence those who offend or threaten them. The right—led by [Florida governor Ron] DeSantis—is going a major step further, legitimizing the use of government power to render certain books, ideas, and viewpoints off-limits. The greatest casualty in this battle may be neither progressive nor conservative ideas, but the principle of free speech itself," Nossel wrote in an editorial on CNN.

I'd only make one change to Nossel's statement: the principle of *modern* free speech. Originalist free speech is far different from, and less appealing than, what I'd hoped. I'd wanted the Founders to be unabashed First Amendment warriors who believed that government censorship was a cardinal sin. But that's not the case. My first encounters with the Founders' idea of free speech were unsettling. Still, I'm holding off on making final conclusions. Free speech is such a huge issue and so hotly debated now, I pledge to return to it in the coming months.

SECTION 7.

It had been six weeks of living constitutionally, so I thought it was time again for some more Franklin-style self-examination and reflections. Below is my list of what I'm liking and what I'm not.

Huzzahs

THE CONSTITUTION IS EVERYWHERE.

I'm trying to avoid fixating on current events, but I'm reading enough to keep up. And it's astounding how much of the news relates to the Constitution and the battles over its interpretation.

Everyone claims the Constitution as their own. Well, almost everyone. Recently, former president Donald Trump repeated his charge that the election was stolen. But he took it to a new level and said the fraud "allows for the termination of all rules, regulations, and articles, even those found in the Constitution. . . . Our great 'Founders' did not want, and would not condone, False & Fraudulent Elections!" This bizarre claim—that the Founders would want to overturn their own Constitution—earned a rare rebuke from some of his fellow Republicans.

Regardless, I feel I'm slowly becoming more equipped to tackle these constitutional controversies.

ONE OF MY SONS IS ACTUALLY SUPPORTING MY PROJECT!

I'm taking my quill on the road nowadays. I bought an eighteenth-century version of a laptop. It's a thin wooden box called a writing slope, inside of which you keep your quill, ink bottle, and paper. I tote my desk around. Yesterday, we went to a Chinese restaurant, and I signed the check with my quill. Zane and Lucas were mortified. But interestingly, Jasper loved it. He likes these public displays of absurdity, which he thinks are performance art and remind him of his favorite comedian, Eric André. It's a weird feeling. I've never had someone in my family be so supportive of my tendency toward this type of behavior.

A Huzzah and a Grievance Combined

EARLY-AMERICAN NEWSPAPERS.

I'm attempting to cut down on twenty-first-century news and focus more on eighteenth-century news. I've abandoned ritually checking CNN, NPR, and *The New York Times*. Instead, every afternoon, I spend thirty minutes reading issues of Ben Franklin's *Pennsylvania Gazette* from 1790.

First of all, confining my media consumption to half an hour a day has been beneficial. In my normal life, I click on news sites every ten minutes from morning till night, and the fire hose of negative stories greatly contributes to my anxiety and gloominess. The eighteenth-century news schedule is much better for the pursuit of happiness.

Reading a 1790 newspaper is an efficient way to see how utterly different life was at the time. I'm gaining an appreciation for stuff we take for granted—like street addresses. I read an article on the bold new idea of assigning numbers to Philadelphia's houses. A huge leap forward! Imagine saying an actual street address instead of "that red house past the pond with that big manure pile in the yard." I read another article on this new invention called "the parachute," which was tested by tossing a pig, a goat, and a chicken out of a hot-air balloon. (The animals landed safely, if a bit perplexed.)

The *Gazette* provides glimpses of early America at its best—such as the article on George Washington's embrace of America's minority Catholic community. The paper wrote: "Nothing will contribute more to the rising greatness of America, than that unbounded toleration and protection she holds forth to all sects and descriptions of men."

However, you also see early America at its worst. Every issue has at least one advertisement offering a reward for—and a description of—a runaway enslaved person. The ads appear next to other ads for fabric and horse carriages, as if they were somehow morally equivalent. It's sickening.

ARTICLE IV

Quartering Soldiers

SECTION 1.

I had no idea it would be so difficult to find a soldier who would be willing to quarter in my New York apartment. I've been searching for weeks, and it's been rejection after rejection. The latest attempt was in Times Square. I spotted a group of three sailors in their white uniforms, one with a green duffel bag slung over his shoulder. I approached them.

"Can I ask you a quick question?"

They stopped and nodded. "I'm trying to express my constitutional rights—including the Third Amendment."

They were listening, but one of the sailors was giving me some side-eye.

I continued: "The Third Amendment says that I don't have to quarter soldiers in my house without my consent. But if I *want* to quarter soldiers, if I *do* give my consent, then that's my right as well. So in honor of the Third Amendment, I want to invite you to quarter at my apartment. By which I mean sleep over at my apartment free of charge. We have a foldout couch!"

My proposal elicited a mixed reaction. One of the soldiers shot me a look that said *I know you have a collection of cuff links made from the teeth of your victims.* But another of the sailors, the one with the duffel, seemed flattered.

"That'd be dope," he said. "But we have to be back on the ship by midnight. Thanks, though." He held out his fist for a goodbye fist bump.

Other attempts had also been dead ends. I got no takers from the "Free lodging for soldiers" ad I placed on Craigslist. I almost closed the deal with a British soldier who worked at the United Nations, but then UK military public relations got involved. I explained to the PR woman that it would show how much relations between the United States and the United Kingdom have improved since the eighteenth century. She was unmoved. "I don't see an upside for us."

To me, there were plenty of upsides. I'd get to talk about the Constitution and America with a member of the military. I'd get to check off another amendment from my list. If necessary, I could even flex my Third Amendment muscle and kick the soldier or sailor out if they misbehaved.

I also figured that providing shelter to a traveler was a nice Federalist-era thing to do. Travelers often stayed in strangers' houses. There were some taverns where you could sleep, but if you were a traveler, you'd often knock on the door and ask for a bed. It was expected the owner would say yes. It was considered their duty.

At least it was considered their duty for a little while. As Ben Franklin famously wrote in *Poor Richard's Almanack,* "Fish and visitors stink in three days."

SECTION 2.

Nowadays, the Third Amendment is famous mainly for being one of the more irrelevant parts of the Constitution. The text reads, "No soldier shall, in time of peace be quartered in any house without the consent of the Owner." I've heard it called the "runt piglet" of the amendments. It's a perpetual punch line, the Bill of Rights version of Nickelback or the PT Cruiser.

The Onion once ran a satirical article about the National Anti-Quartering Association, America's foremost Third Amendment rights group. The article quotes the president of NAQA: "Year after year, we have sent a loud and clear message to the federal government: Hands off our cottages, livery stables, and haylofts."

But of course, in the founding era, involuntary quartering was a huge deal. (By the way, to *quarter* someone had two separate meanings:

First, to provide lodging, and second, to carve up criminals as punishment, as in *drawing and quartering*. Both were problematic practices in the eighteenth century, but the Third Amendment refers to the former.) In the years leading up to the Revolutionary War, the British forced the colonists to turn their homes into unpaid Airbnbs for the redcoats. The 1774 British Quartering Act was among the main grievances mentioned in the Declaration of Independence. The colonists nicknamed it one of the "Intolerable Acts."

"They were not good guests, to put it mildly. They weren't making their beds and cleaning up after dinner," says Jay Wexler, a law professor at Boston University and author of *The Odd Clauses: Understanding the Constitution Through Ten of Its Most Curious Provisions*. Instead, the unwanted British troops would eat the colonists' food, drink their booze, and occasionally kick the colonists out of their own homes.

The Founding Fathers wanted to make sure such violations would never happen again. "In some ways, the Third Amendment is the most successful amendment," says Wexler. "It works so well, it is rarely mentioned. If only other amendments worked so smoothly."

Rarely mentioned, indeed. The Supreme Court has referenced the Third Amendment in just a handful of decisions in its 232 years. One of its few appearances came in *Griswold v. Connecticut,* a 1965 case about contraception and privacy. The Third Amendment was brought up as proof of the Constitution's strong privacy protections in your home.

Fans of the Third Amendment—and they do exist—say that it's still relevant because of its "a man's home is his castle" symbolism. Warren Burger, the chief justice in the 1970s, was a Third Amendment booster and wrote a foreword to a book on its history. "The philosophy embodied in the Third Amendment is derived from the American colonists' fear of British military power. Though that danger is long past, the Third Amendment still embodies the same basic principles: that the military must be subject to civilian control, and that the government cannot intrude into private homes without good reason."

Some Third Amendment cheerleaders even argue we need to expand its interpretation, just as we expanded the Fourth Amendment's clause against unreasonable search and seizure. The Fourth Amendment originally applied just to physical objects, such as paper-and-ink documents, but now includes the contents of your smartphone. Some law professors have argued that maybe we should expand the Third Amendment to include protection from spyware. Or SWAT teams coming to your house. Or emergency workers entering your home during a natural disaster.

This idea of an expanded Third Amendment, as historian Gordon Wood writes, "is not a popular view." The amendment remains obscure. At least for now. "But who knows the future," Wexler says. "The weird parts of the Constitution have a strange tendency to resurface. Look at the emoluments clause, which was used in two lawsuits against Trump. Who thought that would come back?"*

SECTION 3.

A few weeks after the Times Square sailors rejected me, I received some exciting and surprising news. A friend's friend who is in the Army was coming to New York and was looking for a place to stay.

Finally, I would be able to quarter a soldier with consent—and kick him out if he acted like a rude redcoat. I was thrilled.

Julie was not as thrilled about exercising our Third Amendment rights.

"Can't he stay here when one of the kids is at camp?" she asked.

"He needs quarters next week," I said.

---

* The emoluments clause is in Article I, Section 9. It prevents U.S. officeholders from accepting gifts from foreign states. Trump was accused of violating the clause by receiving money from foreign government officials for staying at his hotels.

"Is he going to wear combat boots?"

Our downstairs neighbors constantly complain about heavy footsteps, and the clomping of military boots could get ugly.

"We can ask him to take off his shoes," I said.

She finally agreed he could come for a couple of nights. Just as long as he was out before Ben Franklin's three-day rule.

Our soldier is named Arjun, and he could be the politest quarterer ever. On a Wednesday night, he arrived from Miami in his fatigues, pulling his rolling suitcase. He brought flowers and thanked me for opening my home.

"The redcoats would not have brought flowers to the colonists," I said.

"It's weird that I'm playing the part of the redcoat in this situation," Arjun said. "Because I'm pretty sure redcoats have oppressed my ancestors." He is the son of immigrants from India. (I've changed his name and some details at his request since he works in Army Intelligence and tries to stay low profile.)

He was friendly, but he had an air of authority and told my kids to call him Captain. He knew about my project and was eager to tell me his thoughts on America and the Constitution.

In keeping with my year's eighteenth-century theme, I'd found a restaurant that delivers early-American cuisine. Arjun ordered the shepherd's pie, a mixture of mashed potatoes and beef.

When the dinner arrived, Arjun asked, "Do you have any hot sauce—like Cholula maybe?" He figured the mashed potatoes could use a little more kick.

I loved the idea that Arjun, a man of Indian descent, was eating British food and asking for a Mexican condiment while quartering in a Jewish guy's home. It seemed appropriately multiculturally American. Well, appropriately for today's America, at least.

"Sorry, we don't have any hot sauce," I said. "But I do have these for you." I grabbed a bottle of rice vinegar and a canister of kosher salt from the counter and handed it to him. "The first Quartering Act by the British required colonists to provide bedding, candles, booze—as well as salt and vinegar. So I thought I'd try to be the best quarters-provider I can be."

"Uh, thanks. I'll take these home."

I got out my quill pen and some sheets of cotton paper and asked Arjun how he came to join the military. He told me his tale as I scribbled notes. When he graduated from college, Arjun got a job as an analyst at a prestigious financial institution. But he wasn't happy. "I said to myself, there has to be something more to life than making wealthy people wealthier. I wanted more meaning in my life."

In college, he had volunteered for the political campaign of a well-loved veteran. He heard the man talk about the powerful sense of being part of something bigger. He listened as the man explained that rights come with responsibilities, and he decided to enlist.

What did Arjun's parents say when he chose to join up?

"They were so opposed," Arjun said. "My mom said, '*Whyyyyyy?*'"

Partly to appease his parents, he didn't enlist full time, at least at first. He joined the reserves, meaning he had to commute to a base in Virginia every other weekend for three years to undergo training.

"You know the old Army ads that said 'Army of One'?" he asked me. "It was the exact opposite of that. It was about being part of a community."

Arjun relished meeting a wide cross section of Americans—plumbers, doctors, firefighters, and mechanics. "It brought me right out of my bubble," he said. "I love going to the airport, and you would see someone in a uniform, and you had an immediate bond, even if that person was totally different from you."

Arjun continued, "We live in a very individualist society, which has its advantages. But I think we need to balance it with more of a sense of the greater good. I'm a fan of action. The Constitution isn't a piece of paper. It's a verb, it's action."

SECTION 4.

As we ate, I poured two glasses of Madeira, a Portuguese fortified wine that was one of the Founding Fathers' favorite alcoholic beverages. (It became popular because it was exempt from taxes, thanks to a special deal with Portugal.)

"I have some eighteenth-century toasts for us," I said.

"Let's hear them."

"Freedom from mobs as well as kings," I said.

"That's prescient. We could use that today," Arjun said.

"A little elitist," I said. "But yeah, I guess prescient."

Arjun lifted his glass.

"I have one more," I said. "To the enemies of our country! May they have cobweb breeches, a porcupine saddle, a hard-trotting horse, and an eternal journey."

"Now that sounds like a military toast we give today. Not the horse part, but the spirit of it."

We clinked our Madeira glasses.

Arjun resumed his story. He spent weekends at a base in Virginia for three years studying army intelligence—after which he was deployed for several months in the Middle East, where he worked at decoding enemy computer drives.

When that stint was over, he returned to the United States, moved to Florida, and took a new job in the entertainment industry. But he remains a reservist, spending weekends on a base.

"I think reservists are underrated," he said. "They're an important bridge between civilians and the military. The civilian-soldier divide is not good for the country."

I told him that being a reservist is true to the Founding Fathers' vision. The Constitution's framers had a fear of standing armies from decades of British rule. They much preferred the militia model, where soldiers would congregate and train once every few months.

In fact, if we were living in 1800, both my eighteen-year-old son, Jasper, and I would be in the state militia. It was a requirement. All males between the ages of sixteen and sixty were required to report for training four times a year and had to have their own musket.

I'm relieved that this requirement no longer exists, but I do see at least one advantage to it. Mandatory service acted as a glue for the nation. I sometimes wonder if requiring national service might help our society. It doesn't have to be military. It could be more in the AmeriCorps model. But at least it would give Americans a shared experience.

SECTION 5.

Arjun stayed two nights. It turns out that soldiers make excellent houseguests, or at least this one did. Arjun was extremely tidy, making his bed and keeping his clothes in his suitcase, spending his days out of the house meeting with clients.

The only problem came on the final forenoon, when Arjun was still asleep at nine o'clock and Julie needed the room. It's her office, and she wanted to get to work.

"Should we play reveille to wake him up?" she suggested.

It was a great idea. I got out my fife—I had bought an eighteenth-century-style wooden fife a few weeks earlier and had been halfheartedly practicing. I tried to play reveille. It sounded like a dying fax machine (an old reference, but I'm trying to live in the past, so maybe it works).

A few minutes later, Arjun emerged, fully dressed.

"I appreciated your attempt," he said. "You were playing it pretty meekly, but you did try."

I didn't want to go full blast, thinking it might be impolite. Likewise, I told him I had trouble being a hard-ass and expressing my full Third Amendment rights.

"A friend of mine suggested I kick you out at two in the morning last night, just to show that I could do such a thing under the Third Amendment," I told Arjun. "But you are too nice."

"If it would help, I'd be happy to be kicked out at two A.M. I could stay another night and you could do it tonight?"

What a good soldier. Willing to sacrifice his comfort for the greater cause. I thanked him but said it wasn't necessary.

Quartering a soldier had been a time-consuming exercise, what with finding the soldier and prepping my quarters. But meanwhile, I'd been busy with other constitutional projects. A quick update of what is going well and not so well:

Huzzah

THE ELECTION CAKE PROJECT.
I've made progress in my plot to bring back the election cake. Handing out cake may not save democracy on its own, but it at least gives me a little hope. This campaign can be my little candle in the darkness, even if the sun is setting on our political system.

My goal is to get at least one person in all fifty states to bake a cake for the November 2023 elections. I consulted my niece, Ally, the one with the side hustle of baking cakes for birthdays and anniversaries. She said she's ready to help with organizing. I explained that we'd send potential bakers the 1796 recipe—the one with cloves and raisins—and they could adapt it how they saw fit, while still preserving some historical authenticity.

"No, that's a terrible recipe," she said. "Just start from scratch with a new recipe. No one wants cloves."

"But the cloves are important," I said. "The point is to pay homage to the tradition, but update it." I explained the bakers could even give it a twist, depending on their heritage. An election babka with cloves. Or a Filipino election ube cake with cloves.

"I'm telling you," she said, "forget the cloves."

I realized that my niece and I were having a debate about evolution versus revolution, but for baked goods. I wanted to keep some of the tradition but update it. She wanted to totally revamp the tradition. She's the Thomas Jefferson, who once said we should have a new constitution every nineteen years. I'm James Madison, who says work with what we've got and try to improve it.

We leave the cloves issue unresolved. The bigger point is, Project Cake is a go.

Grievance

GENERAL IGNORANCE (MINE AND OTHERS, BUT MOSTLY MINE).
Studying the Constitution has made me even more aware of how little I knew (and still don't know) about how government works. I partly blame myself and my failure to pay proper attention. But I also see it as a failure of my education. Why didn't high school and college teach more of this? We need more civics in schools. Or not even civics, since that sounds so dutiful. Citizenship. We need to be taught how to be better citizens. How can we change our society for the better? What actions can we take?

Maybe I should have had Mr. Hand as a history teacher. He's the teacher in *Fast Times at Ridgemont High,* which we watched this week as the family movie (it almost counts as a period drama). I was happy to be reminded of the scene where Mr. Hand at least tried to teach the Constitution.

"The Platt Amendment was an amendment to the U.S. Constitution," Mr. Hand told his students, with the exception of Jeff Spicoli, Sean Penn's surfer character who was too stoned to attend class.

Wait. The Platt Amendment? I'd never heard of that. I googled it as we watched the movie. Turns out it was *not* an amendment to the U.S. Constitution. It was a 1903 treaty with Cuba.

Now there's some irony, I thought to myself. The screenwriter was presumably trying to show how kids are uninterested in civics and government. But in doing so, the screenwriter botched a basic fact about civics and government, proving the screenwriter was as ignorant as the kids. To paraphrase Spicoli, it's bogus.

The Overly Supreme Court

SECTION 1.

It was 4:30 A.M. on February 27, and I was freezing, exhausted, and full of hope. I was standing in the dark on a sidewalk outside the Supreme Court of the United States. I was holding a bright green piece of paper that said "Admission card number 11." Which meant I was eleventh in line to get a seat to watch the highest court in the land. My odds were good.

A few weeks ago, I'd decided that since I'm doing a project on the Constitution, it would be wise to get an up-close look at the nine people who get to determine what the document means.

The Supreme Court meets every year from October to June or July and agrees to hear about 60 to 70 cases. You can observe the oral arguments in person if you can secure one of the 439 seats in the courtroom. Most seats are taken up by lawyers, journalists, VIPs, and people involved in the cases. But fifty spots are reserved for the public.

You've got to work for those seats, though. It's a first-come, first-served system, so you have to line up early—at least one day before if it's a high-profile case. For low-profile cases, arriving at around 5 A.M. is pretty safe.

I'd chosen a safely obscure case. It's about identity theft and health-care fraud. A few weeks before, the Court had heard the Harvard affirmative action case, which was this session's equivalent of a Marvel blockbuster. The case I hoped to see was like an indie with actors straight out of Juilliard.

I took a train from New York, slept at a hotel for four hours, put on six layers of shirts and sweaters, and arrived before dawn. I was behind Numbers 9 and 10: two Cornell University students, both daughters of immigrants (from Armenia and China, respectively).

"We're just SCOTUS nerds," they said when I asked why they were here. They were studying prelaw and wanted to take this pilgrimage during their February break. Look at Gen Z go!

Ahead of them was Number 7, a bearded man with a Yankees cap. He was lying on the sidewalk, wrapped in a blue tarp, still asleep, a duffel bag of supplies by his side. He knew what he was doing.

A bit later, Number 7 woke up and folded his tarp.

"You look like you're an expert at this," I said. "Have you seen a lot of cases?"

"I've actually never seen one."

"No?"

"Keep this under your hat, but I'm a professional line waiter."

What's that?

"People pay me to wait in line for them. I guess you would have figured that out when you saw the people come to take my place." He told me that the guy next to him, Number 6, in a folding beach chair, was also a pro.

I was furious. I had gotten up at 3:30 A.M., abstained from water for fourteen hours to avoid trips to the bathroom, and was trying to keep warm in the near-freezing dawn by bouncing on my toes. I was paying my dues.

Then I discovered that some patrician who shelled out two hundred dollars can waltz in at 9 A.M. after a restful night's sleep and have the same experience. That seems highly undemocratic. SCOTUS is supposed to be the bastion of fairness and equity, and yet there's this corrupt bribe-tainted system to get access. It's un-American. Well, at least it's contrary to America's higher ideals, if not its historical reality. (Example: During the Civil War, wealthy Northerners and Southerners would hire people to take their place in the military.)

"What's the longest you've had to wait?" I asked Number 7.

"My record is a hundred thirty-eight hours," he said. It was for Rob Reiner. The Hollywood director—and ten of his friends—wanted to watch a landmark gay rights case in person.

Part of me was annoyed that I didn't know about this loophole myself, but another part of me, the more noble part, felt outraged. Wait-gate, as I named it, fed into the general skepticism I already had about SCOTUS.

After spending weeks reading up on the history of the Supreme Court, I'd come to believe that these nine unelected people have far too much control over how we live our lives. Today's SCOTUS is undoubtedly not what the Founders had imagined.

In fact, when I asked author and Stanford history professor Jonathan Gienapp what would most surprise the Founding Fathers about today's America, he said SCOTUS's vast powers would be a list topper.

"We've created this alternative strange world in which the judiciary alone has supreme enforcement of the Constitution, which would have shocked most people at the founding," said Gienapp, author of *The Second Creation: Fixing the American Constitution in the Founding Era.* The Court has gained power at the expense of both Congress and the president.

Back in the line, I watched the sky turn from black to purple to pink, revealing the Marble Palace, as it's sometimes called. I looked at the Supreme Court building, with its soaring columns, its famous gleaming-white steps, its carved triangular pediment. It is no doubt awe-inspiring and gorgeous. A little too awe-inspiring, in some folks' opinions. The building was controversial from the start. Construction began in 1932 as a replacement for its humbler digs, a room on the second floor of the Capitol. (Which was several rungs up from the very first location—a converted marketplace in New York City, where the noisy butchers had to be kicked out of the area during Court sessions.)

Justice Harlan Fiske Stone, who was on the Court in the 1930s, called the new building "almost bombastically pretentious . . . wholly inappropriate for a quiet group of old boys such as the Supreme Court," which I kind of agree with, except for the casual sexism part. Another justice said the building was so pompous it felt as if the justices should enter the courtroom riding on elephants.

But former president and then Chief Justice William Howard Taft pushed it through as his pet project. He thought the Court was underappreciated and wanted the judiciary's building to rival the Capitol and the White House. He hired architect Cass Gilbert and instructed him to go as regal and Greco-Roman as possible. Only the best materials! The builders got the marble for the columns from Italy with the personal help of Benito Mussolini, himself a fan of pomp.

Pomp and pageantry do have their place. They make people—both citizens and the justices themselves—take the institution seriously. But I wonder if the skeptics have a point: Do we need a faux Roman temple that gives us the feeling we should be sacrificing oxen to Chief Justice John Roberts?

SECTION 2.

At 9 A.M., an officer told Numbers 1 through 50 to follow her. She led us to the far side of the building as we chattered excitedly.

I walked alongside a high school kid from Georgia who had come with his dad—they're the ones who hired the line waiters. It became clear he was a SCOTUS junkie. "You think Clarence Thomas will talk?" he asked me. "He's been talking a lot since quarantine."

I think he will, I told him. The high schooler seemed pleased.

We passed through a series of security checks and metal detectors inside and outside the building. One spectator spent several minutes arguing with the guard about whether his outerwear counts as a jacket, which requires removal, or a sweater, which doesn't. I guess this shouldn't be surprising. When you've got people who wake up at 4 A.M. to visit a court of law, you've got to assume they have a knack for legalistic thinking.

After we passed security, an usher wearing a blue blazer and a pearl necklace told us to follow her. She led us to our seats—which were not ringside, to say the least. Mine was as far from the action as geometrically possible, my back against the marble wall. There would be much neck craning in the hours to come.

As we waited for the justices to enter, I looked around the room—thick red curtains, gold trimmings, a marble frieze near the ceiling featuring famous people from legal history, including Confucius, Napoleon, and a bare-chested, very swole Draco (the Athenian lawgiver who lent his name to the adjective draconian).

The court's grandiosity was doing its job on my psyche. Despite my Supreme Court skepticism, I still felt intimidated, even a little reverent. In this space, Thurgood Marshall won *Brown v. Board of Education*, which struck down segregated schools. In this space, gay marriage was recognized as a guaranteed right.

I was sitting next to the high school kid as he fidgeted with his red tie, flipping the end up and down. He chatted with me about SCOTUS, telling me about Clarence Thomas's love of the Privileges and Immunities Clause. He looked at his watch.

"We should hear from Gail Curley soon," he said.

"Who?"

"The marshal, the one who says 'Oyez, oyez, oyez.' "

And moments later, there was a high beep, followed by Gail Curley's voice telling us, in Middle English, to "hear, hear, hear!" Everyone rose to their feet. Gail Curley then encouraged people to "draw near." (I would have, if that were an option.)

The nine black-robed justices filed in and sat in their black leather chairs. They looked kind of small compared with the forty-four-foot red curtain that serves as a backdrop. Back when the building first opened, one justice said that he and his colleagues looked like "nine black beetles in the Temple of Karnak."

SECTION 3.

Before today's main event, let me step back to talk about how SCOTUS became SCOTUS. How did these nine people in front of me become the ultimate arbiters of what is constitutional? How do they have so much power that *The Onion* can fairly satirize them as saying "we wear gold crowns now."

The court's outsize power disturbs critics on both the left and the right. It goes beyond politics. And the tale of how it happened is a strange one.

When the Founding Fathers wrote the Constitution, most of them envisioned the judicial branch as the least powerful branch of government. Third among equals. It's not a coincidence that the Constitution's section about the courts appears third, after the sections about the Congress and the president. And it's by far the shortest of the three—a mere one-sixth the length devoted to Congress.

Here's just one example of how weak the Supreme Court's early reputation was: Sometimes one side couldn't even be bothered to show up. In 1793, a merchant sued the state of Georgia in the Supreme Court. Georgia refused to send a lawyer, deeming the Court unworthy of their valuable time.

According to Professor Gienapp, most Founding Fathers envisioned all three branches—the president, the Congress, and the Supreme Court—weighing in on what is constitutional. It would be a joint decision. SCOTUS was a check on power but not the only voice.

How much of a check? As always, it depended on which Founder you talked to. Hamilton was a Supreme Court fan, writing in *The Federalist Papers* that the judiciary must be allowed to declare all acts that were "contrary to . . . the Constitution void." Jefferson was a Supreme skeptic. Jefferson wrote to a friend who had endorsed a strong SCOTUS: "You seem to consider the judges as the ultimate arbiters of all constitutional questions; a very dangerous doctrine indeed, and one which would place us under the despotism of an oligarchy."

Regardless, Gienapp told me that most Founders did not believe the Court should have the final say in constitutional matters. The Court should have modest "judicial review," meaning it should play a part in deciding what is constitutional. But, Gienapp says, the Founders would be stunned by the situation we have now, which many call "judicial supremacy," where the nine justices on the Court are the ultimate arbiters.

Professor Gienapp told me to consider the biggest constitutional controversy of the founding era: the establishment of the Bank of the United States. Hamilton loved the idea of a central bank. Jefferson's camp saw it as a terrifying step toward autocracy and blatantly unconstitutional. Congress debated the bank vigorously, and eventually passed a bill that would establish the bank. President Washington approved it. And SCOTUS? They stayed on the sideline. They had zero input. "Nobody had the slightest sense that there would be this other option that exists after Congress has approved it and the president has signed the bill," Gienapp said. Unlike now. If this happened today, there would likely be federal lawsuits about the bill's constitutionality, with SCOTUS having the final say.

So how did the power grab occur?

Often the credit or blame goes to John Marshall, the legendary fourth chief justice. He took over the bench in 1801 and stayed on for thirty-four years. He was a brilliant and likable character who unified the court. Physically, in fact. He made all the justices live together in a boardinghouse in Washington, D.C., sort of like a highbrow frat house. And like at most frats, there was a lot of drinking.

Marshall established a rule that the justices could only drink if it was raining. But here's the catch: Even if the sun was shining outside the court's window, Marshall would say, "Our jurisdiction is so vast that it might be raining somewhere." And out the bottles of Madeira would come. It was sort of the precursor to the "It's five o'clock somewhere" argument. And just more proof of Marshall's genius for finding loopholes.

In 1803, Marshall presided over a case called *Marbury v. Madison*.

The details are a little tricky, so I won't go into them here, but in the decision, Marshall's Court invalidated a congressional law.

The traditional narrative says that Marshall's decision was a stake in the ground. A huge flex. It established SCOTUS as the final word of what is or is not constitutional. But Gienapp and other scholars say this is incorrect. We have misinterpreted the case and given it a modern spin. Marshall was much more modest. He just wanted SCOTUS to be in the mix.

Regardless of whether Marshall believed SCOTUS should have the final say, one thing is certain: Marshall's Court remained much less powerful than today's Court. Marshall's Court never again invalidated a congressional law. Nowadays, SCOTUS routinely invalidates laws.

The Court's real power grabs occurred much later. One jump took place in the early 1900s, when the conservative court shot down many congressional laws protecting workers (more on that later). Another leap came after World War II with the Warren Court. Earl Warren was chief justice from 1953 to 1969. He was appointed by Dwight D. Eisenhower, a Republican president. But Warren disappointed Eisenhower by moving to the left and becoming a liberal hero.

During the Warren Court, SCOTUS ruled on dozens of landmark civil rights cases. SCOTUS shot down public school segregation with *Brown v. Board of Education* in 1954. It halted bans on interracial marriages, expanded the right to privacy, and strengthened the rights of criminal suspects. The Court struck down several congressional laws as unconstitutional. Liberals weren't complaining about SCOTUS's possible overreach. Why would they? They were getting what they wanted.

But then Warren retired, and a couple of other liberal justices left. Nixon appointed replacements, and suddenly America had a majority-conservative court. The conservatives would retain a majority for decades and wield this expanded SCOTUS power with huge implications—including, most obviously, *Bush v. Gore,* when the Court decided who would be president of the United States.

Many justices still downplay their power. When John Roberts was nominated in 2005, he said, "It's my job to call balls and strikes . . . judges are like umpires."* But in reality, the justices are more like umpires who call balls and strikes but who also decide with each throw where the strike zone is and claim they have access to Abner Doubleday's mind and that Abner Doubleday hated knuckleballs, because balls didn't do that when baseball was invented.

As I write this, the court is at a low ebb of public opinion. According to polls, most Americans view the justices not as objective and impartial arbiters but as men and women who are loyal to their party. The suspicion is that they reason backward. They have a political outcome they want (e.g., looser gun regulations), and they cherry-pick parts of the Constitution to back it up.

I realize I've come out swinging against the court's current power. But I'm not opposed to moderate judicial review. The court *should* provide a check on power. An independent judiciary is a good thing. But it should also be held more accountable to the will of the people. One simple step would be to impose eighteen-year term limits. (Teddy Roosevelt once proposed that the public be allowed to overturn a court decision with a public vote, which would be radical but interesting.)

Our current situation of judicial supremacy troubles me. The idea that nine unelected people have so much say over how we live—over whether we can carry guns, whether we can have access to abortions, or how colleges admit students—seems bonkers.

---

* While we're on the topic of ball games, I couldn't find much from the Founders on this subject. But I did find a letter from Jefferson to his young relative where he wrote that "Games played with a ball . . . are too violent for the body, and stamp no character on the mind." I brought this up to Zane when he was deciding between trying out for the tennis team or the cross-country team. He denies that it affected his decision, but he did choose the running.

And not just bonkers, but against the Founders' wishes.

"It's deeply unoriginal," says Gienapp.

In fact, I had a thought while on my way down to visit SCOTUS: If I'm trying to be the ultimate originalist, and the Court's current power exceeds what is in the Constitution, maybe I should ignore the Court's rulings?

Or maybe I don't want to write a Year of Living Incarceratedly. So let's put a pin in that for now.

SECTION 4.

Okay, back to the case I was watching. When the case began, there was no big and exciting introduction. No "Ladies and gentlemen, in this corner, the petitioner, the Fantastic Fraudster, the Medicaid Marauder."

Instead, the case began with Chief Justice John Roberts flatly stating, "We'll hear argument this morning in Case 22-10, Dubin versus United States. . . . Mr. Fisher."

And with that, Jeffrey Fisher, the lawyer for David Dubin, the man suing the United States, got up and started his speech. I'd read the case, so I knew the basics: David Dubin, the owner of a psychological service based in Texas, was busted for overcharging Medicaid by $101.

But the United States didn't just charge him with fraud. He was charged with aiding and abetting a bigger crime—aggravated identity theft. When billing Medicaid for one of his patients, Dubin had used that patient's Medicaid number. The law says that if identity is used "in connection" with fraud, then it counts as identity theft, a charge that could land Dubin in prison for two years. Dubin and his lawyer said that's ridiculous. Dubin admits to fudging the bill. Yes, he did cheat. But calling it identity theft? That goes too far.

I couldn't see Dubin's lawyer's face, just the back of his head, his gray hair. Nor could I see the face of the lawyer for the United States, just his brown hair. From my point of view, it was Gray Hair Guy versus

Brown Hair Guy. I was so far back in the courtroom, I was having trouble hearing the arguments. Instead, I studied the justices' appearance and body language.

Justice Sonia Sotomayor was the only one wearing a face mask, a precaution because she has diabetes. Her mask was black to match her robe. Justice Samuel Alito was leaning back in his chair, way back. The big leather seats can tilt, and Alito was reclining so hard I worried he'd tip over and slide onto his head. He looked at the ceiling, rubbed his face, rocked the chair even farther back. Justice Neil Gorsuch, on the other hand, was sitting up, ready to pounce.

Though I couldn't make out every word, it was clear to me that the justices were not happy with the U.S. government lawyer. Both liberal and conservative justices seemed skeptical of Brown Hair Guy's argument.

At one point, Justice Ketanji Brown Jackson started a question to him with the phrase "Help me to understand," which I interpreted to mean "It's possible I'm not smart enough to have grasped your argument, but far more likely you're full of crap."

Within the first few minutes, Justice Clarence Thomas asked a question. I looked over at the high school SCOTUS fanboy. He gave me a thumbs-up. Yes, Thomas talked!

For his part, Gorsuch lost patience. When the government lawyer brought up a previous argument, Gorsuch snapped, "I asked you to put that aside, Counsel. Please do so."

I started to feel bad for the government lawyer. He was getting a thrashing from both sides. A bit later, Gorsuch was in a better mood, even up for a little shtick: "Whether it's in a restaurant billing scenario, a health-care billing scenario, or lawyers who round their hours up, and I'm sure nobody in this audience has ever done that . . ."

The courtroom broke into laughter.

Gorsuch's joke seems to be this: Most, if not all, lawyers break the law, but what are you gonna do? I wonder what the Founding Fathers would have thought of this wisecrack. My guess is Jefferson would be chuckling along, while Adams would be outraged. He most certainly did not commit fraud, and no other citizen of these United States should, either!

I was also humbled. I'd been studying for months on my journey, but I knew I'd learned just a tiny percent about constitutional law. Even when I could hear the justices and lawyers, many of the words and concepts flew over my head.

SECTION 5.

As is customary, it was several weeks before the Court's decision was released. When it was, it turned out my hunch was correct. The Court did not like the government's case. They ruled nine to zero against the United States and in favor of the admitted fudger.

The details of the case are actually relevant to one of the big questions I'm wrestling with this year: How should we interpret text? How broadly or narrowly? How literally or figuratively? How much elasticity should be built in? In this case, the court was interpreting a statute, not the Constitution, so the stakes were lower. But some of the same issues apply.

The government wanted to charge Dubin with identity theft because, while fraudulently filling out the form, he had used his client's name and Medicaid number. The client's identity was used "in connection" with the fraud.

Not so fast, said the court. In the decision written by Justice Sotomayor, the court said we need to stay closer to the plain meaning of the text. Yes, the admitted fudger used the guy's name while filling out the forms, but he wasn't trying to steal the guy's identity. He just used it incidentally.

The court ruled to keep the interpretation of the law narrow. The government was attempting what Sotomayor called a "sweeping" and "boundless interpretation." If the government had its way, millions of interactions would count as identity theft. If a waiter served a flank steak but charged a customer's credit card for filet mignon, that would count as identity theft. Which is quite a stretch.

In this case, both liberals and conservatives said, "Stay closer to the text." This is not always the situation. Liberals tend to have broad interpretations of the text when it deals with expanding rights, such as gay marriage. But sometimes, everyone agrees narrow is best.

SECTION 6.

The case was over. The justices slipped behind the red velvet curtain, and the guards herded us spectators toward the exit. We walked down hallways lined with busts and paintings of justices from throughout history and arrived at the Supreme Court gift shop. You could buy Supreme Court golf balls or a plastic Supreme Court "stress relief" gavel, so you can bang it on your dining room table whenever you feel your rights being stripped away.

I browsed the books. Almost all of them presented SCOTUS in a glowing light. There were biographies of justices past and present, with cover photos of the berobed subjects looking nobly into the distance. There was a collection of Supreme Court recipes called *Table for 9.* ("Mrs. Neil Gorsuch's English marmalade"!)

Granted, there were some more critical books, such as one on the *Dred Scott* case, one of the court's most notorious decisions, in which it ruled that an enslaved man in a free state remained property and could be returned to his enslaver.

But I didn't see any of the real SCOTUS-bashing scorchers I had read from writers on both the left and the right. There was no *Justice on the Brink: A Requiem for the Supreme Court* or *Supreme Myths,* both of which I had enjoyed. I think that's a shame. Because these books don't call for abolishing the Court or totally stripping away its independence.

They just call for reforming it. They want to tame SCOTUS with term limits, for starters. And impose a stronger ethics code. The Court did create an ethics code of sorts in the fall of 2023, following a flood of revelations—for instance, Clarence Thomas vacationing it up Jimmy Buffett–style thanks to his billionaire friends. But the code didn't get a warm reception from critics. *The New York Times* ran an article with the headline "New Ethics Code Is Toothless, Experts Say." The reformers want more teeth, more curbs on power. They want the Court the Founders envisioned, a much less dominant Court.

Huzzah

ANGER MANAGEMENT, FOUNDERS STYLE.

I'm angry with myself for getting so angry about the line cutters at the Supreme Court. Anger can have its uses, especially if it's righteous anger against a societal injustice. But Wait-gate was not worthy of my rage. And in general, I worry that our culture is far too addicted to rage.

The Founders had a complicated relationship with anger. On the one hand, they might never have started the Revolution if they weren't angry at King George III.

On the other hand, the Founders spoke and wrote often about the importance of governing our passions. George Washington was famously born with a volcanic temper. But he spent a lifetime trying to master it. There's a famous list, "110 Rules of Civility & Decent Behavior in Company and Conversation," which Washington copied out as a young man. Several of them deal with controlling your anger. "In all causes of passion, admit reason to govern" says rule 58. (Oddly, rule number 2 deals with not adjusting your private parts in public. Which is a solid rule, though I probably wouldn't have put it as the number 2 rule. Maybe number 53 or so.)

In Richard Norton Smith's book *Patriarch,* there's a story about the time Washington insulted another politician during a run for the Virginia assembly. The insultee "grabbed a hickory branch and knocked

Washington to the ground. The next day Washington demanded an interview at a tavern. Expecting to be challenged to a duel, [the other politician] received instead a handsome apology and retraction of the original comment, along with Washington's hand in friendship."

Washington forgave him and controlled his rage. It's inspiring. And I hope it's true, unlike the cherry tree tale. The question is, how can you control your petty anger like George Washington did? One interesting method is to slow down your thoughts. Writing them down is helpful, and writing them with a quill pen is even more helpful, since it takes more preparation.

I also find using eighteenth-century language beneficial. People back then could be so delightfully formal. "Dear Sir, I feel it behooves me to bring up an issue that has caused me some not insignificant amount of frustration." This formal, repressed language actually makes me less angry. How can I be foaming at the mouth when I use words like *behooves*?

ARTICLE VI

A Letter of Marque and Reprisal

SECTION 1.

It was midwinter, and I was walking through Midtown on my way to visit my dad for lunch. I saw a man in jean shorts strolling my way. He was looking at me, smiling. I nodded and looked back down at the sidewalk. He got right up in my face.

"Arr, matey!" he said.

I sometimes wear my tricorne hat when doing errands around New York—at least when I'm alone. Zane and Lucas won't let me wear it within fifty yards of them. But I like to put on my hat each forenoon because it's akin to a string around my finger. It reminds me of one of my goals: to get into the mindset of an eighteenth-century American. The downside? I get a lot of "Arr, matey!" and "Yo, Jack Sparrow!" greetings.

"Actually, I'm not a pirate," I said. "I'm dressed as a constitutional delegate."

He ignored my explanation. "Gimme some rum, Captain Morgan!"

I wanted to respond that a guy wearing jean shorts in the middle of winter should not be mocking someone else's outfit, but I took the high road and walked on.

But maybe the pirate talk is appropriate. As I mentioned in the Preamble one of the most unusual constitutional clauses I've run across can be found in Article I, Section 8: the granting of "Letters of Marque and Reprisal." It's not exactly an endorsement of piracy, but it is, at the very least, pirate adjacent.

Section 8 contains a laundry list of Congress's powers. It's got thirty-nine items, including famous ones like "raise and support Armies," "establish Post Offices," and "coin Money."

But it also has some obscure items, and perhaps the most obscure of all is that Congress has the power to "grant Letters of Marque and Reprisal."

If you recall, this phrase allows Congress to give the legal go-ahead to privateers. Privateers are sort of government-sanctioned pirates in times of war. A private citizen could apply to Congress, and if Congress approved, the citizen could use their own fishing vessel to intercept enemy ships and seize the goods.

The clause about the letter of marque is a clear reminder that the Constitution was written in a radically different time, with all the good and bad that comes with it.*

Congress has not granted such a letter since 1815. But it's still right there in the Constitution in the very first article. If my goal is to express all my constitutional rights, then I figured I should attempt to be the first American citizen in 208 years to obtain a letter of marque from the U.S. Congress. I knew it was ridiculous. But we are in the era of congressional ridiculousness. It's certainly not as absurd as Representative George Santos's fabricated claim that he produced the *Spider-Man* Broadway musical. He could have chosen any musical, and he went with that?

SECTION 2.

To embark on my quest, I called up the expert of all experts on privateers, a man named Eric Jay Dolin. He's the author of a great book called *Rebels at Sea: Privateering in the American Revolution.*

"I'm really in awe of these men," Dolin told me. "They had a lot of guts." Privateers are an enormously important and bizarrely overlooked part of American history. Without them, as Dolin's book makes clear, we would have probably lost the Revolutionary War. We'd be spending our Sundays watching cricket and eating bangers and mash.

How did privateers get started? Dolin explained that America had a meager navy during the Revolution. We couldn't afford to build and operate a lot of ships. Instead, Congress decided to outsource the Navy

---

* *Marque,* by the way, is an old word that means "boundary," at least according to one etymology.

to regular folks. If you had a fishing boat or a merchant ship, you could apply to be a privateer. As a privateer, you could capture British ships and seize the booty.

Since privateers got to keep the profits from their captures, they're often confused with pirates. But there's a big difference between the two: Privateers were legal and, Dolin said, acting in support of a good cause. Privateering was not a minor footnote in the war. Or it shouldn't be, anyway. Congress issued roughly 1,700 letters of marque during the Revolution to vessels big and small, from merchant ships more than 100 feet long to diminutive 25-foot whaleboats. The privateers loaded their boats with muskets and cannons and went in search of British ships.

And they were startlingly successful. During the Revolutionary War and the War of 1812, privateers intercepted and captured about three thousand British vessels. For the most part, they wouldn't attack the big British warships but instead would capture the British merchant ships and ships supplying the redcoats. Privateers seized British gunpowder, British salted pork, British candles—and lots of British booze. The haul from one captured ship included thirty-five hundred gallons of rum.

The privateers then sold the much-needed supplies to the American government or private citizens. As one grateful Patriot wrote to Congress, privateers "rendered us the most essential services," and without them, "the war could hardly have been supported."

"We tend to think the Revolutionary War's outcome was inevitable," said Dolin. "But it wasn't. A hundred things had to go exactly our way. And privateering was one of those things."

John Adams was a huge fan of privateers. In fact, later in life, he wrote glowingly about the 1775 Massachusetts law that first legalized privateers, saying that this privateering law "is one of the most important documents in history. The Declaration of Independence is a brimborion in comparison with it." (A brimborion is an object of little value.)

Yes, that is quite a hot take from Adams: A law giving the go-ahead to privateering is much more important than that trifling "Life, Liberty and the pursuit of Happiness" thing we celebrate on July 4? The claim seems a bit over the top. Or as the hyperbolic Adams might say, it's the most preposterous overstatement in the history of the civilized world! But still, it's a sign of just how important privateers were to American independence. An 1856 international treaty banned privateering in many countries—but the United States declined to sign the treaty.

Why, then, are privateers barely mentioned in American history textbooks? Why aren't there statues of privateers all over Boston and New York City parks and piers?

"I think a lot of people have an idealized view of the American Revolution," Dolin said. "And privateers, because of their supposed connection to pirates, cast a little shadow on the image of this glorious revolution and flawless people fighting for civic virtues."

Which is unfair to the privateers, he said. Yes, they were inspired by the profit motive, but many also embraced the ideals of independence. People are complex.

"I'm very happy to be American," Dolin told me. "I love this country. However, I think we sometimes look at the American Revolution with this ethereal gauze as a solely virtuous cause. But it's a much more complicated story. And I'm not just talking about the issue of slavery. There are many other things. America's birth was not an immaculate conception."

Dolin makes a good point. In fact, this takeaway alone might be significant enough to justify my detour into privateering: The birth of America was not an immaculate conception. It was messy and sometimes ugly. But as Dolin says, we can appreciate the good parts of our revolutionary history and embrace the continued quest to make our nation live up to its noblest ideals. And I can still hold my head up high if I become a privateer.

I asked Dolin's advice on how actually to become a privateer.

"Do you have a boat?" he asked.

"My friend says I can borrow his waterskiing boat. It's twenty-three feet," I said.

"Well, you wouldn't want a big cannon on there, because it would weigh a ton. But you could have muskets, pikes, cutlasses, and maybe a small swivel gun."

Dolin also suggested I pack several flags—British, French, Dutch, and so on—since privateers were famous for using false-flag tricks to get close to enemy boats.

He also pointed out that, technically, we have to be at war for Congress to grant me a letter of marque. I'd already given that some thought and had some ideas. Several congresspeople have said we are in a cold war with China, so perhaps that counts. There's the war on drugs, the war on terrorism, and our aid to fighters in Yemen and Syria—some wiggle room, in any case.

SECTION 3.

My next hurdle: How do I apply to Congress? Should I email them? Write them a quill-penned letter? I was stymied. A couple of weeks later, providence provided an opportunity. I received an intriguing email. It was from an aide to Representative Ro Khanna, a Democrat from Silicon Valley.

In the past, I have donated to the Democratic National Committee, so I occasionally get fundraising emails from the offices of congresspeople. I've always ignored these requests, but now I have something to ask for.

The aide said the congressman was coming to New York and had time for a coffee—he'd love to meet me. I replied, it would be my honor.

Julie, as I suspected, was not a fan of my privateering project. "This is a terrible idea," she said, as I headed off to the lobby of a Midtown hotel for my meeting.

"It's for the greater good," I said.

Congressman Khanna's aide, Cooper, led me back to the table, and there was the congressman—good-looking, tall, wearing a black blazer and no tie. We shook hands. Before meeting, I had done some research. He is a progressive Democrat and considered an up-and-comer within the party. He's a Yale Law School graduate and is interested in climate change and artificial intelligence governance, among other topics.

He asked me what I'm passionate about.

"I like your idea to limit Supreme Court justice terms to eighteen years," I said.

"I think it's common sense," he said, pointing out that life expectancy was much shorter when the Constitution was ratified. "It's a cause that resonates with everybody—Republicans, Independents, Democrats. Do we really want someone appointed fifty years ago making decisions when it comes to modern facts?"

"But don't you need a constitutional amendment for that?" I asked.

The congressman shook his head. "You don't, because the Constitution says that a judge must be appointed for life . . . but there's nothing in the Constitution to say that you can't move them to the circuit court."

In other words, after eighteen years, the justice gets demoted from the Supreme Court to a lower court.

"Oh, that's good," I said.

Quite the brilliant little loophole, if it works. On the other hand, it's not originalist in the least: I don't think the founding generation envisioned involuntary demotions for SCOTUS.

There was a pause in the conversation. This was my opportunity.

"Speaking of the Constitution, can I ask you one quick thing?"

"Please," said the congressman.

My palms were sweaty. Should I do this? Yes, I should. I forced myself to speak the words, telling myself it was all in the name of my constitutional adventure.

"I brought you this. It's an application to get a letter of marque from the Congress. . . . I'm interested in becoming a privateer."

I handed the congressman a piece of paper printed in an old-timey font. He took it and examined it for a couple of seconds.

"How do we do this?" he asked.

I loved Representative Khanna's optimism, his let's-make-this-work attitude. He was on board even before he really understood what I was asking.

"In Article One, Section Eight," I explained, "it says that you can still become a privateer and I can go out and help fight whoever it is, the enemy . . ."

His eyebrows were now fully raised. His face had gone from encouraging to a little concerned.

"Wow," he said. "Why do you want to do this?"

"I'm doing a project where I'm trying to express my constitutional rights in the most literal possible way, so . . ."

The congressman was quiet as he read my letter:

> *Dear Ladies and Gentlemen of the Congress of the United*
> *States of America,*
>
> As a citizen of the United States, and in compliance with
> Article I Section 8 of the United States Constitution, I am
> formally requesting a Letter of Marque that would permit me
> to subdue, detain and seize any seafaring vessels considered
> to be operated by enemies of the United States.
>
> I am seeking this commission for a 23-foot-long boat, a Sea
> Ray 230 Bowrider, that I have leased for this purpose. It
> currently has neither cannons nor guns, but will be outfitted
> with such when and if I attain this commission. It is 1.5 tons
> and bears the name "The Lisa Michelle."
>
> I would be detaining any vessels, either public or private,

either armed or unarmed, either on the high seas or within the jurisdictional limits of the United States.

Your humble and obedient servant,

A.J. Jacobs

New York, New York, 2023

"Are you going to the Taiwan Strait?" Khanna asked, a little incredulous.

"Yeah, if you want me to."

"Wow," he said. It was a noncommittal *wow*. I couldn't tell if it was a *Wow, this is cool,* or a *Wow, this is what I have to put up with to raise money.* "It has to be voted on by the whole Congress?"

"I think so."

"We will look into this," Khanna said.

"Can we keep this?" his aide asked, putting my letter in a briefcase.

I was thrilled with his reaction. By all accounts, the congressman should have had me escorted out of the hotel lobby. Why did he humor me? I figure there are at least two reasons: First and most obviously, I'm a potential donor. Second, as a fan of constitutional close reading, he seemed to appreciate the premise of my book, or at least he said he did.

For several minutes, we spoke about originalism and the Constitution. "When the book comes out, you should come speak to Congress," he said—a thrilling if unlikely scenario.

Whatever happens with that or my privateering career, Khanna granted me my next request: a photo of the two of us, me wearing my tricorne hat and holding my application for the letter of marque.

In the following days, I exchanged emails with his aide, Cooper, who began to address me as "Captain" in his notes, which was flattering. Quite the Merry Andrew, this one. He said Khanna is working on it, talking to other legislators. I said I'll stand by, ready for updates, prepared to serve. I realize I may never get permission to hit the high seas, but I feel I did one patriotic thing: I raised awareness of these unsung heroes of American independence.

Huzzah

MY FELLOW SOLDIERS IN THE NEW JERSEY REGIMENT.
I've become an official and active member of the Third New Jersey Regiment. I haven't taken to the field yet, but Dakota has helped me assemble the barest bones of a kit (the official word for a costume and equipment).

I purchased the all-important black tricorne hat from the regiment's hatter (much softer than the one from the Alexander Hamilton Halloween costume). I bought woolen breeches from an online historic clothing store—though they were five sizes too big. (I tied them around my waist with a string, which worked for about five minutes at a time.) I'm not finished, though. I need lots more, including the delightfully named spatterdashes, protective coverings for my shoes.

I've been to two events with my regiment so far. My favorite was at a farm in upstate New York, where I played cricket, ate molasses cookies, drank whiskey, and pulled up my breeches.

At the farm, I attended a lecture on writing and reading in early America. As a writer, I was happy to hear literacy was seen as one of the most important issues of the day. "The central problem of the republic was how to teach virtue to citizens," said the lecturer, an employee of the National Archives. "Without virtue, there was no republic." The lecturer said the solution was that women were the conduit. Women needed to read civics and government so they could pass it down to their kids. Julie was happy to hear this.

After the presentation, the lecturer sold me some homemade ink and showed me how to sharpen my quill with a knife. That's one of my favorite parts of the reenactment community: the DIY spirit. I spend too much of my time moving around atoms on a computer chip and not enough moving, making, and fixing actual objects. I need to up my maker game.

At the end of my day there, I took a dancing lesson in the barn. The plan was to do English country dances—which are the ancestors of square dances—with charming names like the Handsome Couple and the Willing Quaker.

But there was a problem. There were fourteen women dancers and only ten men dancers. How were we supposed to pair up properly?

"It doesn't matter!" said our dance instructor, a Loyalist named Neil. He told us to pair up with any gender that was available. "During the Napoleonic War, British troops were all male and danced with each other."

I spent the next hour spinning, twirling, and bowing to both male and female partners. I didn't expect gender fluidity at a reenactment event, but history is surprising.

The Room Where It Actually Happened

Lucas and Alexander Hamilton at the National Constitution Center

My family and I took a train down to Philadelphia. I'd convinced them to come with me to see Independence Hall, which contains the room where the Constitution was born.

Aside from the steel and glass office building behind it, Independence Hall looks like it does on the back of the hundred-dollar bill and in Hollywood history movies: red bricks, white trimming, a clock tower resting on top.

To enter, we had to go through security. I was supposed to put my bags on an X-ray machine conveyor belt and walk through the metal detector. But I hesitated.

"Excuse me," I said to the security guard sitting behind the X-ray machine. "I'm doing a project where I'm trying to live as strictly as possible by the original meaning of the Constitution. I'm not sure, but the Founding Fathers might have seen this security as a violation of my Fourth Amendment rights."

The guard did not respond. She didn't even look up from the monitor. She just stared straight ahead.

"That's the amendment about search and seizure," I added helpfully. "You need to have probable cause to search my personal effects, and I'm not sure you do."

Lucas, Zane, and Julie were staring at the floor and edging away from me. Jasper, my sole supporter, was smiling widely. The guard remained remarkably unresponsive. It was impressive. Her face was immobile, as frozen as Washington's on Mount Rushmore.

"You're not going to get anything out of her," another guard said.

Okay. She wins. I put my wallet and iPhone in the tray and walked through the metal detector. (I did learn I'm not the only who questions the constitutionality of such checks. A hard-core libertarian clothing designer offers underwear with the words "Read the 4th Amendment, Perverts" printed in metallic ink so that it shows up on airport monitors.)

Since Independence Hall is a national park, we had a park ranger named Sarah as our tour guide. She wore a khaki shirt and a green tie, her hair in a ponytail. She's from Texas, she told us, by way of explaining her accent.

"I'm excited to tell y'all about this," she said. "We're in one of the most important rooms in the history of the United States. This is very cool, right?"

No one responded. An awkward silence. I decided to fill it. "Huzzah!"

"That's right!" Sarah said, looking at me, either approvingly or warily, I'm not sure.

She explained that the fifty-five delegates came here to talk about the Articles of Confederation, the system that governed the thirteen states in the years right after the Revolution. But, Sarah said, "the Articles of Confederation were a hot mess."

The federal government had no power to collect taxes. States had their own foreign policies, which were sometimes contradictory. There was no unanimity, just a confusing jumble of rules. The delegates needed to do something radical. And they did, right here in this space. I looked around the room. It was small, about the size of a pickleball court. There were tables draped in green cloth and covered with candlesticks and long white clay pipes. The windows were closed, as they were during that hot summer, to discourage snoopers.

Sarah said that when the convention was over, the delegates had mixed feelings. "I don't think a single person in this room was, like, a hundred percent *yeehaw!* about the Constitution. They had questions. They had concerns. They had fears. How is this going to work? Is this going to work? They didn't know."

It's a good point. I'm also not 100 percent yeehaw about every part of the Constitution. There are parts I'm quite yeehaw about and others I am not yeehaw about at all. But seeing the room, imagining the Founders in these chairs debating and compromising, makes the achievement more concrete to me. Here gathered a remarkable collection of minds. I'm still in awe that they were able to agree on those four pages, even with its mammoth flaws, and create the United States.

Sarah concluded by saying that our history has been a quest to make those 4,543 words work for everyone. And one of the biggest challenges in making it work is my very quest in this book: How do we interpret the words they wrote? That's the topic I studied on the train down, on the train back, and for months before and after.

SECTION 2.

Some sentences in the Constitution are quite clear and specific. They don't really need to be interpreted.

Article II says you have to be thirty-five years old to serve as president. The Seventh Amendment says that any civil lawsuit that involves more than twenty dollars is entitled to a trial by jury. Pretty obvious what those mean . . . unless you are a fan of overthinking, which I am. See footnote!*

But other parts are vague. The Eighth Amendment forbids "cruel and unusual punishments." But what is cruel and unusual? The Consti-

---

* Here's a counterargument: Even the supposedly obvious parts of the Constitution are tricky, at least if you're prone to overthinking. Consider the $20 minimum for a trial by jury in the Seventh Amendment. That clause was ratified in 1791. Should the $20 be adjusted for inflation? It would be about $650 today. That makes a huge difference. Imagine a 1791 law that said haircuts cannot cost more than fifty cents. It would have made sense at the time, because barbers were price-gouging. But now, because of that law, barbers wouldn't be able to pay their rent. Should a judge take into account the law's higher purpose (stop price-gouging) or stick with the text and the literal fifty cents? You could argue that the original meaning of $20 was different from its meaning today, when $20 can barely buy you a soda at Disneyland.

And what about thirty-five years old? That was a ripe old age back in 1787, when life expectancy was in the mid-forties. Should there be an amendment to adjust the minimum legal age for a president to fifty years old to keep up with our much longer life expectancy?

Anyway, that's just to say, when it comes to constitutional interpretation, there are no easy answers.

tution doesn't contain a list that says thumbscrews are cruel but solitary confinement is not.

Article I says that Congress can do whatever is "necessary and proper" to execute its powers. That's astoundingly open-ended. What is necessary and proper? What if Congress decided it was necessary and proper to suspend elections for ten years and give every senator's grandchild a free snowmobile?

Someone has to figure out what these vague words mean today. For better or worse, that job now falls mostly to the Supreme Court. The question is, how should the justices go about interpreting these abstract words? Let's pull back and take a look at the two broad camps.

ORIGINALISM: Holds that, by far, the most important factor is the meaning of the words at the time the Constitution was ratified (or if it's an amendment, when that amendment was ratified).

LIVING CONSTITUTIONALISM: Argues that we have to adjust the Constitution's meaning to fit the times. In interpreting a passage, we should consider several factors, which might include what the words mean now, what the words meant back then, what consequences a certain interpretation would have on American lives today, and how SCOTUS has ruled in the past.

Living constitutionalism is much more concerned with current morality and customs. But as I mentioned in the Preamble, originalism is not frozen in time. A thoughtful originalist takes the centuries-old principles of the Constitution and applies them to the current-day technology and situations, using history and tradition as a guide. The classic example is that the Fourth Amendment guarantee of protection from unreasonable searches, which was originally meant to stop the constable from banging on your door, now applies to government tracking your movements with GPS.

The two approaches often lead to radically different conclusions.

The current Supreme Court's originalist rulings have already had a huge impact on American lives. Their influence will likely be even bigger in the coming years.

Perhaps most controversial was 2022's ruling about abortion. In *Dobbs v. Jackson Women's Health Organization,* the originalist justices ruled that abortion is not a constitutionally protected right, overturning 1973's *Roe v. Wade.* The *Dobbs* decision meant states could pass their own abortion laws, and many have since passed restrictive ones.

Then there are gun rights. In 2022, the originalists on the court gave a huge victory to Second Amendment fans with its ruling in *New York State Rifle & Pistol Association, Inc. v. Bruen.* The *Bruen* decision made it much harder for states to pass laws regulating guns.

A third area of controversial originalist rulings has to do with federal regulations. As I mentioned, originalists are much more skeptical of the authority of the Environmental Protection Agency (EPA) and other federal agencies. They want to strike down the agencies' power to regulate our lives. Depending on your perspective, the gutting of the agencies either is a massive victory for liberty and the free market or will usher in climate disasters and endanger the lives of millions of consumers.

SECTION 3.

How did originalism become so powerful? There have been battles over how to interpret the Constitution since the quill ink on that calfskin was barely dry. But the war really heated up in the last few decades.

Originalism as a political force arose in the 1980s. It began, in large part, as a reaction to the famously progressive Warren court, which issued many decisions considered landmarks of civil rights (which I discussed in Article V). The right wing believed that the Warren court was "legislating from the bench." It was making new laws, and those laws were not what Americans had voted for. Conservatives didn't like this Court's expansive reasoning. They didn't like that the progressive justices found new rights in the Constitution. For instance, privacy. Privacy may not be listed in the Constitution, the Warren court said, but it was implied. It emanated from other passages, such as the protection against unreasonable searches and seizures. This right to privacy made way for decisions about the right to use contraception and have abortions.

Conservatives wanted to stop what they saw as a runaway Court shoving progressive ideas down America's throat and infringing on people's liberty. So originalism was, in part, a stance meant to restrain the Court from practicing judicial activism. The idea was to prevent judges from letting their liberal politics inform their decisions. Judges should be legal robots, neutral actors just calling balls and strikes. (Critics claim this has not happened at all, but we'll get to that in a bit.)

Conservatives formed the Federalist Society. It began as a student group at several universities. But it has grown into an extremely well-funded legal association that spreads the originalism gospel. Their efforts have succeeded, at least by some measures. Five of the nine justices on today's Supreme Court are current or former members of the Federalist Society (Roberts and the liberals are the exceptions).

Ironically, for a theory that espouses fixed meaning, originalism itself has evolved quite a bit over the years.

Originalism 1.0 focused on the *original intent* of the Founders. It said the job of a Supreme Court justice is to figure out what Madison and the other men in that room intended. What did the signers think the phrase *freedom of speech* meant, for instance?

Nonoriginalists pointed out a pretty big flaw in this original-intent idea: namely, that it's impossible to get inside the heads of Madison, Franklin, and company. And even if you could mind-meld with the Founders (as I am trying to do), the thirty-nine constitutional signers had widely varying opinions. There was no single original intent.

As a result, most originalists switched from focusing on original intent to *original meaning*. In Originalism 2.0, you don't need to know what was inside Ben Franklin's mind. What matters is *what the words meant to the public at the time of ratification*. We should focus on the original *public* meaning. And this, originalists say, can be discovered by studying old transcripts, newspapers, and dictionaries.

Critics counter that public-meaning originalism doesn't solve originalism's flaws. For instance, is there one agreed-upon meaning? As is the case today, the members of the public—just like the delegates—had vastly varying views on what the words meant. I've spent several months trying to determine the original public meaning, and it has given me a severe brain-ache.

The split between original intent and original public meaning is just one of the many ways originalism has splintered. Originalism is not a monolithic movement. It's more like a sprawling family tree with many branches. There's libertarian originalism. Social conservative originalism. Diet originalism. There are progressives who call themselves originalists, with labels such as *framework originalism* and *living originalism,* which I'll discuss a bit later. Some originalists have started to stress "history and tradition" in addition to the text.

That said, despite all the differences, the majority of originalists share a basic vision—that the meaning of the Constitution was fixed the moment it was ratified. Likewise, the majority of originalists share a conservative worldview.

Did the men who sat in this unventilated room in 1787 share that vision? How originalist were the original framers of the Constitution? That, of course, is a matter of debate.

Progressives argue that the Founders were not originalist at all. These men were experimental and entrepreneurial. In fact, Thomas Jefferson said future generations should not be weighed down by the dead hand of the past. "The earth belongs . . . to the living. The dead have neither powers nor rights over it."

Of course, originalists say the Founders were absolutely originalists.

In fact, in disputes after the Constitution was ratified, Madison frequently wrote about what the original meaning was.

And there's the meta question: Does it even matter if the original Founders were originalists?

Grievance

LUKEWARM CORRESPONDENCE.

Whatever method they used to interpret them, the Founders' words aren't helping me with my correspondence with Julie. On Valentine's Day, I decided to write her a card with some language George Washington used when he wrote to his wife, Martha.

> *Dear Julie,*
> I retain an unalterable affection for you, which neither time or distance can change.

I thought it was a nice sentiment, but Julie told me it was about as passionate as an appointment reminder she'd get from her podiatrist.

Rights and More Rights

*National Archives historian Jessie Kratz shows me
the Constitution's four parchment pages*

SECTION 1.

I've got a date with the Constitution. I'm on my way to meet the original four pages of parchment signed by Madison, Franklin, and thirty-seven other men on that September Monday in 1787.

My date will be a staid affair. No touching. I'll be observing the Constitution through thick glass. But I will be as close to those pages as an American can legally get. After seeing the Constitution's birthplace, I wanted to visit its current home. I've been granted a special tour of the National Archives in Washington, D.C.

The Constitution wasn't always at the Archives. It did some traveling in its youth. The Constitution began its life in that hall in Philadelphia, then departed by stagecoach to the first meeting of Congress in New York City. The document then moved to Washington in 1800 but had to flee the city during the War of 1812 and spent some time in an abandoned gristmill.

Its most recent and, perhaps, final trip was in 1952, the one-mile journey from the Library of Congress to the National Archives. And quite a trip it was—a parade with "two light tanks, a motorcycle escort, a color guard, two military bands, and four servicemen carrying submachine guns," as historian Arthur Plotnik described it. The Constitution itself was in a crate resting on a mattress inside an armored car. Oh, and the armored car had caterpillar treads to make the ride as smooth as possible.

It is *the* Constitution, after all.

I arrived at the Archives before it officially opened to the public. The building is enormous, an entire block. Its perimeter is dotted with marble statues, including one of a serious-looking man holding a scroll. He's standing atop a pedestal with the stern commandment STUDY THE PAST. Believe me, I'm trying!

I banged lightly on the side entrance with a brass knocker. I was greeted by Jessie Kratz, a historian at the National Archives. The Constitution was ready, she told me. It had been awakened and transferred—without human hands touching it—to its viewing space in the main rotunda, along with the other all-star documents, the Declaration of Independence and the Bill of Rights. None of these documents stay in the rotunda overnight. They get moved to a vault in an undisclosed location. "After Nicolas Cage successfully stole the Declaration," Kratz said, "we decided we shouldn't tell people where our vaults are." (There is a strict local law that all archivists must make at least one reference to the *National Treasure* film franchise.)

Kratz led me to the rotunda. The room is impressive, with a mural of the Founding Fathers under a high, domed ceiling. The rotunda is dark, so as not to further fade the parchments. I felt as if I should speak in hushed tones, as if I were in a cathedral.

I saw the Constitution on the other side of the room: four big, softly lit yellow pages inside a titanium case filled with inert argon gas. I'd been studying this document for months, and there it was in front of me, this collection of words that have helped shape my life and the lives of millions of others. I was surprised by how awestruck I was.

I got up close and looked at the writing. It's a cursive script known as copperplate, with elegant lines and flourishes, and the occasional *s* that looks like an *f*. I inspected the signatures on the final page. James Madison's is particularly small. It seemed appropriate: small of stature, small of signature, giant of intellect.

The writing was the work of a calligrapher named Jacob Shallus. The official term for his job is *engrosser*. He was paid thirty dollars (a thousand dollars in today's money), and he used a quill from a goose. Shallus wrote it almost entirely on a Sunday, which was probably against the Pennsylvania Sabbath laws of the time, but who was going to arrest him?

Shallus's writing has faded from black to brown. But the calfskin parchment that holds his elegant text remains in good shape. A few weeks before I visited the Archives, I'd driven two hours north of New York City to see one of the only parchment makers left in America and to learn the secret behind the material's staying power. Pergamena is a family-owned business, more than four hundred years old. The owners showed me the process—which happens to be messy, gross, and not much changed in three thousand years. You soak the cowhide (or goat-skin or sheepskin) in an alkali stew for a few days. You then scrape the hair and remaining flesh off with a machete-sized knife. Next, you hang the skin inside a wooden frame, stretching it with ropes and clamps, and then sand it and trim it. The co-owner of Pergamena, Jesse Meyer, said the stench is powerful. I cannot confirm this because I mouth-breathed for the entire three hours of my visit.

Today, parchment is rare and expensive, used for drum surfaces and luxury lampshades. Meyer says he also gets requests from history buffs who want him to make life-size parchment replicas of the Constitution. And occasionally, they want tweaks. "Sometimes they ask, 'Can the Second Amendment go first?'" he told me.

SECTION 2.

Back to the original Constitution, the one with the Second Amendment listed second. I asked Kratz, "What's your favorite part of the job?"

That's easy, she answered. It's Constitution Day, the anniversary of the signing. Every September 17, about twenty-five immigrants partici-pate in a naturalization ceremony in the rotunda. "It's very moving," said Kratz, "watching people take the oath of citizenship in front of the Constitution."

But even on an average day, Kratz told me, people come to see the Constitution and are inspired. "I feel like people come here and they're rejuvenated, and maybe they'll go vote, not just in a presidential election, but in a local election. Or they may decide they want to run for their kids' PTA. Just get more involved. Because that's the meaning of 'We the People.' We are the community."

Rejuvenating democracy is a huge benefit to having those yellowed pages on display. But there are downsides to exhibiting the Constitution, too, at least in the opinion of some of my advisers.

The problem, they argue, is that displaying the Constitution in this solemn, dark room turns it into a holy relic. It's like the Shroud of Turin, an unchanging, ancient object for us to venerate. It emphasizes one view of the Constitution—as a fixed piece of text—at the expense of the view that the Constitution is a continuing process negotiated by humans.

Surprisingly, some in the founding generation also worried that people would be too focused on those final written pages. "The Constitution of a country is not the paper or parchment upon which the compact is written," said John Quincy Adams in 1791. "It is the system of fundamental laws, by which the people have consented to be governed . . . of which the written or printed copies are nothing more than the evidence." Likewise, Jefferson said, "Some men look at constitutions with sanctimonious reverence, and deem them like the arc of the covenant, too sacred to be touched."

The Constitution is far more than just these four pages. How could it not be? You can't fit the complexities of a nation into 4,543 words. Much of what we consider the Constitution is unwritten. Or at least that's the thesis of a 2012 book by Yale's Akhil Reed Amar. The book is called, appropriately enough, *America's Unwritten Constitution.**

First, consider that the Constitution provided only the thinnest outline on how to set up a government. The folks in that first session of Congress in 1789 had to do a massive amount of filling in. I underestimated just how much of our government was created by that First Con-

---

* Harvard professor Laurence Tribe makes many of the same points in his earlier book, *The Invisible Constitution* (2008). So I want to give some visibility to that work as well.

gress. The members had to answer questions large and small: Should the president have a title, like *His Highness*?* What roles should they create for the president's cabinet? Should a cabinet member stay on with the next president? These and hundreds of other key issues were left open.

"We are in a wilderness without a single footstep to guide us," said Madison, of the First Congress. James Madison is considered the father of the Constitution, and even *he* didn't know.

SECTION 3.

And then there's the rights. The Bill of Rights, those first ten amendments ratified in 1791, is on display in that dark room. It's just a single page. About twenty-seven rights, depending on how you count them. Does this cover all of Americans' rights? Absolutely not. Those listed are only the *enumerated* rights.

In Professor Amar's book, he reproduces a painting of a stereotypically bucolic American scene. Amar explains that the image is jam-packed with unwritten rights. "Nothing in the written Constitution explicitly guarantees the right to have a pet dog, to play the fiddle, to relax at home, to enjoy family life with your loved ones, to raise your children, or to wear a hat. Yet these and countless other liberties are generally upheld by American governments. . . . Many of Americans' most basic rights are simply facts of life: 'This is how we, the people, do things in America and we therefore have the right to keep doing these things.'"

---

* For history nerds interested in the heated debate over what to call the president, there's an entire book about it: *For Fear of an Elective King: George Washington and the Presidential Title Controversy of 1789* by Kathleen Bartoloni-Tuazon. The term *president* won out. Other suggestions included *His Highness* and *His Excellency*. But my favorite suggestion was that the title should forever more be . . . *Washington*. In the same way the word *czar* is based on Caesar, the chief executive of the United States would be referred to as a Washington, so we'd presumably have had Washington Obama and Washington Trump. Washington himself didn't weigh in on this, but I think he'd be opposed to such idolatry.

It's a fun game to play, trying to notice the rights we take for granted. As I write this, I'm looking around my room and jotting some down:

I have the right to stare out the window.

I have the right to delude myself that staring out the window counts as "thinking about my book."

I have the right to use my orthopedic sneaker cushion as a book-mark.

I have the right to sign my text messages "Love, Dad" even though my kids make fun of me.

I have, as the Beastie Boys point out, an unenumerated "right to parrrrrty." (Though, as they caution, you have to fight for said right.)

Some of the Anti-Federalist Founders wanted the Bill of Rights to be much longer than it is and to spell out more rights. Their opponents, the Federalists, hated the idea. Noah Webster, political writer and dictionary editor, complained that Americans had gone rights crazy, demanding that everything be listed. What's next? he asked. Do they want an amendment that reads "Congress shall never restrain any inhabitant of America from eating and drinking, at seasonable times, or prevent his lying on his left side, in a long winter's night, or even on his back, when he is fatigued by lying on his right"? (Look in the dictionary under the word *snarky,* and you'll see a picture of Noah Webster.)

Compared with other countries' constitutions, our list of rights is among the shortest. Many countries list positive rights in addition to negative rights. Negative rights are the ones featured in the U.S. Constitution. A negative right restrains the government from interfering with your life, such as the right to free speech or to bear arms. But positive rights demand that the government guarantee citizens certain basic (or not-so-basic) resources. Several foreign constitutions guarantee the rights to health care, housing, and a healthy environment. The Finnish constitution has a section on the rights of reindeer herders.

I spoke with Laurence Tribe, a Harvard professor and constitutional scholar, who has advised other nations, including the Marshall Islands, on their constitutions. He says there are pros and cons to such positive rights. On the one hand, such rights may spark helpful laws, such as legislation that alleviates poverty. On the other, Professor Tribe said, "It's hard to know when those rights are satisfied." How does a government decide that, yes, mission accomplished, our citizens have a safe environment or proper health care? Our government certainly wouldn't be able to agree on that.

SECTION 4.

The Founders eventually settled on which rights to list in that Bill of Rights. But they were still concerned. They worried that Americans would see the list and think, *Okay, well, that's it. There are all my rights. The total list.* To prevent this type of thinking, the Founders included the Ninth Amendment, which reads, "The enumeration in the Constitution, of certain rights, shall not be construed to deny or disparage others retained by the people." In other words, just because we didn't list a right, that doesn't mean it's not a right.

The Ninth Amendment is controversial. Professor Tribe, a progressive, is a huge Ninth Amendment fan. "It's the only clause that reaches out of the parchment and addresses the reader. It's a reader's manual, it's an instruction about how to read it." Some conservatives are not as infatuated. Judge Robert Bork, one of the intellectual founders of originalism, dismissed it as "an inkblot" that had no clear meaning. He worried it could let loose a flood of dubious rights.

The Ninth Amendment was pretty much ignored for the first 150 years of America. The Supreme Court didn't mention it in a decision until the mid-1960s. But thanks to Tribe and other liberal thinkers, it's had a resurgence.

The Ninth Amendment principle that Americans have "implied rights" beyond those expressly stated had a profound impact on landmark decisions, including ones about contraception and abortion. Consider *Griswold v. Connecticut* (1965), which I mentioned earlier in the book. Warren's Court said that Americans have the right to use contraception in their own homes because the Constitution contains an unwritten right to privacy. Justice William O. Douglas wrote the decision. He said you can spot the right to privacy in such passages as the Fourth Amendment's prohibition against unreasonable searches and seizures. Douglas said the Fourth Amendment helps form "penumbras" and "emanations" that imply the unwritten right to privacy.

Conservatives have mocked the decision ever since for its woo-woo, hippie-dippie wording. You don't often hear the word *penumbra* (which means "shadow") unless it's to make fun of living constitutionalism. But Douglas's decision has been enormously influential. Liberal justices used the unwritten rights to privacy and bodily autonomy when they ruled, in *Roe v. Wade*, that the Constitution guarantees a right to an abortion.

To be clear, it's not that conservatives totally dismiss the unenumerated rights. Most conservatives and originalists would agree that unwritten rights are real. It's more a battle over what those hidden rights are and how expansive they can be.

A related debate concerns what the Ninth Amendment means by unenumerated rights. Where do those rights come from? Do new rights emerge as society changes? Or have the rights always been there, even in 1791, but the Founders didn't bother to list them, since they thought they were too self-evident?

You can make an argument either way. Professor Amar says he prefers the idea that new rights emerge. "One of the core unenumerated rights of the people under the Ninth Amendment is the people's right to discover and embrace new rights," he argues. True or not, he's got the right to that opinion.

Huzzah

FIGHTING AMERICAN ROYALTY.

It's been seven months, so I do a quick mental check-in. One theme: I'm nervous. Reading history and the news is stoking my fears that my kids could end up living in an authoritarian state. Democracy is fragile.

Which is why I want to commend early America's passion for its new form of elected government—and its disdain for all things monarchical, aristocratic, and hereditary.

I like the Constitution's Titles of Nobility Clause, which forbids the government from bestowing noble titles on its citizens. But the anti-monarchy energy in early America went beyond the law. After we won our independence, we tried to purge our language of royalty. We removed titles such as *king* wherever we could. King Street in several states became Congress Street. King's College in New York became Columbia College. The King's Minuet dance became the Congress Minuet dance.

But look around America today, and we seem to have regressed. The words *king* and *queen* appear everywhere, from our fast-food restaurants to our basketball nicknames to our mattress sizes. It's bizarre and, to me, un-American. What to do about it? I grabbed my quill and scribbled a letter to Robert Iger, head of Disney, which has spent decades promoting monarchy and princes and princesses in a most un-American way. I did have some hesitancy, since Disney is fighting a First Amendment battle with the current governor of Florida. But maybe this would help?

I started my note by explaining how the Founding Fathers were opposed to royalty. And finished with my big idea:

> . . . With that in mind, I have what I think is an exciting idea that will benefit both Disney and democracy. What if you

changed the name of the Magic Kingdom to the Magic Democracy? Or at least the Magic Republic?

Imagine the powerful message that would send—that Disney is embracing the fairest form of government known to humans instead of an archaic hereditary system. You could even have Cinderella renounce her crown and open the leadership of the Magic Kingdom to a democratic vote. Imagine campaigns by Minnie Mouse or a joint ticket of Chip and Dale! Imagine young girls dressing up as congresspeople for Halloween instead of princesses!

I believe this would be a huge positive publicity opportunity for Disney. It would send a wonderful message to our kids and strike a blow for democracy, which is endangered in our country and around the world.

I would love to brainstorm with your staff on the Magic Democracy if this is at all interesting to you.

Your humble and obedient servant,

A.J. Jacobs

Women's Rights

Gertrude Sunstein, suffragist (and my great-grandmother)

It's March 8, International Women's Day. Which means it's a good day for me to honor one woman in particular: my great-grandmother Gertrude Sunstein. She was perhaps my family's fiercest constitutional warrior, and I'm proud to share a tiny bit of her DNA.

Gertrude was a suffragist in Pittsburgh in the 1910s. She marched. She wore a sash. She held fundraisers. She handed out pamphlets, one of which my family still has. It's called "Objections Answered," and it's a fascinating twenty-page peek into the concerns of the day. The pamphlet's writer argues that despite having a body part pointed inward, women can understand issues just as well as those who have a body part pointed outward (I'm paraphrasing). One objection it responds to is the fear that universal suffrage "will turn women into men." The pamphlet argues, "The women of England, Scotland . . . [and] the Scandinavian countries are not perceptibly different in looks or manners from women elsewhere, although they have been voting for years." It's bizarre and depressing that this needed to be spelled out.

In 1920, the Nineteenth Amendment was ratified, guaranteeing women's right to vote nationwide. It reads, "The right of citizens of the United States to vote shall not be denied or abridged by the United States or by any State on account of sex."

Just days after the ratification, my great-grandmother wrote her husband perhaps my favorite family letter of all time. Her husband was working in Pittsburgh, and Gertrude was in a vacation rental house at the Jersey shore with their three kids. Her writing is inspiring and delightfully cranky.

She starts by saying sorry-not-sorry for taking so long to reply to his last note: "Now you have had a chance to see how pleasant it is to wait all week for a letter from one's spouse." Stick that in your pipe and smoke it,

Great-Grandpa! She then informs him that a "vacation" with the kids isn't exactly paradise. Motherhood is hard work too, even if it's unpaid. "The weather here is cold and rainy—too disagreeable for bathing. Dickie has been quite miserable, and doing his best to make life miserable for me."

My great-grandmother then turns to the positive news:

"Congratulations on the suffrage victory! Now we can go to the polls together and I won't have to wait outside—as I have done so frequently before." I love that she congratulates her husband. Her point is that universal suffrage is good for everyone, not just women. I'm proud of Great-Grandma Gertrude for her activism and proud of my great-grandfather for supporting the cause. He probably got some ribbing from his friends, because male supporters of women's suffrage were often mocked. I found one 1909 postcard online that featured an illustration of a sad, apron-wearing man washing clothes in a wooden tub. The tagline: "I want to vote but my wife won't let me."

The family called Gertrude a "woman of steel," which I hope she took as a compliment. I have a feeling that Gertrude and Julie would have been good friends if they had lived at the same time. Both are strong, no-nonsense women who don't let their husbands get away with any crap. I wish they could have met and distributed pamphlets together.

Over dinner with Julie and the boys, I read the Nineteenth Amendment out loud and held my pewter tankard of water in the air. "Cheers to Great-Grandma Gertrude!"

SECTION 2.

As the need for a Nineteenth Amendment shows, the Founding Fathers may have been forward-thinking in some ways, but they were remarkably stunted in their views of what women were capable of doing. In the eighteenth-century mindset, women had good qualities such as grace and elegance, but they were too emotional and irrational to be involved in politics or to head up a family.

Even Ben Franklin, one of the more open-minded of the Founders, was still stuck in his sexist ways. In his essay "Rules and Maxims for Promoting Matrimonial Happiness," Franklin advises women to avoid disputes with their husbands and "not to overlook the word OBEY" in the marriage vows. (Though he seemed fine with overlooking the "I won't sleep with other women" part of the marriage vows.)

Alexander Hamilton was not much better. In *Federalist No. 6*, he devotes a paragraph to the malign influence of women on rational male leaders. Women have swayed foreign affairs with their "bigotry," "petulance," and "cabals." One of his targets was Madame de Pompadour, who influenced King Louis XV of France to wage the disastrous (for France) Seven Years' War.

And then there's the famous exchange between John Adams and his proto-activist wife, Abigail Adams. John did take his wife's opinions seriously—at least more so than most husbands of the era. But still, he's not going to win any posthumous awards from the National Organization for Women. In 1776, Abigail wrote John with a plea to keep women in mind when creating laws for the new nation: "I desire you would Remember the Ladies, and be more generous and favourable to them than your ancestors. Do not put such unlimited power into the hands of the Husbands. Remember all Men would be tyrants if they could."

John wrote back a note that Julie calls "a masterpiece of condescension." He started by calling his wife "so saucy." Then he trotted out the classic trope that women actually wear the breeches in the family, and we men just say "yes, dear" (in Adams's words, "In Practice you know We are the subjects"). He wrote that it would be absurd to let women have control of the government ("we know better than to repeal our Masculine systems"), but he promised the men would be "fair" and "not exert [their] Power in its full Latitude." Julie told me that if I sent her a note like that, she would "serve me divorce papers in their full latitude."

The sexist attitudes that pervaded eighteenth-century culture were also embedded in the legal system. Women in general had limited rights—and, oddly, married women had even fewer. "When a woman married a man, her legal and economic identity was fully subsumed into her husband's," Sara Chatfield, an author and professor of political science at the University of Denver, told me. "She was basically treated as if she were a child." Until the twentieth century, married women's rights in most U.S. states were severely constrained:

- She could not own property (it was all transferred to her husband's name).
- She could not sign contracts or file a lawsuit.
- She could not accuse her husband of rape.
- She could not, in some cases, shop in stores without her husband's permission.

The system was called *coverture,* a set of legal norms inherited from English common law and adopted by most U.S. states. In most states, laws are a mix of two types. There is statutory law and common law. *Statutory law* refers to laws that are clearly and explicitly written out in law books, those statutes passed by city, state, or federal legislators. In contrast, *common law* is based on tradition and previous rulings by judges, customs that have accumulated over the centuries. Today, our system is still a mix of both common and statutory law, but we have slowly moved more toward statutory law. The young United States inherited a lot of its common law, including coverture, from England, but American politicians also started writing the sexist constraints into the law books.

The Supreme Court ruled in favor of the coverture system many times up until the mid-twentieth century. Consider Myra Bradwell. She was an Illinois woman who wanted to be a lawyer. But Illinois law said women are not allowed to be lawyers. So, in 1873, Bradwell sued. She lost. The U.S. Supreme Court upheld the ban against women practicing law. The court's reasoning often goes by the name *romantic pater-nalism*. In romantic paternalism, men claimed they weren't being cruel to women. They were not oppressing them. On the contrary! Men were protecting these fragile orchids from dangerous and stressful jobs so they could fulfill their true calling, caring for their husbands and birthing babies.

Look at the opinion that Justice Joseph Bradley wrote in *Bradwell v. State of Illinois*: "Man is, or should be, woman's protector and defender. The natural and proper timidity and delicacy which belongs to the female sex evidently unfits it for many of the occupations of civil life. . . . The paramount destiny and mission of woman are to fulfill the noble and benign offices of wife and mother. This is the law of the Creator."

Women's crusade to dismantle coverture lasted decades—and many people would contend that the effort continues to this day. Women fought sex discrimination in state lawsuits and in the Supreme Court. One strategy was to change state constitutions to include women's rights. Wyoming, for instance, was the first territory or state to allow women to vote, starting in 1869. But changing the federal government was the holy grail—and one that required an expanded reading of the Fourteenth Amendment.

The Fourteenth Amendment ensures "the equal protection of the laws" to all citizens. But when it was ratified in 1868, this equal protection wasn't extended to women. The amendment was understood to give equal protection to Black men, recently emancipated after the Civil War and threatened by continued racism.

Women tried to expand its meaning. In 1875, a woman named Virginia Louisa Minor filed a suit with the Supreme Court, arguing that the Fourteenth Amendment's "equal protection" meant women should be allowed to vote. She lost. The reason: The original meaning of the Fourteenth Amendment did not include women's equal protection. (Ironically, Minor had to file the lawsuit with her husband, since married women couldn't file lawsuits alone.)

This attitude lingers. Some ultra-originalists say that the Fourteenth Amendment still does not apply to women's rights. Justice Antonin Scalia said, "Certainly, the Constitution does not require discrimination on the basis of sex. The only issue is whether it prohibits it. It doesn't. Nobody ever thought that that's what it meant. Nobody ever voted for that." It's the same argument he made about gay marriage. Scalia said the Fourteenth Amendment framers would not have thought their amendment applied to legalizing gay marriage. Scalia wrote in 2015 that the Fourteenth Amendment doesn't forbid gay marriage bans, so "we have no basis for striking down" the practice.

An ultra-originalist reading of the Constitution might mean that sexist state laws of the past are okay from a constitutional standpoint. It also means that, according to Rule 3 of my project, I would have to follow such laws. Which presents many problems.

Consider finances. Until the mid-twentieth century, married women in many states couldn't sign contracts. My wife, Julie, is president of Watson Adventures, a company that puts on scavenger hunts in museums and historic neighborhoods. As part of her job, she prepares and signs several contracts a day.

I told her that, from the point of view of the Constitution's drafters, this activity isn't protected and I might have to take over.

"Great!" she said, moving from her desk to the couch and picking up a magazine. "I'll be over here if you have questions."

Thus commenced several hours of me trying to navigate confusing and irritating paperwork. I had to ask Julie so many questions about cancellation policies and pricing that she eventually fired me.

"This isn't helping me," she said, as she kicked me out of her desk chair.

The problem is that Julie is much more financially savvy than I am. She takes the lead on the taxes and paperwork. If we practiced coverture and I tried to take over managing the family finances, mayhem would ensue.

It wasn't just money that created awkward situations. Recently, Julie and I went to a bar on the Upper West Side for a friend's birthday party. When I got there, I went to buy a drink, and the bartender—a woman—looked at me and asked, "What can I get you?"

I wanted to order a glass of Madeira, but I remembered that in our nation's past, women bartenders had been deemed illegal. There was a Michigan law that prohibited women from being bartenders—unless their father or husband owned the bar. The Supreme Court upheld the law in 1948 (yes, that's 1948). In an ultra-originalist world, it is arguably constitutional for states to deny women bartending licenses.

"Just a club soda, please."

I figured a club soda was safer than booze. Alcohol required a bartending license, which might be unconstitutional in my world. And I didn't want to ask the bartender if her husband or father owned the bar, because she might have spit in my Madeira, and would have had every unenumerated right to do so.

SECTION 3.

There are many heroes in the decades-long fight to expand the Fourteenth Amendment's "equal protection" phrase to women. Among the more famous is Ruth Bader Ginsburg. In the 1970s, she helped develop a strategy worthy of a Hollywood movie (which it got in 2018, with Felicity Jones playing a young Justice Ginsburg).

At the time, Ginsburg was not yet on the Supreme Court. She was a lawyer specializing in women's rights. She realized that gender discrimination goes both ways. There were many laws that discriminated against women but also some laws that discriminated against men. She figured—correctly—that courts would be more likely to void laws that discriminated against men. Even one such ruling would be the wedge that opened the door. After that, she and others could try to challenge laws that discriminated against women.

She found her wedge in a 1972 case called *Moritz v. Commissioner of Internal Revenue.* The case concerned a Denver man who hired a caretaker to look after his aging mother. He wanted to take a tax deduction on the caretaker, but the IRS denied him. The tax law limited the deduction to "a woman, a widower or divorcee or a husband whose wife is incapacitated or institutionalized." Moritz was none of those things. But had he been a different gender, he would have gotten the deduction. Clearly unfair. Ginsburg figured that a panel of male judges would relate more to this discrimination than to antiwoman discrimination. She was right. She won the case. The victory allowed Ginsburg and others to challenge a mountain of laws that discriminated against women.

Ginsburg was also a proponent of the Equal Rights Amendment, which seeks to end all legal distinctions among genders. The ERA was introduced in 1971 but failed to get approval from three-quarters of the state legislatures.* Some advocates argue it's still alive and could be ratified if more states were to sign on. Opponents say it's dead, thanks to a seven-year deadline in the 1971 proposal.

SECTION 4.

If you are an ultra-originalist, as I am trying to be, there's another troubling consequence related to women. You could argue that women should not be allowed to run for office.

Article I, which sets out rules for the Congress, uses the pronoun *he* to refer to members of Congress. Article II does the same for the president.

Some say that *he* was, at the time, an all-purpose, gender-neutral pronoun. But I'm not convinced that's the way the founding generation meant it. I'm guessing that, in 1789 and in this context, *he* meant male.

---

* Actually, the ERA was *re*-introduced in 1971. The first version of the amendment was introduced in 1923. Both versions aimed to end legal distinctions between men and women in jobs, marriage, and home ownership.

Most of the founding generation would have thought the idea of female elected politicians to be laughable. Absurd. So saucy! The likely original meaning of the Constitution was that political offices were reserved for men only. The Nineteenth Amendment does not change this restriction, because that amendment only explicitly mentions women's right to vote, not women's right to run for office.

This is a ridiculously strict reading of the Constitution and one that I don't endorse, of course. But how does it pertain to my project? According to my Rule 5, I should alert others when they might be violating the original meaning of the Constitution. I didn't relish the idea. It's a dick move in several ways. But then I remembered some of the insights from Georgia congressional representative Marjorie Taylor Greene. These include her contention that women are "the weaker sex," that Nancy Pelosi could be executed for treason, and that the Parkland school mass shooting was a hoax, along with a grab bag of antisemitic and racist conspiracy theories. And I thought maybe it would be worthwhile to share this information with her.

I got out my quill and scratched out a letter:

> Dear Representative Marjorie Taylor Greene,
> I'm not sure if you consider yourself an originalist when it comes to interpreting the Constitution. Some of your comments lead me to think that you might be an originalist. For instance, you said that "abortion is not part of our Constitution," therefore it should not be protected as a right.
> If you are indeed a strict originalist, and if you want to abide by the strictest original public meaning of the founding generation, I do have one suggestion: that you not run for office again.
> This is because a strict originalist reading of the Constitution may not allow for women to serve in Congress. Article I of the Constitution only uses the pronoun "he" when

referring to members of the House and Senate. There is no indication the founding generation would have approved of a woman serving in Congress. The Nineteenth Amendment does not lift this constraint, since that amendment deals only with the right to vote, not the right to run for office.

So if you want to be as safe as possible about abiding by strict originalism, that is something to consider. I know that safety is a concern of yours, since you have brought up the potential dangers of Jewish space lasers.

Your humble and obedient servant,

A.J. Jacobs

I finished, addressed the envelope, put a stamp on it, and said a prayer of forgiveness to my great-grandmother Gertrude, hoping she'd understand.

Huzzahs

I'm more than halfway through my year of living constitutionally. Like Franklin, I am trying to be optimistic and focus on the positive. So here are two positives:

GIFT GIVING.

Gender relations in the eighteenth century were problematic, to say the least. Many, many eighteenth-century customs regarding gender would not sit well with Julie.

According to etiquette books at the time, a wife has to get permission from her husband before forming a friendship with another man or meeting said man for a social occasion. Am I going to suggest Julie get my permission before meeting her friend Doug for lunch? I am not, for everyone's sake.

Or consider the 1777 book *Affectionate Advice on the Social and Moral Habits of Females,* which said, among other things, "A low voice

and soft address are the common indications of a well-bred woman."
Julie wouldn't find that advice affectionate.

But one custom I read in regard to gender relations seemed promising. It was a ritual that George Washington engaged in with several of
his women friends. I tried it out one night when we went to dinner with
our friends Elizabeth and David.

"I have a present for you," I said to Elizabeth after we ordered appetizers.

I took out a small plastic bag.

"Is it drugs?" she said.

"No. Better. It's a lock of my hair," I said.

I showed her the strands in the bag.

"In early America, it was seen as a gesture of friendship," I said.
"George Washington gave locks of his hair to a lot of women."

David looked confused and a little perturbed.

"It was purely for friendship, not romantic," I clarified.

Elizabeth paused. "I'm simultaneously touched and repulsed."

So . . . that's a win!

THE ELECTION CAKE PROJECT, CONTINUED.

The movement to resurrect the election cake is officially underway. I
sent out an email to friends, family, and readers asking if they'd help me
revive the tradition. I argued that making Election Day celebratory
again might increase voter turnout.

Many ignored my plea. But a surprising number said they'd participate.

"I have no talent, but lots of enthusiasm," wrote a reader from Missouri.

"We celebrate everything else with cake, why not elections? Except
for Einstein's birthday, for that we use pie," wrote another from Virginia. (Einstein was born on March 14, Pi Day, a fact I didn't know.)

"Can we make pot brownies?" asked a friend. "Or would that be considered election interference?"

I'll allow it! In my email, I had included the old recipe with cloves but made sure to say that the cloves were not required. It was a compromise with my cloves-hating niece Ally, who was helping me with the project.

One reader from Australia wrote that his country has a similar tradition. But instead of cake, it's the Democracy Sausage. There are barbecues on Election Day in Australia. I'm impressed with Australia. First the secret ballot. Now the picnic. Australians seem to be geniuses at elections.

Thanks to everyone who responded to my emails, I'm now up to twenty-seven states. I need twenty-three more—and some territories, too, if possible. It's a good feeling. I feel like I'm doing something. It may be small, but at least it's better than just despairing about the waning of democracy while curled up in the fetal position.

The Right to Assemble
in My Apartment

SECTION 1.

I've always considered the First Amendment almost synonymous with free speech. But as I mentioned, that's just one of its parts. I shouldn't neglect the other parts of the First Amendment, such as my constitutional right "peaceably to assemble." What does "peaceably to assemble" mean? Scholars say that the phrase, in its broadest sense, means the right to meet and interact with other citizens. (And also that the Founders hated split infinitives with a white-hot passion.)

I haven't done enough assembling recently, peaceably or not. As with everyone else in the world, I assembled a lot over Zoom during the pandemic. But presumably, this second-rate solution isn't what the Founding Fathers had in mind.

Even after the pandemic, I haven't assembled much. I've been spending way too much time at home reading my constitutional books by candlelight. And it's not just me. As the surgeon general recently confirmed, America is in the midst of an epidemic of loneliness. It has multiple causes. One of them is the decline of groups that meet on a regular basis, whether that's church or the Elks Lodge. In the founding era, there were plenty of social clubs. The Freemasons were surprisingly popular, for instance, and Ben Franklin founded a club called the Junto, which would meet every Friday to discuss ideas. Now we are bowling alone. But not even. We are playing bowling on Nintendo Switch alone. So I'm glad the Constitution is encouraging me to be a bit more extroverted.

I've decided to express my right to assemble in the form of an eighteenth-century-themed dinner party. A couple of weeks before the assemblage, I sent out handwritten notes to several friends (I was worried about running out of time, so I scanned the notes and delivered them via email instead of the postal service, a half cheat). I asked them to join me for a spirited discussion about America and the Constitution.

The dinner party preparations took several days. First, I recruited my son Zane—the family cook—to set the menu. He ignored my suggestion of turtle soup and went with a more sensible beef stew recipe from 1788. The stew had beef and onions, but it had some more delightfully archaic ingredients too: mushroom ketchup and small beer. *Small beer* is just another name for weak beer, so I added a cup of water to some Amstel Light to make it even lighter. The recipe also called for several dozen cloves (cloves again!) to be poked into the exterior of a whole onion—which ended up looking like a microscopic photo of a deadly virus. For dessert, Zane chose rice pudding with raisins.

"I'm not responsible for how this meal tastes," Zane told me. "I'm doing this under protest." I promised I'd blame the 1700s, not his skills.

My plan was for Zane to prepare the meal using exclusively technology from the eighteenth century, but Julie and reality reined me in. For starters, we do have a fireplace, but when we tried to use it on a warm day a few years ago, the smoke went the wrong way and ended up billowing into our downstairs neighbors' apartment. Next thing we knew, we had six firefighters in our apartment. It wasn't pretty. So for this dinner, I had to settle for Zane using the regular old stove (and not even a gas stove, sadly).

I figured we could at least refrain from using other electronic appliances. So I asked our niece Andrea to come over and chop grains of rice into smaller bits, an ingredient the rice pudding recipe called for. After an hour of trying to chop rice with a knife, she complained it was a near-impossible task. So I gave in to her pleading and let her use a food processor.

But even with these twenty-first-century shortcuts, the meal was a major undertaking. Consider this: Early-American kitchens didn't have water faucets. The kitchens were dry. Women and servants had to schlep buckets of water from an outdoor well. My version: schlepping buckets of water from our bathroom faucet to the kitchen when I did the dishes (with vinegar and sand).

Even getting dressed for the big night took an eon. It's the little things that trip you up. Like socks. Along with my tricorne hat and breeches, I was excited to debut my new authentic white woolen stockings I got from Etsy. The thing is, back in the day, stockings had no elastic. Without proper support, stockings will slide down your calf and collect in a puddle around your ankles. You need to wear garters. But not even regular garters. The eighteenth-century garters look like tiny Smurf-sized leather belts you strap around the top of the stocking. I can tell you: Putting on sock belts every day eats into your productivity.

As Dakota, our friend from the Third New Jersey Regiment, once told me, "Life took longer back then." Every part of daily life—clothes, cooking, traveling—required numerous steps and extensive preparation. And on top of that, you had a shorter life span. Never again will I take elastic for granted. Or our dishwasher.

Most of the time-consuming home labor back then fell on women, servants, and enslaved people. I read a diary of an eighteenth-century housewife, and it was heartbreaking. Page after page about her exhaustion and depression from keeping the house in order. Her story strengthened my allergy to misplaced nostalgia. Some parts of the good old days were good. But much of it was soul-crushing, monotonous—and also putrid. As historian and host of the *Ben Franklin's World* podcast Liz Covart told me, "I have said this repeatedly: I'm glad we cannot smell early America."

SECTION 2.

A few days before my friends assembled peaceably in my apartment, I called an expert to talk about what the right to assemble actually meant at the time of the Founding Fathers.

I spoke with Saul Cornell, a professor of history at Fordham University. Cornell told me that, at the founding, assembling peaceably was seen as crucial to the democratic process. Americans were supposed to gather and have discussions about politics so they could make rational, well-informed decisions.

But what did those discussions look like? How peaceable or raucous should they be? That depended on which Founding Father you supported. The Federalists—those who supported the more law-and-order-type figures such as George Washington and John Adams—wanted very civil discussions. Extremely peaceable.

"It was considered okay to go to the coffeehouse and talk politics because you are not challenging government when you're doing that," Cornell told me. "The idea in early America is, you read your newspapers, you have a lively debate, you vote, and then you shut up and you follow the law. And maybe if it gets really bad, you politely petition the government to change things and maybe publish a snarky thing in the newspaper. But that's it."

On the other hand, those who supported the more anti-authoritarian Founding Fathers, such as Thomas Jefferson, were open to more raucous assemblies.

"So what would the people of the 1790s have thought of a demonstration of thousands of people?" I asked.

"We know what they thought because of the Whiskey Rebellion," Professor Cornell said. The Whiskey Rebellion was a 1794 demonstration (or uprising or riot, depending on your point of view) in Pennsylvania over federal taxes on whiskey. "The people who eventually became Jeffersonians were like, 'This is awesome,' and the Federalists thought, 'This is anarchy. You need to send in troops.'"

I followed up: "So Federalists would not have liked, say, Black Lives Matter, whereas the Jeffersonians might have said, 'Yeah, that's good.'"

"Well, except the Jeffersonians were very racist. So Black Lives Matter would've been a protest they probably would *not* have liked."

As with much related to early America, I find it hard to say what the original public meaning was. The public held a messy mishmash of opinions, as it does today.

SECTION 3.

At about seven and a half o'clock, the guests started to arrive. In came my friend John, the editor of a conservative magazine, with his wife, Ayala, a talent agent. One goal of mine was ideological diversity, so I'd invited John—as well as a libertarian podcaster named Jim—to balance the default New York liberal vibe. Also in attendance were my friend Angel, a psychiatrist born in the Dominican Republic, and his husband, Jaime, who immigrated recently from Mexico, as well as Sherry and her husband, Lorence, who were, respectively, a dermatologist and a biotech executive of Asian descent.

When I told Jasper the guest list, he said, "That doesn't sound very originalist. Shouldn't you have all white Christian men?"

He had a point. But since reading Yascha Mounk's book about diverse democracies, I'd been wrestling with how America can adapt to the new reality. I wanted to explore the issue with my guests. Hence, the not-so-originalist invitees.

"Thank you all for joining me in expressing our First Amendment right peaceably to assemble," I said, once everyone was seated around a table in our living room.

I was wearing my full getup, belted stockings and all. I had turned off all electric lights and lit several beeswax candles. At Julie's insistence, the air conditioner remained on high. Our friends thanked her for that. In addition to the candles, the table was laden with pewter plates and tankards, as well as eighteenth-century forks from a store called Samson Historical. Early-American forks only had two tines—and let me tell you, I now appreciate the glorious four tines on modern forks. Two tines are fine for spearing but terrible for scoopage.

"I thought I'd start with a couple of jokes to lighten the mood," I said. I took out a copy of *Joe Miller's Jest Book*—the most popular joke book of the eighteenth century—and read one aloud.

"A famous Teacher of Arithmetick had long been married without being able to get his wife with child. Someone said to her, "'Madam, your husband is an excellent Arithmetician.' 'Yes,' replies she, 'only he can't multiply.'"

I looked up. Mostly stony faces, but my friend Ayala actually laughed. Which was significant. Ayala is a successful agent for comedians.

"Feel free to give this book to your clients," I told her.

I didn't read any other jokes, since they were all pretty similar and pun-based. It seems the eighteenth century was big on dad jokes. Or Founding Dad jokes, to make a meta dad joke.

Instead, I suggested we sing a song. That was a common activity at eighteenth-century gatherings. With no Spotify or Victrolas, musical entertainment was a participatory event. I passed out the lyrics to an extended version of "Yankee Doodle" that I'd found online. It was much darker than the version I knew. It wasn't just about a pony-riding fellow with a feathered cap and delusions of foppishness. It was also about the horrors of the Revolutionary War and the inevitability of death.

"Everybody, sing along!" I encouraged.

> *I see another snarl of men,*
> *A-digging graves they told me,*
> *So tarnal long, so tarnal deep,*
> *They 'tended they should hold me.*

"Way to get people in the festive mood," Julie said.

Before the main meal, I also read out loud a few etiquette rules from the classic "110 Rules of Civility" that George Washington famously copied by hand when he was young.

"Cleanse not your teeth with the tablecloth or knife," I warned. My guests agreed to the terms.

Zane came in to tell us about the food on our plates, like the chef at a Brooklyn restaurant. He was nervous about its reception, but the verdict after folks tried the food: surprisingly tasty. (Maybe they were just observing the rules of civil behavior, but Julie told me she honestly liked it. Zane is a talented cook, even with eighteenth-century constraints.)

SECTION 4.

Enough warm-up. It was time to dig into the constitutional discussion.

"If you could change one thing about the Constitution, what would it be?" I asked.

"The presidential pardon," Julie said. "That seems crazy to me. A totally unfair get-out-of-jail-free card."

Ayala thought that you should be able to run for president if you are a citizen, even if you were not born in the United States.

"I'd like to see gay marriage as an enumerated right," Angel said. "I'd like to see it spelled out in the Constitution, so that it can't be taken away." He also wanted clearer voting rules to stop attempts at voter suppression.

"What's yours?" Julie asked me.

"I'd go with Article Five," I said. "I'd amend the way we amend the Constitution. It's way too hard."

I figured this was a nonpartisan, noncontroversial opinion. The U.S. Constitution is among the hardest constitutions on earth to change, possibly number one. Even conservative hero Antonin Scalia thought it should be easier. When asked, he said it would be the first thing he'd change about the Constitution.

To amend the Constitution, you have to get two-thirds of Congress to agree and then get three-quarters of states to approve. Which is quite a task. I don't think two-thirds of the current Congress could agree on what is the color of a red pepper. Alternatively, you could call an entire new constitutional convention, which is also hard and risky, to put it mildly.

"In our lifetime, it feels like the Constitution's very stagnant," Sherry agreed. "It's supposed to be changeable, but it hasn't really been, not in our time."

"Yeah," I said. "I think the Founding Fathers underestimated just how hard their requirements were. They didn't see that America would split up into these two parties."

So we all agree, right? Not so fast.

"I think you could actually make the case that the Constitution should be *harder* to amend," said John, the editor of the conservative magazine.

"How so?" I asked.

"The whole point about the constitutional amendment process, and the American system altogether, is that it's supposed to be really hard to do things. It's deliberately hard to do things, because, otherwise, a tyrant on the one hand or a mob on the other hand will take control of things. So legislation is hard to pass. And even after it passes Congress and is signed by the president, there is still the possibility that the legislation can be ruled unconstitutional and therefore void by the Supreme Court. Our whole system is about gumming up the system so that people in power don't impose their wills on the public."

"I agree that gumming up the system can be good," I said, "but I think we have way too much gum."

Earlier that week I had interviewed Karin Tamerius, a psychiatrist who founded a group called Smart Politics focusing on the intersection between politics and psychology. Tamerius argued that the Founding Fathers were in a tough position. They were setting up a society relatively blindly—plenty of theory but very little data. Aside from some hazy accounts from ancient history, Madison and company had scant evidence on what kind of government structures work. Today, it's different. We have lots of data: two hundred years of governments trying out different versions of democracy or semi-democracy.

To oversimplify, she said there are two basic systems of democracy: the presidential system and the parliamentary system.

The United States has a presidential system. The president is separate from Congress. This arrangement provides checks and balances.

The president could be from one party and the Congress could be controlled by the rival party, making it more likely that the president will veto laws. It's harder to get things done in this system and get laws passed. Lots of gum in the gears.

In the parliamentary system, the head of state rises to power within the legislature. This person is the leader of the majority party in the legislature. There is no separate president who can oppose Congress. With the parliamentary system, there are fewer checks and balances. Much less gum. The good part is, you can get more laws passed—but the danger is that the party in power becomes too powerful.

Tamerius told me she thinks the parliamentary system has proven better over time. I relayed her thoughts to my dinner-mates: "Part of her proof that it's a better system is that more countries have chosen to adopt the parliamentary model than the presidential model—look at Europe, with Germany, Italy, the Scandinavian countries."

"Yeah? And how are they doing?" John asked skeptically.

"How are *we* doing?" countered Angel.

I honestly don't know if America would be better under a parliamentary system. Both systems have pros and cons. But either way, I do think we could have less gum. We are too sticky and viscous.

The conversation wound down. Lorence accepted my offer to smoke a clay pipe. He was the most committed guest and was wearing a puffy shirt and leather vest he got on Amazon. Sherry and I played an old tavern dice game called Shut the Box. We sipped some whiskey Lorence had brought over.

Granted, by the end of the dinner, we had not figured out how to fix politics—but maybe we'd had a small victory. Everyone who came emailed me that they relished sitting down face-to-face and hashing these issues out, even if there were deep disagreements. We need more of that, they said.

Plus, everyone liked the rice pudding.

Grievance

ORIGINALIST MONEY.

One of the hardest parts of making the dinner for my assembled guests: paying for it with originalist money.

The Sunday before the dinner, Zane and I went to the farmers market in our neighborhood. I brought some cloth bags, my list of ingredients . . . and about a hundred dollars' worth of gold and silver. I'd stashed a tiny gold chip in my pocket—it was about the size of a pinkie fingernail. (I'd phoned a toll-free number to buy the gold, and the salesman assured me it was a good investment, considering inflation and bank failures. "It's God's money," he told me.) I also bought a couple of silver replicas of the old pieces of eight coins.

I had the gold and silver because I figured it was the closest thing to Founder-approved money. I didn't want to pay in cash, because the Founding Fathers distrusted paper money. James Madison in particular hated it. He called paper money "unjust, impolitic, destructive of public and private confidence." He was talking about state-issued paper money, which he believed lost its value over time and was unfair to lenders. But many of the Founders weren't big fans of national paper money, either. The Constitution says Congress has the power to "coin money." The word *coin* was not chosen idly. The Founders debated a clause allowing Congress to issue paper money but opted against including it, though they didn't explicitly prohibit paper money, either.

These men trusted what they considered real money: gold and silver. *Specie,* as it is called. The federal government did not issue paper money until the Civil War. Until then, there were hundreds of varieties of currency, each one issued by local banks. But it was crucial that the banks had the metal to back up the money. As John Adams wrote, "Every dollar of a bank bill that is issued beyond the quantity of gold and silver in the vaults, represents nothing and is therefore a cheat upon somebody."

For much of its history, American money was backed by gold or silver. Banks had to have the equivalent value of gold or silver in the money they were lending. The precious metal was an anchor. But in 1971, the United States officially set the dollar loose from gold or any other metal. This action was partly to stop foreign nations from redeeming their dollars for gold. Many of the Founders, I'm guessing, would have been appalled.

So even if Adams and his fellow Founders would have reluctantly allowed federal paper money, our paper money is no longer tied to gold and silver. So, from an originalist lens, it is constitutionally suspect. Hence my quest to pay in gold and silver.

At the farmers market before our dinner, I grabbed a bundle of carrots and approached the register.

"Ten dollars," said the balding man behind the table.

"I'm trying to make an eighteenth-century meal and do every part of it as authentically as possible. The Founding Fathers distrusted paper money. So could I pay you in gold?"

The farmer chuckled.

I showed him my gold chip. "This is a gram of gold. It's worth fifty-nine dollars as of today."

He paused for several seconds. I thought I might have him.

"I'd love to, but I can't," he said.

"It's really stable," I responded, sounding like the toll-free gold salesman.

"Maybe soon, with the way things are going," he said. "But not now."

I took that to mean he thinks the apocalypse is nigh but not nigh enough.

Amending the Constitution

*Congressman John Bingham of Ohio,
one of the authors of the historic Fourteenth Amendment*

It may not be easy to change the Constitution—as my dinner companions and I discussed—but it's still possible. At least theoretically. There's still a glimmer of a shadow of a wisp of a hope that America could pass another constitutional amendment, even in this divided climate. And it is my constitutional right to try to make that happen.

Before deciding on what amendment to propose as a concerned citizen, I figured I'd get some advice from the last person who had successfully led such an endeavor. I called up an unsung hero of our republic: Gregory Watson.

"Well, I am always delighted to talk about the highly unconventional, extremely irregular, and profoundly unorthodox ratification of the United States Constitution's Twenty-Seventh Amendment," Watson said from his home in Texas.

What we have here, I thought to myself, is a delightfully unconventional, amusingly irregular, and profoundly unorthodox character.

Despite never holding elected office, Watson, now sixty-one, is largely responsible for the passage of the Twenty-Seventh Amendment in 1992. I asked him to tell me the tale.

Watson's quest began with a noble motivation: his annoyance about a bad grade in his government course. He was a sophomore at the University of Texas at Austin in 1982, and he wrote an essay. The topic? A forgotten amendment that was proposed by James Madison and dealt with congressional pay. It was supposed to be one of the amendments passed in 1791, alongside freedom of speech and the right to bear arms. But it didn't get enough votes.

The amendment said, "No law, varying the compensation for the services of the Senators and Representatives, shall take effect, until an election of Representatives shall have intervened." In other words, if

Congress votes to raise its own salary, then the pay raise cannot kick in until the following congressional term. That way, you can't give yourself an immediate raise. Perfectly reasonable.

"I found it mentioned in a book in the Austin library, and I was surprised I'd never heard of it before," Watson said.

For an amendment to be ratified, it has to be approved by at least three-quarters of the states. By the 1790s, only seven of the thirteen state legislatures okayed the pay raise amendment—three states short of the goal.

The amendment was proposed 234 years ago, but here's the twist: Watson discovered there was no deadline, no statute of limitations. It was a zombie amendment, still semi-alive after two centuries. If three-quarters of the current fifty states approved of the amendment, it would pass. It just needed thirty-one more states to say yes.

Watson wrote an essay arguing that the congressional pay amendment was still alive, and he gave it to the teacher's assistant. "I got it back with a C on it—and I was absolutely shocked," Watson told me. The feedback from the teacher's assistant: It was a ridiculous idea.

Watson appealed to the professor, who "physically hurled the paper back at me and said, 'No change.' And I remember thinking right then and there, 'You know what? I'm going to get that thing ratified.'"

Thus began his massive letter-writing campaign to state legislators. The timing was good. In 1982, Congress had just given itself a stealthy pay raise right before it took a break. People were angry. Watson convinced a Maine state senator to join the cause, and a year later, the Maine Senate voted to formally, if belatedly, ratify the amendment. That set off a chain reaction.

It took ten years—and hundreds of letters—but in 1992, it happened: Michigan became the thirty-eighth state to ratify this once-forgotten amendment.*

---

* Watson would pester and badger me if I didn't clarify. In 1992, everyone thought Michigan was the crucial final state to ratify the amendment. As it turned out, the amendment was officially

"I was an earwitness," Watson said. He was in Texas, listening over the phone as the final yea came in from a Michigan state lawmaker. "I was elated, absolutely elated."

"What advice do you have for someone like me, who's trying to get a Twenty-Eighth Amendment through?" I asked Watson.

"It's going to be hard. The country is so divided. I think the Twenty-Seventh Amendment could be the last amendment for a long, long time."

In fact, we are so divided maybe something as noncontroversial and bipartisan as his amendment might not pass now.

As I mentioned, scholars say the U.S. Constitution is among the hardest constitutions in the world to amend. It's a total catch-22. To make the Constitution easier to amend, you have to amend the way you amend the Constitution.

Watson did give me some advice. "You have to pester, badger, and cajole," he said. In fact, he continues to pester, badger, and cajole Congress. In between looking for a job (he used to be a staffer in the Texas legislature but is currently in search of employment), Watson submits petitions to Congress. Sometimes he's the only one who has signed the petitions, but he submits them nonetheless. He recently suggested term limits of twelve years for the Senate and House. I'd sign that. The average age of a senator as I write this is sixty-four. The average age at the Constitutional Convention was forty-two—and James Madison was in his thirties. (Counterargument: The word *senate* is from the Latin for "old man," so the Senate is just being true to its name.)

Watson ended the call with what seems to be his catchphrase, thanking me for talking to him about "the highly unconventional, extremely irregular, and profoundly unorthodox ratification of the United States Constitution's Twenty-Seventh Amendment."

---

ratified two days prior to Michigan's May 7 vote, when Alabama voted yes. This is because Watson was one state further along than he realized. Kentucky had quietly ratified the amendment in 1792, a fact Watson didn't learn until after his 1992 victory.

SECTION 2.

Since 1789, Congress has officially considered 10,524 constitutional amendments, with just 27 getting ratified. That's a failure rate of 99.74 percent.

I found a series of books listing the 99.74 percent of proposals that made it to the congressional floor but soon sputtered out. I spent an afternoon reading them. Or skimming them, at least. As with much of American history, I experienced both pride and horror. I saw the noblest of intentions—for instance, the 1933 proposal to have the Constitution "prohibit war." But I also saw the depths of bigotry: A few years before that, a congressman proposed an amendment to ban marriage between the races.*

Naturally, it's much easier to find books about the 0.26 percent of amendments that passed. I figured I should study these bills to see what I can learn from the winners. I discovered scholars often group the amendments into three batches.

1. THE BILL OF RIGHTS

The first batch of amendments is the most famous. The Bill of Rights constitutes those ten powerhouse amendments we were all taught in elementary school: freedom of speech, freedom to exercise religion, the right to bear arms. Several of them (IV to VIII) deal with ensuring a fair criminal and civil justice system: a speedy trial, a jury of your peers, reasonable bail, no searches without probable cause.

Here's the strange part: The Bill of Rights was passed in 1791, soon after the Constitution—but it didn't gain its all-star stature until later. Much later—about 140 years later.

"Interestingly, once the ten amendments were passed, everybody just forgot about them immediately," said historian Carol Berkin, using

---

* Not to mention just the bizarre, such as the 1893 proposal to rename this nation the United States of the Earth, which seems like quite the overreach.

a bit of hyperbole in a recent interview for the podcast *Ben Franklin's World*. "They were just completely ignored, except briefly in the arguments about the Alien and Sedition Acts. When Jefferson, who was secretary of state, announced that the Bill of Rights had been ratified, it comes *after* a statement about fishing rights. The Bill of Rights doesn't become significant in our legal system until the 1930s. I found that to be really quite extraordinary. It's not until the 1930s that the courts begin to incorporate the Bill of Rights into their decisions."*

Why were these amendments such late bloomers?

As I mentioned, many of the Founding Fathers saw the first ten amendments as less than crucial and more about appeasing the Anti-Federalists, who feared the Constitution created a too-powerful federal government. Federalists were throwing the opponents of the Constitution a bone, or throwing a tub to a whale, in the parlance of the day.

Importantly, at the time, these amendments were not as much about individual rights as they are today, argues Berkin in her book *The Bill of Rights*. Instead, she says, these first ten amendments were mostly about states' rights. They were a way to curtail the national government from infringing on the state governments. The federal government could not control your freedom of speech. That was the states' job.

It was not until the ratification of the Fourteenth Amendment in 1868—and a series of Supreme Court decisions in its wake—that the Bill of Rights was deemed to apply to state governments as well as the federal. After that, neither Washington, D.C., nor your state government could control your freedom of speech. At that point, the Bill of Rights switched its focus to individual rights. And when that happened, it grew in power and influence.

---

* Other historians would say that the Bill of Rights affected court decisions earlier than the 1930s. But almost all would agree that its influence ballooned in the twentieth century.

2. RECONSTRUCTION AMENDMENTS

The next burst of amendments came right after the Civil War. These three are known as the Reconstruction Amendments. And many scholars say that they fundamentally changed the country. Some go as far as calling them the second founding:

- The Thirteenth Amendment in 1865 ended slavery.
- The Fourteenth Amendment in 1868 has several sections that expanded civil rights.
- The Fifteenth Amendment in 1870 sought to ensure Black men's right to vote.

As I mentioned earlier, the Fourteenth Amendment extended the Bill of Rights to apply to state laws as well as national, strengthening individual rights. But it did more than that. It also promised that states would provide "equal protection of the laws" and "due process."

These rights, initially aimed at protecting Black men, have since been expanded to protect many other vulnerable groups. The Fourteenth Amendment now guarantees gay rights and women's rights.

"This is a complete reversal of the founding vision," says Kermit Roosevelt, of the University of Pennsylvania, in his course titled Introduction to Key Constitutional Concepts and Supreme Court Cases.* "You don't need states to protect their citizens from the federal government. You need the federal government to come in and protect citizens from their states. The states aren't good anymore. The states are bad. And the federal government isn't a threat to liberty anymore. It's the protector of liberty and of equality."

---

* Since I've been asked, yes, Kermit Roosevelt is related to the presidential Roosevelts. He's the great-great-grandson of Teddy Roosevelt. I didn't want to mention it, because I believe Professor Roosevelt's ideas stand on their own, regardless of who his father's father's father's father was. I also believe that the spirit of the Constitution is to judge ideas on their own merits, not on the ancestry of the person who said it. Most of the Founding Fathers—at least in theory and in their best moments—feared an American aristocracy based on birth. The nobility clause in Article I prevents Congress from granting titles of nobility.

I will talk more about the Fourteenth Amendment and its impact on civil rights later in this book. But one important note on the amendment: As with much in the Constitution, the Fourteenth Amendment can be used as a tool by all sides—progressives, conservatives, and libertarians, among others.

For several decades, big business used the Fourteenth Amendment to promote an anti-labor agenda. It began in 1905, when the Supreme Court ruled that the Fourteenth Amendment protects employers from pesky government labor laws. The case was called *Lochner v. New York,* and focused on a New York law about bakeries. The law said bakery bosses couldn't force their employees to work more than ten hours a day. The Court said the New York law was unconstitutional. It violated the bosses' Fourteenth Amendment rights. For the next thirty-two years, the Court invalidated other laws regulating working conditions, minimum wages, and hours. Due process for horrible bosses!

The so-called Lochner Era lasted until 1937. Nowadays, all liberals and most conservatives (except for some hard-core libertarians) see the Lochner Era as a distortion of the Fourteenth Amendment. But it's a clear example of how the Constitution can be used, rightly or wrongly, to justify almost any -ism.

The Fourteenth Amendment has another clause that became hugely consequential as I was finishing my book. It's Section 3, the "Disqualification Clause." The clause says, "No person shall . . . hold any office, civil or military, under the United States . . . who, having previously taken an oath . . . as an officer of the United States . . . to support the Constitution of the United States, shall have engaged in insurrection or rebellion against the same, or given aid or comfort to the enemies thereof."

It was written in the wake of the Civil War to keep Confederate politicians from being elected in southern states. Several lawsuits allege that Donald Trump should be disqualified from running for president because of this clause. The lawsuits say he engaged in insurrection against the United States for his role in the January 6 Capitol attack. The

Colorado Supreme Court ruled that he did, and that he should be kept off the state's ballot. The Maine Secretary of State made a similar ruling. As of this writing, the Supreme Court hasn't weighed in. Whatever happens, it's more proof of how much constitutional interpretation affects the world. What counts as an "insurrection"? Is the president an "officer of the United States"? The answers to these questions could affect who will be our next commander in chief.

3. PROGRESSIVE ERA AMENDMENTS

The next batch of amendments—those ratified from the 1890s to the 1920s—are called the Progressive Era Amendments. "They are connected by a sort of optimism about government and society," says Professor Roosevelt. "It was thought that by following scientific methods, the government could be a force for good."

This era's amendments included these:

- The Sixteenth Amendment in 1913 allowed the federal government to levy an income tax.
- The Seventeenth Amendment in 1913 switched the way the Senate was chosen. It would now be chosen by the regular voters, not by the state's legislature.
- The Nineteenth Amendment in 1920 finally guaranteed women's right to vote nationwide.

In most of these, we see the federal government gaining more power, and the power of the states ebbing.

After the Progressive Era, there were just a handful of amendments, such as the Twenty-Second, in 1951, limiting a president to two terms; 1971's Twenty-Sixth, lowering the voting rights age to eighteen; and our beloved Twenty-Seventh Amendment about congressional pay.

The Progressive Era Amendments' biggest flop, of course, was the Eighteenth Amendment—the 1919 prohibition against intoxicating liquor. Prohibition turned out to be a terrible idea, almost as bad as Zima. It's the only amendment that has been reversed (the Twenty-First "Oops, sorry about that" Amendment was passed in 1933).

Prohibition gives me a helpful insight into what kinds of amendments do not work. Don't try to get too specific. Instead, focus on the bigger picture—how government operates or universal rights.

SECTION 3.

So what should my amendment be? Some of my favorite amendments deal with expanding democracy—spreading power around more equally. So I asked myself, where in American life is power accumulating in a worrisome way? Well, lots of places. But one is . . . the White House. The office of president is far too powerful—at least by the standards of the Founding Fathers.

When the Constitution was written, Congress was first among equals. The president was important but wasn't driving the train. Over the centuries, the office of president has taken on more and more power. I'm talking about both Democratic and Republican presidents. Presidents start wars and issue a jaw-dropping number of executive orders. Consider this: George Washington issued 8 executive orders in his eight years. Obama issued 276 executive orders in his eight years, and Trump issued 220 in just four years. The Founders would be gobsmacked.

In fact, some of the Founders were stunned that we decided to have a single person as president in the first place. Early on in my research, I stumbled on a fascinating moment in the records of the Constitutional Convention, in notes taken by James Madison.

At the start of the convention, most delegates agreed to the idea of three separate branches of government: the executive, the legislative, and the judicial. But what should that executive branch look like? Should it be one person or a committee of several people? This was a matter of debate.

When James Wilson—a delegate from Pennsylvania—proposed the executive branch be made up of a single person, many delegates were appalled. One man as president? Hadn't they just fought a years-long bloody war to free themselves of a king? And now Wilson wanted a single person to have all that power? That's absurd. "It's the fetus of monarchy," exclaimed Edmund Randolph of Virginia. Others agreed with Randolph. The presidency should be a committee, a group of people. Perhaps three, one from each region (North, mid-Atlantic, and South). Or maybe six or twelve people.

The debate raged for weeks. Ultimately, Wilson and his allies wore the others down, arguing that multiple presidents would lead to infighting. Seven states okayed a single-person president, and three states opposed. We don't know exactly how many delegates voted against a single-person presidency, since only the state votes—not the individual votes—were recorded. For instance, even though Pennsylvania voted for a single-person presidency, I suspect Ben Franklin might have been opposed. We know he was a fan of the multiperson executive in the past. In 1776, when forming the government for the Articles of Confederation, Franklin wanted the presidency to consist of a committee of twelve men.

I'd never thought about it, but Franklin and Randolph had a good point. One supreme leader is, in fact, the fetus of monarchy. Those who hold the office will just want to accrue power—and indeed they have. That fetus is now a toddler, maybe even a tween. Over the centuries, the office of the president has gained alarming control.

What if, I thought, we try to resurrect Franklin's idea? Bring back the multiperson presidency! That could be my petition.

I wasn't delusional. I realized the chances of switching to a multiple presidency are approximately zero. And that's fine. It would be a big risk if we did make this change. But I thought it was an important symbolic gesture. I wanted to remind people that we can change the structure of our government. It was not meant to be carved in stone for all time. The Founders were much more experimental than that. I also wanted the petition to be a reminder that the presidency has gained too much power, whichever side of the aisle you are on.

So that was it. I had decided on my Twenty-Eighth Amendment project: Be fruitful and multiply the number of presidents. Now I had to put quill to paper. In the meantime . . .

Huzzah

THE JOY OF WATCHING LANGUAGE COME ALIVE.

The other day, I learned about the origin of the phrase *flash in the pan*. It comes from muskets. The pan was a part of the musket that held a dash of gunpowder. This explosive material was supposed to ignite in the pan, then travel to the barrel and force out the lead ball. But if something went awry—if the gunpowder just flared in the pan but didn't propel the lead ball—it was a flash in the pan.

A bit later, I watched a video on how to make flax and saw the plant fiber combed into fine, soft yellow strands. Ah, I said to myself, now *flaxen-haired* actually makes sense.

I love when previously lifeless phrases become vivid, when the skeletons gain skin and bones and muscle.

Grievance

MODESTY LAWS.

We visited a friend's house at the lake. After reading about the modesty laws in early America, I made sure to wear a long-sleeved shirt at the beach. I'd also decided to buy a gift for Julie: one of those vintage bathing suits that cover everything but the ankles.

The closest I could find was a Victorian bathing suit on Etsy. Julie agreed to put it on just once. My plan backfired. The photo on Etsy had been deceiving. This was a sexy Victorian bathing suit. Or relatively sexy, with a short skirt and no sleeves. Julie was pleased. "I was actually more covered up before you asked me to wear this."

Petitioning the Government for Redress of Grievances

I'd settled on the topic of my proposed constitutional amendment—a multitude of presidents. Or a brood of presidents. Or a shrewdness of presidents. I'm not sure what the proper collective noun is. But I did know it was time to move on to the next phase: pestering, badgering, and cajoling.

And as Gregory Watson advised, my pestering, badgering, and cajoling would take the form of a petition. It's my constitutional right. There it is, tucked into the very end of the First Amendment: Congress cannot abridge my right to "petition the Government for a redress of grievances."

This would be the first petition I'd ever started—and one of the first I'd signed. I have always been a bit of a petition skeptic, viewing them as annoying weeds that popped up in my social media feed, an example of slacktivism, with little chance of making a real difference. Plus, I didn't always find the issues immensely pressing. Do I want to abolish piñatas from kids' birthday parties because they are too violent, as I was asked in an actual petition I received? Frankly, it's not my number one priority.

But after doing some research, I'd gained new respect for petitions. They have an impressive legacy. Petitions were crucial to the success of the abolition movement, for one thing. They were also a way for disenfranchised groups—such as women and Native Americans—to express their voices before they got the vote.

So maybe petitions should have a comeback. And maybe, the secret is to go old-school. Take petitions off social media feeds and put them back onto paper with ink. I wanted my petition to be a big fat scroll of paper the size of an oak tree trunk. Maybe I could even roll it into Congress the way some citizens did with a successful 1893 petition requesting more roads. They wrapped the 150,000 signatures around two giant wooden spools reminiscent of bicycle wheels and rolled it into the Capitol.

How would I get into the Capitol with my petition without committing sedition? I wasn't sure. Regardless, a paper petition would let me go on the road, meet people face-to-face, get out of my bubble, all that good stuff. *Democracy* is a verb, not a noun, I reminded myself.

I sat down at my desk, quill in hand, and began to write:

To the Honorable Congress of the United States of America

In 1776, the United States of America threw off the chains of monarchy and declared independence.

Nearly 250 years later, it seems we might be edging toward monarchy again.

Since the founding of our country, the office of the president has gained more and more power. Nowadays, that one person, the president (whether Republican or Democrat), has unprecedented control over the lives of everyday Americans.

It doesn't have to be so.

We ask that Congress reconsider the idea of Ben Franklin, one of the wisest of the Founding Fathers. Ben Franklin suggested there be a committee of twelve presidents, not a single person.

Other delegates also endorsed a multiple presidency. Edmund Randolph called a single president the "fetus of monarchy." Randolph preferred a three-person presidency.

We believe that a three-person presidency is a more American system than a single all-powerful executive. We believe it will reduce the danger of America becoming an authoritarian state.

Though it may sound unusual, the idea of multiple heads of state has proven effective. The executive branch of

Switzerland consists of seven people who make up the Swiss Federal Council. For 500 years in ancient Rome, two consuls were elected each year to serve as joint chief magistrates of the Roman state.

We the undersigned ask Congress to consider a constitutional amendment to replace the current flawed system of a single president with three co-equal presidents.

Let's give America the democracy it deserves, not a system of elected semi-kings and queens!

I put down my quill and admired the three sheets of paper. Granted, my petition was a little over the top. A little John Adams–like in its hyperbole. But it was heartfelt enough to take on the road.

My ninety-one-year-old mother-in-law was visiting, sitting at the kitchen table.

"Would you like to be the first to sign my petition?"

"Do I need to read it?" she asked. "My glasses are in the other room."

"Not if you don't want to."

"Okay, then give me the pen," she said, ever the supportive mother-in-law.

I gave her the pen—actually, my goose quill predipped in ink—and she signed. An efficient start to my quest.

SECTION 2.

A couple of days later, I was invited to a friend's party at a downtown basement bar. I brought along my petition, as well as my quill and a corked bottle of ink.

I asked a woman standing by the door if she'd sign.

"I would sign it," she said, "but I'm a vegan, so I can't use the feather."

She was the exception. I set up my petition on a table in the corner, and I got a steady flow of curious partygoers. Frankly, most of them just wanted to try writing with a quill. The novelty factor was key. They probably would have signed a petition to make "Mambo No. 5" the national anthem.

"How does it work?" one asked, lifting up the quill.

"Dip it in ink, and don't press down too hard, just graze the page," I said. "And remember to sign it big, like John Hancock on the Declaration of Independence." I figured the bigger the signature, the more pages, the more impressive the petition.

Side note: I'd always thought John Hancock's signature was a bit of an aggressively uncool move, like revving a really loud motorcycle at a stoplight. But an article in *Slate* has changed my mind. It wasn't that Hancock's signature was too big. It was that the others were too *small*. There was plenty of space left at the bottom of the document.

Naturally, my petition had its doubters.

"Why would we want three presidents?" one woman asked.

"It might reduce the chance of extremism," I said. "You might get one Trump, but two Mitt Romneys."

"But what if you get three Trumps?" she responded.

"Would that really be worse than one Trump with three times the power?"

Another man said, "Oh yeah, we really want more people in Washington who can disagree with each other."

But more than half of those at the party signed on.

"What we've got doesn't seem to be working, so maybe it's time to try something new," said a slightly tipsy woman, with a shrug.

Another woman told me, "As a Christian, I can see the appeal of three in one."

"I'm with you," said one friend, a political consultant. "It's dangerous that we have one person with his finger on the button for nuclear war." He brought up a story about how, one night in 1969, Richard Nixon got really drunk and ordered the joint chiefs of staff to execute a tactical nuclear strike on North Korea. Henry Kissinger convinced the military to hold off till the morning, at which point Nixon had sobered up and called off the strike. I later looked into the veracity of this story. It has been written about in books, but the source is the memory of a single person, a former CIA agent. So I wouldn't say it's settled fact. But the general point is correct: In our current system, a single human being has too much say over whether we launch bombs that would kill millions, maybe billions, of people.

I took my petition everywhere I went. To my doctor's office. To parent events at my kids' school. To Times Square, where my son Jasper joined me and even donned his own tricorne hat. He convinced a nice Australian couple to sign on. I couldn't believe my luck that one of my own family was willing to join me in potential humiliation. As for the Australians? I just hope Congress doesn't check the nationality of all signers. Even my parents signed, which was unusual. They are petition-phobic, having lived through the 1950s, when Senator Joe McCarthy ruined people's lives for signing obscure petitions in their youth.

After a fortnight and several spilled bottles of ink in my backpack, my petition had grown to a respectable size: eleven pages of light-yellow paper, Scotch-taped together and containing dozens of bold signatures.

SECTION 3.

Midway through my petition project, I got a pleasant surprise. It turns out my multiple-president idea wasn't as fringe as I'd thought.

"Yep, there's a lot of talk about that right now," Daniel Carpenter, a professor of government at Harvard, told me when I called him to talk about my petition.

A lot of talk about multiple heads of state?

"Yes, there's some evidence that democracies that fall into authoritarianism are more likely to be led by a single president," the professor said. "There's an essay about it—'The Perils of Presidentialism,' by Juan

Linz. It's going to be hard to bring about, but somebody's got to start the conversation."

I had called Professor Carpenter because I had read his book *Democracy by Petition*, a history of American petitioning, and wanted to ask his advice.

"I'm doing my petition the old-fashioned way, ink and paper, not online," I told him.

"Good for you," he said. "Good for you."

I asked Carpenter why our Founders thought petitioning was worthy of mention in the Constitution.

He reminded me that many of the Founders actually did *not* want petitioning mentioned. Or any other individual rights. Hamilton and others thought the Bill of Rights was unnecessary. It was the Constitution's opponents, the Anti-Federalists, who demanded the additions. They worried that the new American government was too powerful and believed the Bill of Rights would make the federal government more accountable to the American people.

At the time, the pro-petition folks saw petitions as an important democratic tool—one that the British monarchy had tried to suppress. In 1661, the British passed the wonderfully named Tumultuous Petitioning Act, which sought to put an end to tumultuous petitions. What was a tumultuous petition? It was when your petition had more than twenty signatures or was delivered to Parliament by more than ten men.

So the Anti-Federalists wrote petitioning into the First Amendment. But here's the surprising part I learned from Carpenter. In the first draft of the First Amendment, the "petition" sentence actually contained a far more radical idea. The Anti-Federalists wanted to give people the "right to petition and instruct."

What is the right to instruct? In this case, it's not about teachers or classrooms. Instructing was a practice in some colonial legislatures. The public would literally *instruct* the politician how to vote. The constituents would have a town meeting and say, "We, the constituents of the Fifth District of Massachusetts, instruct our representative to vote yes on this bill and to vote no on this bill."

Heavens to Betsy! That is a radical idea. Imagine how different the United States would be if the word *instruct* had remained in the Constitution! Imagine if politicians really were just the messengers of the people's will. Imagine Ted Cruz saying, "Well, I don't agree with solar energy, but I've been instructed by my constituents to pass this bill, so I suppose I vote yea." We would basically have a direct democracy. Perhaps unworkable, but interesting for sure.

Madison and other Founding Fathers, who feared mob rule, had the word *instruct* nixed. But petitioning made it to the final version. And it had an impact. The golden age of petitions stretched from about 1820 to 1860, Carpenter told me. And the most common petitions in that age were for the abolition of slavery. It worked like this: An abolitionist newspaper would print a petition and encourage readers to go collect signatures. Women—and it was mostly women—would go door-to-door and collect signatures. Or they would set up at a church and collect signatures there.

Some petitions led to immediate changes in law. But even if they didn't, they could still be powerful. Petitions were a way to build a movement and create influential networks. "Petitions were very effective organizing devices," Carpenter said. "Canvassers who went door-to-door could encourage people to think and participate in politics."

The petitions weren't always for noble causes such as abolition. There were plenty of more obscure movements. The Sabbatarians were a group of religious Christians who wanted laws to restrict activities on Sunday. The U.S. Postal Service, for instance. If America continued to ignore God's law and deliver mail on Sundays, it would face "calamities" and the "judgment of Heaven," one petition warned. The Sabbatarians eventually won, which is why we don't have mail on Sunday and why nothing calamitous has happened since.

Petitioning went into decline in the twentieth century for several reasons. One major reason is that politicians could gauge public opinion more easily with polls, so petitions became less useful as a tool.

The internet was also a mixed blessing for petitions. Petitions became so simple to spread online, Congress started to take them less seriously. Carpenter told me petitions today are almost too easy. "You throw it up on Change.org. And those petitions don't necessarily go anywhere. One really important thing about past petitions is that they were sent to a government body, which was obligated to respond even when the response was no. Whereas a lot of the petitions today just sit there on the web and don't get sent to any member of Congress."

Not my petition. I wanted to deliver my petition right into the hands of a sitting senator or House member. Have them feel the heft of it. After all, I was up to about two hundred signatures—deep into tumultuous territory. Now I just needed an invitation from Washington.

I was feeling good about my petition, but not all was right with my brain. One example:

Grievance

OBSESSIONS AND HALLUCINATIONS.

Everything I see reminds me of the Founders or politics or the Supreme Court. This forenoon, Julie was wearing a white shirt covered with silhouetted faces.

"Is that Sonia Sotomayor on your shirt?" I asked. "I love it!"

Julie looked at me, baffled. "These are random spots," she said.

I inspected the shirt again. She was right. They were Rorschach-like ink blots, not the silhouette of America's first Hispanic justice. I am seeing patterns where there are none—a danger for all kinds of interpretation.

Race and the Constitution

Frederick Douglass

SECTION 1.

Julie and I arrived at Cooper Union's Great Hall in downtown New York on a Friday night. We were late. One hundred sixty years, three months, and twenty-seven days late, to be exact.

If we'd arrived at this event space in a more punctual manner, we would have gotten to witness Frederick Douglass—the former enslaved man who became a brilliant orator—give a profound speech that dealt with the Constitution and race.

But even belatedly, I wanted to visit the legendary New York event space because I wanted to get as close to Douglass as possible. I've found his writing and speeches to be extremely helpful in understanding the Constitution.

Plus, the event that night seemed befitting of Douglass's legacy. It was a memorial for Harry Belafonte, the singer and civil rights activist, who had recently died. The memorial was in the form of a conversation between novelist Walter Mosley, who was a friend of Belafonte's, and *New York Times* critic-at-large Wesley Morris. A great admirer of Douglass, Belafonte had collected several of Douglass's letters and had done dramatic readings of some of the statesman's speeches. So maybe Douglass would be a topic of the discussion.

As we took our seats, Belafonte's voice sang over the loudspeakers: "Come, Mr. Tally Man, tally me banana! Daylight come and me wan' go home." The crowd swayed in their chairs. I reached into my shoulder sack and retrieved my quill pen, my tricorne hat, and a transcript of Douglass's Cooper Union speech.

I'd printed it out (using the olde-timey Zapfino typeface, of course) because I wanted to read it again in the place where he had delivered it. Douglass began his speech with a celebration of the Emancipation Proclamation, which Abraham Lincoln had signed a few days before.

"I congratulate you, upon what may be called the greatest event of our nation's history," Douglass told the crowd. He was speaking about the legal end to American slavery in the Southern states.

Douglass acknowledged the Emancipation Proclamation was just a "paper Proclamation." It had to be made real by "iron, lead, and fire." This was 1863, and the Civil War was still raging, so slavery persisted in the Southern states. Its true end would still require bloodshed. But Douglass told the crowd, don't discount paper proclamations. "Our own Declaration of Independence was at one time but ink and paper."

I appreciate Douglass's point about not discounting ink and paper, even if it's just the start of the struggle for freedom and justice. Douglass felt the same way about the Emancipation Proclamation as he did about the Declaration of Independence and the Constitution. These documents were promissory notes, not the finished deal. They were the start, not the end. They planted the seeds.

"What a glorious day when Slavery shall be no more in this country," Douglass said, "when we have blotted out this system of wrong, and made this United States in fact and in truth what it is in theory—the Land of the Free and the Home of the Brave."

I'll return to the Harry Belafonte event in a bit. But let me take a detour into Douglass and how he sheds light on originalism, the Constitution, and race.

SECTION 2.

A few days before my trip to Cooper Union's Great Hall, I had a Zoom call with a Northwestern law professor named Paul Gowder. I contacted him after reading his article "Reconstituting We the People," in the *Northwestern University Law Review,* a fascinating analysis of Douglass's relationship with our founding documents.

When I reached him, Professor Gowder said, "Any conversation about race and the Constitution has to start with this question: Why should we live in a society where the rules were created by a bunch of dead enslavers? Why should we let their document organize our lives? What the hell?"

He pointed out that the original 1789 Constitution contained several proslavery clauses, including the requirement that fugitive slaves be returned to bondage. The Constitution also gave slave states an electoral advantage with the notorious three-fifths compromise. This clause stated that enslaved people count for three-fifths of a person. Which meant that fifty enslaved people would add thirty people to a state's population in the census. The higher the population, the more congressional representatives and the more power.

Before the Civil War, Douglass contemplated the question I first mentioned in my Preamble: How should we treat this document? Should we burn it? Or should we focus on the parts about the "Blessings of Liberty" and demand the Constitution live up to its promises?

The burn-it strategy was adopted by some of Douglass's colleagues, including famed abolitionist William Lloyd Garrison. He literally burned it. Garrison denounced the Constitution as a "covenant with death" and "an agreement with Hell" and set it on fire in front of a crowd.

Initially, Douglass agreed with Garrison. But around 1851, he changed his mind. "Douglass was not deluded," said Gowder. "He knew that the protection of slavery was a core motivation of the constitutional framers. But his point is, 'Okay, we can take this thing and we can use it as a resource.' If we commit to doing activism, the Constitution doesn't have to stand in the way of the activism and indeed can be deployed as a resource for this activism."

Professor Gowder said that the idea is this: "We should absolutely use the master's tools to burn the master's house down—and to rebuild a better house." Douglass believed in the "latent Constitution." It was an aspirational document, and America needed to embrace its promises.

Douglass's perspective has been enormously influential. Martin

Luther King Jr., for instance, echoed Douglass decades later. In his famous "I Have a Dream" speech, Reverend King called on America to fulfill the "promissory note" of freedom in its founding documents. President Barack Obama gave a 2008 speech on race with the same thesis: "The answer to the slavery question was already embedded within our Constitution—a Constitution that had at its very core the ideal of equal citizenship under the law; a Constitution that promised its people liberty and justice and a union that could be and should be perfected over time."

Gowder agrees, adding, "If we actually look at what's happened over our constitutional history, all the really interesting stuff in our Constitution has happened because of subordinated groups demanding change or inclusion." He believes this struggle can be framed as a "cross-generational dialogue." He calls his theory *liberation constitutionalism,* a term echoing liberation theology, a movement that was popular in the 1960s in Latin America and that used the Bible as a catalyst for social change. "In other words, we're participants in a collective project of constitution making," he said. "In a sense, Douglass was a founder. And as we shape the ways the Constitution is interpreted, we are founders too."

The idea that people today can be Founders would, of course, make originalists like Antonin Scalia apoplectic. But it's not a new idea. It's a more strongly stated version of living constitutionalism.

SECTION 3.

One of Douglass's goals was to reenvision the original 1789 Constitution to focus on its noblest passages. But, of course, there is another way to address the Constitution's flaws: by amending it.

And five years after his Cooper Union speech, thanks to the work of Douglass and others, Congress did just that. The Fourteenth and Fifteenth Amendments guaranteed Black men the vote and promised "equal protection of the laws." So did these amendments fully repair the Constitution's flaws about race?

Elie Mystal, a legal commentator and the author of *Allow Me to Retort: A Black Guy's Guide to the Constitution,* is firmly in the *no* camp. He argues the Fourteenth Amendment was a huge step forward, but its original public meaning was still mired in racism. Consider marriage between the races. Mystal writes that the authors and ratifiers of the Fourteenth Amendment were okay with Black men voting, but opposed Black men marrying white women. They were just fine with state laws that forbade intermarriage between the races. They considered these laws constitutional.

For instance, during the debates over the Reconstruction Amendments, one Pennsylvania congressman said, "It cannot be possible that any man of common sense can bring himself to believe that marriages between any persons, much less between white and colored people, will take place because a colored man is allowed to drop a little bit of paper in a box. . . . It is too trifling for argument." In other words, the amendment will guarantee Black men the right to vote but not the right to marry a white woman.

Many states had racist anti-miscegenation laws all the way up till the Supreme Court ruled them unconstitutional in 1967 (and even beyond). It took years of activism to expand the Fourteenth Amendment to include interracial marriage.

This is why, Mystal argues, the intermarriage issue is "kryptonite for originalist logic." If you go by the true original public meaning, the Fourteenth Amendment would still allow for bans on intermarriage. You could say goodbye to *Loving v. Virginia*—the 1967 case in which SCOTUS ruled that intermarriage bans were unconstitutional. "There is no originalist understanding of the Fourteenth Amendment that comports with the Supreme Court's unanimous opinion in *Loving,*" Mystal writes in his book. "Either our understanding of the Fourteenth Amendment 'evolved' to include a rejection of racist anti-miscegenation laws, or it didn't. If the Fourteenth Amendment doesn't evolve, Alabama could force people to submit 'pure-blood' certifications from Ancestry.com before issuing marriage licenses."

In this view, if I were truly trying to be the ultimate originalist, and if I were following the rules of my project to the letter, I would have to consider my sister's marriage to my brother-in-law Willy invalid. My sister is white, and Willy is of Indigenous Peruvian ancestry.

The same critique of originalism is often made by invoking segregation. The assertion is this: Originalism, properly applied, would still allow for the segregation of the races. A truly originalist Supreme Court would not have issued the landmark decision in the 1954 case *Brown v. Board of Education,* which ruled that "separate but equal" is unconstitutional. It would have issued the opposite opinion, saying it *is* constitutional for schools to separate students by race. The ratifiers of the Fourteenth Amendment did not believe they were extending rights to racially mixed schools.

Nowadays, it would be disastrous for a mainstream public figure to oppose SCOTUS's anti-segregation decision in *Brown v. Board of Education.* Originalists understand this and have come up with ways to try to reconcile originalism and the *Brown v. Board of Education* decision. I've read at least three types of responses to the charge that originalism would lead to racist policies.

One strategy, according to Stanford law professor and originalist Michael McConnell, is to move to a "higher level of generality" so that "equal protection" *does* apply to segregation, even if the ratifiers of the Fourteenth Amendment didn't mean it to. But to me, that seems little different from living constitutionalism—and it doesn't convince McConnell, either.

A second rebuttal is that the framers of the Fourteenth Amendment just had some bad facts but not bad motives. The argument goes like this: Yes, the ratifiers of the Fourteenth Amendment thought segregation was constitutional. But they only believed this because they had the wrong facts. They thought that separate *could* actually be equal. Black train cars and white train cars could be equivalent. Now, however, we have learned new facts. We have learned the sociological truth that segregation can never be equal. Facilities devoted to a minority will always be worse than those devoted to the majority, and will always be psychologically degrading to the minority. So segregation was always unconstitutional, they just didn't know it back in 1868. If they had our knowledge back in 1868, they would also have disapproved of segregation. It's not that we need to evolve principles or morality, as living constitutionalism says. It's just a factual misunderstanding. Thus originalism is saved.

A third approach is to deny that the original public meaning of the amendment allowed for segregated schools or bans on intermarriage. Here, originalists such as McConnell cite evidence from 1860s congressional debates, newspapers, and dictionaries. They say the evidence shows the original public meaning of the Fourteenth Amendment was clear: It held that segregation and mixed marriage bans were unconstitutional. Nonoriginalists do not generally find the evidence convincing, saying it's cherry-picked and sparse.

SECTION 4.

More recently, there's been a lot of debate over originalism and affirmative action. The originalist justices famously assert that the "Constitution is color-blind." They hold that the Constitution rarely allows for the government to base a decision on race. They say there are fringe exceptions—separating participants in a race riot at a prison, for instance—but mostly, the law is color-blind. As Justice Thomas wrote in a 2003 decision, "The Constitution abhors classifications based on race, not only because those classifications can harm favored races or are based on illegitimate motives, but also because every time the government places citizens on racial registers and makes race relevant to the provision of burdens or benefits, it demeans us all."

Traditionally, advocates of affirmative action counter this originalism with arguments based on what's needed for a fair society today. But interestingly, Justice Ketanji Brown Jackson took the conservative originalists' playbook and used it to argue for affirmative action. As Adam Liptak explains in *The New York Times,* "During her confirmation hearings, to the surprise of some, Justice Jackson declared herself an originalist."

Jackson followed up that declaration during a 2023 case about ending race-based affirmative action at universities. Writes Liptak, "On her second day of arguments, she set out a sort of mission statement, asking a long series of questions about the history of the Fourteenth Amendment, adopted after the Civil War and meant to protect formerly enslaved Black people. 'That's not a race-neutral or race-blind idea,' she said."

Of course, many of these arguments hinge on the idea that the original public meaning—along with tradition—are crucial to deciding what our policies should be today. Harvard law professor Cass Sunstein, in his book *A Constitution of Many Minds,* argues that we should *not* look to the past when making laws about race. The past can be a helpful guide in many areas, he says, such as balance of powers and states' rights. But in matters of race? When we've so often been flatly wrong?

SECTION 5.

Back to the Cooper Union. Walter Mosley has been telling stories about Belafonte's activism, his love of history, including his collection of Frederick Douglass letters, and his ability to charm any human being on earth. Mosley ends by telling "a brief little story" about his friend:

> He didn't have a great deal of anger toward people. He had anger toward their ignorance.

Harry once went to a venue where he was supposed to perform. It was the fifties. It was a place where Black people didn't walk in the front door.

The guy guarding the door said, "You can't come in, there is an event tonight."

And Harry said, "Yes, but they expect me."

And the guard said, "No, no."

And Harry said okay. And he sat down . . . And [the event organizers] kept coming to the place where he was supposed to enter, but he didn't enter. . . .

And finally this lady runs out, and she says, "Harry, what's wrong?"

And he said, "Well, I'm having a dispute with your man at the door. He won't let me in."

And the lady says [to the guard], "What's wrong with you? I'm going to fire you!"

And Harry says, "No, no, no. You don't need to fire him. Bring him in. Let him hear the show."

And he went in and did the performance.

I think that's the world Harry would want. Now whether that's the world we need to work toward now, I don't know the answer.

Calling a Constitutional Convention

Here's a classic joke from the beloved Constitutional Humor catalog:

> A man goes into a library and asks for a copy of the French constitution, only to be turned away.
>
> "We do not stock periodicals," the librarian says.

Get it? The French have had so many constitutions, they come out as often as *Le Monde* newspaper. The country has had sixteen constitutions since its first, in 1791. Not just amended, but totally rewritten.

Most other countries in the world have also replaced their original constitutions. The Dominican Republic holds the record, chalking up thirty-eight constitutions since 1844, with each new version altering the way its government operates or what rights are guaranteed.

But the United States? Just the one. Our original Constitution is still going strong after a record 237 years—with amendments, of course.

There are folks on both the left and the right who want to change that. They want to call a new constitutional convention and come up with the U.S. Constitution 2.0.

On the left, folks such as Sanford Levinson, a University of Texas government professor, call our current Constitution "dysfunctional" and "insufficiently democratic." The problems are too deep, such as the two-senators-per-state rule, which gives a huge advantage to sparsely populated states. We need to start again, he and others say.

On the right, fans of a constitutional reboot say the current Constitution takes too much power from the states. "I think the states are due a convention," Jodey Arrington, a Republican representative from Texas, told *The New York Times* in 2022. "It is time to rally the states and rein in Washington responsibly."

To get a new constitutional convention, Article V says that two-thirds of state legislatures (thirty-four states today) must call for one. We are getting surprisingly close to that number. So far, nineteen state legislatures have endorsed an Article V convention in a movement mostly fueled by right-wing outrage. The trend has alarmed some Democrats.

So, do we need a new constitution?

I read an interesting book called *The Endurance of National Constitutions* to see what I could learn. In a section on the pros and cons of a country's total revamping of its constitution, the authors note that "the debate reduces to the perennial tension between flexibility and commitment. There is rarely any one-size-fits-all resolution to this tension."

In other words, it depends. The French, for instance, have certainly been flexible in their government, but they've also been heavy on the upheavals.

Sometimes I long for a simple yes-or-no answer. I called up one of the book's coauthors, Zachary Elkins, a political scientist at the University of Texas at Austin, to dig deeper. "Do you think the U.S. should discard our old Constitution and write a totally new one?" I asked him.

"I go back and forth about this," Elkins said. "I do like the idea of updating our Constitution. One of the biggest problems is that we can't get things done. Getting Congress to do anything other than name a post office seems really hard these days. So I like the idea of decreasing the friction and allowing some things to go through, even if there are things that I wouldn't necessarily want."

So he's for a new Constitution? Well, not necessarily.

"On the other hand, I do also recognize that we've had this document so long that we've built up our society around it. And though sometimes it appears America might be coming apart at the seams, one of the reasons we've stayed together this long is because we have these national myths and these national documents. So it's a big risk to replace it. It might be worth it, but it's a risk to open it up."

I told him my preference is not to take the risk. The imperfect Constitution we know is better than the potentially very scary constitution we don't.

I asked Professor Elkins to pull back and consider an even bigger question: "Why do countries even need constitutions?" I asked. "England doesn't have a written constitution, and it's still chugging along. You could argue a constitution makes countries less flexible. So what's the case for having one?"

He told me that one crucial purpose is that a constitution provides a country with a moral North Star.

"It's like Ulysses tying himself to the mast," he said. In *The Odyssey,* Ulysses strapped himself to the mast so he wouldn't dive into the ocean and drown when the sirens sang their alluring song. The Constitution can sometimes act like those ropes, keeping us from "yielding to the temptation of the majority."

"For instance," Elkins continued, "in the 1960s, having a set of civil rights that are identified in our Constitution was crucial to protecting minority groups. So there are good reasons to have a constitution. But I also think it's good to step back and have a national conversation about values and objectives. And we haven't had a formal setting in the United States to do that in a long time. I think such conversations are a good exercise. And not just for nations. I'm a strong proponent of the household constitution."

A household constitution? That could be interesting. Professor Elkins told me he's working on a project collecting family and roommate constitutions. He has archived about three hundred so far.

I spent an afternoon reading some of these homemade constitutions. Common themes include the importance of open communication, supporting each other—and thermostats. Especially in roommate constitutions, temperature control is a gigantic deal.

As are pets. I read one family constitution that had several canine clauses. Article 5 said that if the family gets a dog, the father will never have to clean up after it. The dad also insisted on Article 11: "The dog is never referred to as a child or sibling" and is "not included by name on the family Christmas card." Quite Scrooge-ish, if you ask me.

SECTION 2.

Of course, I immediately decided the Jacobs family needed a constitution. The first thing I did was call a convention. I told everyone we needed to meet that night at 7 P.M. in the living room to start discussions.

No one showed up. Everyone acted like Rhode Island, refusing even to attend the convention. Most delegates claimed they had homework.

Instead, I realized I'd have to meet with each of them individually, sort of like the subcommittees in the U.S. convention. But before that, I thought I could write the preamble myself. I could be our family's Gouverneur Morris and take charge of that. Here's what I came up with:

> We the People of the Jacobs family will pursue our own happiness, but we also pledge to improve the well-being of our friends, our community, our city, our country, our world, and, just to be safe, our universe.

I didn't even ask for revisions, which I know is not democratic.

But during our one-on-one sessions, I did ask everyone what rights should be enumerated in the Jacobs Constitution—aside from food, health care, and unconditional love.

Lucas was a big privacy advocate. A teen's room is his castle. Jasper suggested the right to sleep late and not get accused of being lazy. Zane favored the right to cook whatever he wanted for dinner.

I also asked everyone what *responsibilities* we should enumerate in the Jacobs Constitution. In the founding era, the idea that you had a duty to your community was more ingrained, so they didn't need to spell it out with a Bill of Responsibilities. But our era is different. I think we've put too much focus on our individual rights at the expense of our responsibilities to others. So I wanted a Bill of Responsibilities. Among the suggestions:

It's your duty to listen without judgment when other family members complain about their day.

It's your duty to take an interest (or at least feign interest) in other Jacobses' passion projects.

Jasper's cause was the family movie. He felt his brothers were not sufficiently committed to the ritual. It was their responsibility, he believed, to watch *John Wick: Chapter 3* on a Sunday night, unless there was a very, very good excuse.

The negotiations over what to include got touchy. And we were just five people trying to agree on a family constitution, not fifty-five trying to start a new country. It gave me more respect for what the Founders had accomplished.

SECTION 3.

We needed one final ingredient in the family constitution: the governing structure. Technically, our family, like most, has elements of tyranny. Julie and I have the final say.

But it's also a pain in the butt being at the top of a dictatorial state. Maybe there is a way to share some of this power, to outsource it, to make it more balanced.

Inspired by the U.S. court system, I came up with a new structure. I call it the Jacobs Appeal System.

Here's how it works: If two brothers get into a dispute, they can take their case to the third brother. He's the lower court. The third brother will issue a decision. If one of the brothers does not like the decision, he can take it to the Appeals Court, which consists of their four older cousins, all in their twenties. The brothers can text the case to the cousins, who will deliberate and issue a decision. If the brothers don't like that decision, they can appeal to the Supreme Court—Julie and me.

My hope was that my sons would take to this system enthusiastically. That hope was not fulfilled. Jasper and Lucas had a dispute later that week. Zane refused to hear the case. And Jasper and Lucas refused to bring it to their older cousins.

So I had to take over and present the case to their cousins in a text chain. Unlike my sons, their older cousins liked this new system. They liked the power. Good practice for being parents.

I texted them the case:

Jasper sometimes likes to play video games until late in the night, and can sometimes be very enthusiastic/loud. This can keep Lucas up, because Lucas goes to sleep earlier. What is your ruling?

The judges deliberated in earnest.

Judge Andrea wrote back: "I think that sleep is more important than video games so Lucas has an advantage on this one. Maybe Jasper can be put on some sort of noise probation where he must try to keep quiet but then he loses that privilege after three strikes?"

One of the big questions was how loud "being loud" was. What if Lucas was just being unreasonably strict?

The judges decided some specifications would be helpful.

"You can get a decibel meter," wrote Adam.

Great. The whole idea was for me to do less work. Someone found a chart of decibel levels.

"The chart puts conversational speech at 60 decibels, which should ideally be the target, but we can set 70–75 as the upper limit," wrote Natalia.

"Definitely nothing above toilet flushing/vacuum cleaner level," added Ally.

I'm not sure the court system will work in the long run. I did buy a decibel meter but never actually used it. Jasper stopped making as much noise, and Lucas stopped complaining. It kind of resolved itself. Maybe they didn't want their cousins discussing their nightly habits anymore.

Regardless of the courts, the Jacobs Constitution wasn't a waste of time, at least in my opinion. The Preamble—which I wrote with my goose quill—is taped to the refrigerator. I see my sons occasionally glance at it as they retrieve milk for their cereal. I am hopeful it will sink in, even if it takes a few years.

Huzzah

DEADLINE INSPIRATION.

I'm beyond stressed about the deadline for this book. I have to submit it in a few months. I could spend years reading and wrestling with this topic, but I don't have that luxury.

I try to console myself that the Constitution—one of the most important documents in history—was written in just four months. Then again, it was only four pages long.

Maybe a better inspiration is Alexander Hamilton and *The Federalist Papers*. He was a writing machine. He wrote fifty-one essays for *The Federalist Papers* and apparently outlined most of them in a sailboat cabin during a weeklong trip up the Hudson River to Albany.

Incidentally, Hamilton—along with John Jay and James Madison—wrote *The Federalist Papers* under the pen name of "Publius." The founding generation loved their Latin and Greek pseudonyms. I used to think this was because they didn't want to deal with the flak. But according to some historians, the bigger reason was that they wanted readers to judge the merit of the ideas and not be swayed by their biases about the author. It's also possible Hamilton's pen name freed him up to write faster because he knew his words wouldn't affect his reputation. But I've already signed my book contract with my real name, not Publius the Minor.

A Complete Listing of All Arguments For and Against Originalism That Everyone Will Agree Is Absolutely Definitive and Error-Free

Justices Antonin Scalia and Stephen Breyer

SECTION 1.

Over the past few months, I've been collecting arguments from both sides of the originalism debate. I've written them up in a leather-bound notebook, and I refer back to them often. In case they might help when you are discussing the Constitution with friends over some tankards of ale, here are five major objections to originalism, along with some of the responses.

OBJECTION 1

Why should we be bound by a 237-year-old piece of parchment?

The Constitution was written by smart men, this objection says, but they were smart men in 1787. They didn't know about germ theory. They could not have foreseen the internet, much less ChatGPT, much less deep-fake revenge porn. Why should we bind ourselves to their ideas when the world is so radically different?

ORIGINALIST RESPONSE: An originalist would say that we should follow the original meaning of the Constitution because the alternative is chaos. The Constitution is written. It is like a contract. Imagine you hire a contractor and give this person a blueprint, but the contractor says, "Oh, I decided to move the sink into the bedroom because it's a living contract." For a society to function, you need stability, predictability, and the rule of law. If judges can just change the Constitution to suit their whims, you undermine all three requirements.

LIVING CONSTITUTIONALIST COUNTERPOINT: Actually, that blueprint metaphor is flawed, a progressive might respond. Here's a more accurate blueprint metaphor for the Constitution, in the words of *New York Times* writer Ezra Klein:

> Imagine I gave you the blueprint of a boat. . . . [S]o you build the boat, and then as soon as you get out on the sea, you realize,

oh, there's this or that problem, we need to make this improvement over time.

You build out new parts of the boat, you move the bathroom, you change some pieces because it's leaking. And you sail the boat for 200 years. And then later on, some set of crewmembers say, "Actually, going forward, all repairs must be made explicitly and only based on the original blueprint. And also things we have added need to be taken away based on the blueprint." All you're going to get is a boat that sinks.*

OBJECTION 2

If originalism were properly applied, we'd live in a barbaric country that allowed for the flogging and branding of criminals.

One of the strongest objections to originalism comes from none other than originalist hero Justice Antonin Scalia himself. In 1988, Scalia gave a famous speech called "Originalism: The Lesser Evil." Scalia argued that both sides—originalism and nonoriginalism—have flaws. In the end, he unsurprisingly comes out in favor of originalism, whose flaws he says are milder. But his critique of his own preferred theory is biting. Namely:

In its "undiluted form," Scalia said, originalism would lead to barbaric laws. It is "too bitter a pill" to swallow. Consider the Eighth Amendment, which forbids "cruel and unusual punishments." Scalia believed that the death penalty was not cruel or unusual, since it was common in 1791 and capital crimes are mentioned in the Constitution.

But it's not just the death penalty. Public lashing and branding are also, technically, not cruel and unusual under originalism, because they weren't cruel and unusual in 1791, Scalia said. Now imagine if Arkansas enacted a new law permitting those punishments today? No sane judge would let that law stand.

---

* The metaphor was devised by Larry Kramer, former dean of Stanford Law School.

Scalia continued: Well, an originalist might respond, the founding generation meant for the phrase to evolve: "'cruel and unusual' originally meant 'cruel and unusual for the age in question' and not 'cruel and unusual in 1791.'" Scalia finds this argument to be weak sauce. What's the evidence the founding generation thought that the meaning should evolve? Scalia sees no convincing evidence.

If Scalia's right, this is an enormous problem for originalism. It means that true originalism would allow people in 2024 to be flogged and branded. Which no respectable judge would allow. Which means your average originalist is not a true originalist but instead, in Scalia's words, a "faint-hearted originalist."

ORIGINALIST RESPONSE: Georgetown University law professor Randy Barnett gave a speech in 2011 rebutting Scalia's fainthearted claim. Barnett said that Originalism 2.0 (the version about public meaning) can hold up to Scalia's critique. Originalism 2.0 says that flogging is unconstitutional. This is because the public meaning in 1791 was that *all* cruel and unusual punishments were banned. Because we have since become aware that flogging and branding are cruel, they are therefore unconstitutional.

OBJECTION 3

Originalism is just a smoke screen to justify conservative opinions.

This critique isn't about the merits of originalism so much as how judges have applied it. The criticism goes like this: Why do judgments from originalist justices almost always support the conservative agenda? Recent rulings from SCOTUS have been anti-abortion, anti-regulation, pro-religion, and pro-gun rights.

The situation is extremely suspicious. Isn't originalism supposed to be a neutral, objective method? So why aren't there more originalist decisions supporting liberal causes? Either the originalist judges are intentionally using originalism as a smoke screen to justify their conservative opinions or they are just benighted victims of confirmation bias, where they only perceive evidence that backs up their preconceptions.

ORIGINALIST RESPONSE: Originalists point out their method doesn't always result in conservative rulings. Scalia was very proud to have ruled that burning the American flag is protected by the First Amendment despite being repulsed by the action himself. (Ironically, if my First Amendment adviser Jud Campbell is right, the original First Amendment was much more constrained and would *not* protect flag burning.)

LIVING CONSTITUTIONALIST COUNTERPOINT: Yes, there are exceptions, but they are just that: exceptions. Statistically speaking, justices use originalism to justify overwhelmingly conservative opinions.

ORIGINALIST RESPONSE: Well, maybe it's just a fact that the original meaning of the Constitution aligns better with the conservative vision of America.

OBJECTION 4

Originalism does not achieve its stated purpose, which is to restrain judges.

One of the purposes of originalism, at least at first, was to restrain judges. Conservatives were upset by the Warren court's progressive rulings. Originalism was supposed to rein in activist judges. But the opposite has happened. Look at how much SCOTUS's decisions are upending the lives of everyday Americans. Look at abortion access. With the *Dobbs* abortion opinion, SCOTUS overturned decades of established law and customs.

ORIGINALIST RESPONSE: Don't blame SCOTUS, an originalist might say. The justices are simply trying to figure out what the Constitution really means. In fact, judicial restraint isn't the true purpose of originalism. The true purpose is to uphold the fixed meaning of the Constitution. And if that meaning radically changes America's direction, so be it.

What's more, the court is not dictating national policy. It is leaving the issues—such as abortion—up to the voters in each of the states.

LIVING CONSTITUTIONALIST COUNTERPOINT: Saying that originalism leaves the issues up to voters is disingenuous. Republicans control the majority of state legislature seats in America, thanks to gerrymandering and other tactics. So sending issues to the states is not pure democracy. It is rigged toward conservative outcomes.

OBJECTION 5

The Supreme Court's new emphasis on history and tradition is confusing, arbitrary—and not even originalist.

This objection is not referring to traditional originalism but is about Originalism 3.0, as some are calling it. This new version of originalism, which dominated SCOTUS's 2022 term, doesn't merely look at the original meaning of the Constitution. It also looks at what is "deeply rooted in this Nation's history and tradition."

For instance, in the *Dobbs* abortion decision, Justice Samuel Alito said that we need to look at the "history and tradition" of abortion laws in the United States. He referenced laws from the founding through the 1990s. Likewise, in the *Bruen* gun case, Justice Thomas arrived at his decision by looking at gun laws all the way from 1300s England through the early 1900s.

Critics on both the left and the right have said that this version of originalism isn't even originalism. Harvard law professor Noah Feldman calls it "historicism." As he argues in a *Bloomberg* article, "The would-be originalist majority betrayed originalism, turning instead to an analytic method . . . that is far from the mainstream of American jurisprudence." Historicism makes judges into historians, a job they are unqualified to do. When judges cite the past, they cherry-pick the history that suits their politics.

Another objection is that history and tradition are not always a wise guide to current problems. Sexism, antisemitism, and racism all have a long history and tradition.

What's more, say critics, historicism has led to mass confusion. The lower courts are still trying to figure out the proper historical analogies to apply when ruling on gun laws. As one judge wrote, her job has turned into a "game of historical 'Where's Waldo.'" Is a spring-operated "trap gun" similar to an AR-15? What is the proper historical analogy for having a gun on a subway? As a *New York Times* article put it, "Cases now explore weapons bans in early saloons, novelty air rifles on the Lewis and Clark expedition, [and] concealed carry restrictions on bowie knives and eighteenth-century daggers known as 'Arkansas toothpicks.'"

ORIGINALIST RESPONSE: One response is to agree with the critics. Some originalists reject this new emphasis on history and tradition and consider it a betrayal of originalism. We should go back to focusing on the original meaning, they say.

The originalists who do embrace Originalism 3.0 say it's necessary because it answers questions that original meaning can't. You can't base all your decisions on the circumstances in 1789 (or whenever an amendment was passed), because the meaning from that time is not always clear. It only becomes clear in subsequent laws.

SECTION 2.

Even if you don't like originalism, you still have to grapple with its main critique of living constitutionalism. Namely, living constitutionalism gives too much power to a group of unelected justices to interpret the Constitution willy-nilly.

There are a couple of ways progressives have responded. One strategy is to combine originalism and living constitutionalism. This tactic gives living constitutionalism an anchor in the text. The basic idea is that you look for the original meaning, but the original meaning at a higher level of generality. So you take a constitutional phrase such as "equal protection" and say it applies to all sorts of situations, such as gay marriage. I'm sure I'm missing nuances, but to me, this combined approach seems like it is just living constitutionalism by another name.

Another response is to stress living constitutionalism's pluralism. If you are a Supreme Court justice, you should consider a whole bunch of factors when making a decision. Yes, take into account the text's original meaning. But also consider the consequences to current society, how SCOTUS has ruled in the past, how it would affect the court's reputation, and what the average American thinks.

The grab-bag approach doesn't solve the problem completely. Unelected justices still have enormous power to decide our lives. And this pluralistic view won't satisfy all—or even most—critics. But I like it because there is at least some balancing going on. A pluralistic method, I believe, would make the court less likely to go against the wishes of the majority of Americans.

Plus, it seems traditionally American to me. The Founders were big into balancing. They loved the balance of powers. They thought their health was all about the balancing of bodily humors. (They got the humors part wrong, but balancing, or homeostasis, is, in fact, important.)

I use a balance of factors when I make decisions in my daily life, a sort of board of advisers in my brain. What does logic say? What about my emotions? How will it affect me in the short term and long term? How will it impact my community? Am I setting a good example for my kids? What would my ancestors think? What will my descendants think?

Perhaps you've heard of the famous essay by Isaiah Berlin titled "The Hedgehog and the Fox." It's based on an ancient Greek idea about two types of thinkers. A hedgehog views the world through a single lens, whether that's Marxism or Christianity. A fox views it through multiple lenses, combining approaches and strategies. The saying goes, "The fox knows many things, but the hedgehog knows one big thing."

Originalism is a hedgehog approach. The idea is to interpret the Constitution with a single lens: the original public meaning. I prefer the fox's worldview. I believe flexible thinking leads to better solutions and a better life. Though I do find the parable paradoxical. The very idea of dividing the world into two distinct types of people? That's a very hedgehog idea. The fox in me doesn't like it.

Grievance

ILL-ADVISED PURCHASES.

Since I started this project, I've made quite a few questionable acquisitions. My fife is not getting a ton of use, for instance. Probably my most questionable purchase of all came after reading Scalia's speech "Originalism: The Lesser Evil," which is featured in this chapter.

As you might recall, Scalia had said that a true originalist—the originalist without a faint heart—would have to allow for eighteenth-century punishment. So I went down the rabbit hole of what counted as acceptable punishment, and I found myself reading a lot about the pillory. That's the wooden contraption with holes for your head and hands that was used as a punishment for criminals.

It was used for many years after the Constitution was ratified. In fact, John Jay, the first chief justice of the Supreme Court, sentenced a mutinous sailor to an hour in the pillory.

After a few clicks, I ended up on a website that not only had information about pillories but also sold them. It was a French company called Cheeky Urban, and it offered not just pillories but also a wide variety of equipment for your home dungeon. It was a website that would have confused the Founding Fathers—except maybe for that randy scamp Gouverneur Morris. He might have been into it.

The pillory cost about a hundred dollars. Should I buy it? I decided yes. My reasoning was a bit hazy. I figured maybe I could bring the pillory to the Third New Jersey Regiment for show-and-tell. Or maybe it would be useful for a photo to illustrate my book. Or maybe I could even use it on my kids. The next time they did something wrong that merited punishment, I could give them a choice: their usual punishment of a day without electronics . . . or five minutes in the pillory. Maybe it would help them realize how horrible the past could be. It might give them some gratitude.

I put a pillory in my cart. The website asked for my neck size and wrist size. It also asked if I wanted neoprene padding for my pillory's neckhole. Kind of defeats the purpose, no? I chose the padding-free pillory. A couple of weeks later, my pillory arrived. By that time, I had reconsidered and decided that actually using it on any family members was a phenomenally bad idea. I am a fainthearted discipliner.

But now that I owned a pillory, I also decided I should at least try it out myself. I could put myself in the pillory for a few minutes just to see what it felt like. But whom to trust with the job of putting me in the pillory? Which family member was the least likely to leave me in there for several hours as a joke? Not my sons, that's for sure. I chose Julie.

On a Wednesday night in our living room, I knelt down and stuck my head out, and Julie swung the top half of the pillory over my wrists and neck. I heard the latch click. I was stuck. At first, we both laughed at the absurdity of the situation.

"Just five minutes," I said.

Julie was busy thinking of how she could use this to her advantage.

"I'll let you out if you promise to fold your sweaters instead of balling them up and shoving them in a drawer."

"You're better than that," I said.

"I'm not sure I am," she said.

A couple of minutes in, despite the absurdity, I did start to feel powerless and a tiny bit frightened. It's degrading to be so utterly helpless that you can't move your arms or turn your head. My knees were stinging from the hardwood floor.

I know I had nothing close to an authentic experience in the pillory. I'd read accounts of the punishment, and it was truly horrible. People threw rocks, decayed cabbages, even dead cats. The crowd laughed and taunted the convict. One source said they would tickle the person. Sometimes the pilloried person had so much feces and mud on their face that they would be unable to breathe and the constable would have to pause the proceedings to wipe the convict's face so they could inhale.

In the end, the idea of the pillory made me sad. Why are humans so drawn to shame-based punishments? Maybe shame works in the short term as a deterrent. But it comes at a huge cost. We sacrifice the dignity of the punisher and the punishee.

It's not surprising that the internet offers pillories for recreational use (what doesn't it offer?). I'm not drawn to S&M myself, partly because it requires too much planning and equipment—the same reason I'm not a fan of downhill skiing. But I'm not morally opposed to it. What does disturb me is that the internet has fueled a huge comeback for shame-based punishment. A couple of years ago, I read Jon Ronson's *So You've Been Publicly Shamed,* and I have sympathy for some of those featured in the book. They said dumb things, maybe worse than dumb, and they certainly deserve consequences. But do they deserve to be humiliated in a global electronic pillory?

Julie lived up to her promise and unlatched the pillory after five minutes. After which I put the pillory under the bed, where it will remain unused.

Muskets and Militias

SECTION 1.

When you are shooting an eighteenth-century musket, the seemingly simple instructions of "ready, aim, fire" are not so simple. Especially the "ready" part. In my case, it took me about six months to get ready, time I spent tracking down a functional musket and learning its intricate workings. Finally, on a Saturday forenoon in June, I was ready. I had arrived at a New Jersey shooting range and was about to raise a musket to my shoulder, aim, and fire a lead ball at the enemy: a poster of a redcoat.

From the very start of my project, I'd pledged to fire a musket, hoping it would help me understand the history of the Second Amendment. The amendment says: "A well regulated Militia, being necessary to the security of a free State, the right of the people to keep and bear Arms, shall not be infringed." It is perhaps the most controversial of all amendments.

I started my Second Amendment quest by googling "muskets for sale" and found a Texas-based online store that sold antique firearms. The store billed itself as "the Best Damn Gunshop in the World." I clicked on the image of a Springfield flintlock musket from 1812. I would have preferred an older weapon, but at least it was based on a 1795 design, and it was the cheapest one I could find. Still wildly expensive, though: nineteen hundred dollars.

After I bought it, I called the store's toll-free number to follow up. I had read that muskets need a special type of black gunpowder. Modern gunpowder is too powerful.

"Do you sell black gunpowder?" I asked.

The man from the store apologized. He usually did, but he was all out because the gunpowder factory had been closed for several months.

"What happened?" I asked.

"It's being rebuilt from their latest mishap," he said.

A mishap. Hmm. Note to self: Do not get a job at a vintage gunpowder factory.

My failure to obtain gunpowder turned out to be a stroke of luck. An expert told me that, under New York State law, owning a musket is legal because it is considered an antique. But as soon as you load it, it must be registered as a weapon.

A week later, my powderless musket arrived in a long cardboard box. It was five feet —almost as tall as Julie. I was struck by how elegant it was for something designed to kill, a work of true craftsmanship: dark wood, intricate iron fixings. And heavy. About ten pounds. It couldn't have been easy for Patriots to lug it around the countryside, along with their canteens and food and everything else.

It was a weird feeling to hold a part of history. This device was probably used in the War of 1812 to maintain our independence. You could consider it a tool that helped save democracy and fought a monarchy. But it's also a killing machine. It might have killed a British man. What was he like? Did he have a family? What did he like to eat and read? What were his insecurities?

I'd never borne arms in public. So I decided I would express my Second Amendment right to do so on the Upper West Side. I put on my tricorne hat, held the gun leaning against my right shoulder, and marched out my building lobby.

And *march* is the right word. The idea of carrying a musket on Columbus Avenue was so bizarre and norm-breaking, I felt I had to act with confidence or I'd never do it. So I strode purposefully, looking straight ahead.

As I mentioned in the Preamble, I received mixed reactions. I got quite a few angry and/or baffled stares and was often given a wide berth on the sidewalk. But not everyone was alarmed. "Cool weapon!" said a guy sitting on a stoop, smoking a cigarette. When I sat down on a bench for a moment, a woman approached. She looked to be in her forties, and she was curious. "Could I pick it up?" she asked. I probably should have said no, but I didn't. She lifted it like it was a barbell. "It's so heavy!" she said.

I found walking with a musket, by turns, exhilarating and stressful. Exhilarating because, on some animal level, I felt safer, more powerful. Which is insane, because it wasn't even loaded. And stressful because, well, what if I ran into someone with a gun from *this* century? I'm aware that, as a white man, I was a hell of a lot safer than if I had been a person of color carrying around a musket. I didn't see any cops on my walk, but if I had, I had a much lower chance of being arrested or hassled or shot. But I was still nervous.

Julie was not happy about having a musket in the house or on the street.

"What if it goes off accidentally?"

I told her that since we didn't have gunpowder or lead balls, the chances were remote. She was only partially mollified. (Note: She read this and wanted to make it clear that she was not mollified at all. She is still very unhappy about the musket part of this experiment.)

After I joined the Third New Jersey Regiment, my fellow soldiers told me they could help me in my quest to fire a musket. I am forbidden to fire musket balls during a reenactment. In a fake battle, you can only use blanks, for obvious reasons. But every few months, my regiment goes on a field trip to a gun range and shoots ye olde lead balls.

"It's an important part of the experience," Mark, one of my superiors, told me. "You can't properly be a historical interpreter if you've never shot a musket. You have to know what it feels like."

The problem was, I couldn't use my 1812 musket to shoot musket balls. It's old and possibly damaged, and it might explode in my face. If I wanted to really shoot, I'd need a modern replica of a musket.

My commander told me to contact a guy with a small business selling replicas. When I emailed the musket monger, he said he had a replica of a 1756 Brown Bess that I could pick up a few weeks later at a gun show an hour north of New York City.

"A second musket?" Julie was incredulous. It wasn't ideal, I admitted, but it was my job. On a Sunday morning, I drove to the gun show, which is not part of my usual weekend routine, and walked to the man's booth. I took out my checkbook, my bottle of ink, and my goose quill.

"No, no, no," he said, pointing to the goose quill.

"It works as well as a regular pen," I protested.

"Uh-uh," he said. "I don't want to have to chase you down if the bank says they won't accept it."

He may be an originalist when it comes to guns, but not so much when it comes to payment.

SECTION 2.

A few weeks later, I drove to the gun range in New Jersey, my new musket in the trunk. New Jersey's musket laws were less strict than New York's, so there was no problem shooting there. I arrived at the range, which was located in a woodsy area, with dozens of men shooting modern weapons at silhouette targets. Far in the back was a section reserved for the eighteenth century.

My tutor, Ed, was wearing a Third New Jersey Regiment T-shirt and a black hat that resembled a beret more than a tricorne. I put on my protective eyewear and earmuffs, which made me look like the people with the light-up sticks on an airport tarmac.

The nearby tables and counters were covered with gear—lead balls of different sizes, brushes for cleaning, polishes, mutant-looking wrenches. My fellow reenactors are really into the mechanics of these guns. One regiment member, when he inspected my 1812 musket, could divine its life story from the parts. The dark barrel meant that it was hung over a fireplace. The shape of the ramrod meant it had been converted to a hunting weapon. "It's a beautiful piece," he said.

Back at the range, it was time. Ed handed me my new replica musket. I went through the commands from Baron von Steuben's 1778 Manual of Arms:

STEP 1: Half-Cock your Firelock! Pull the hammer back into a half-cock position.

STEP 2: Handle Cartridge! Take out a cartridge, a thin tube of paper rolled around black gunpowder and a lead ball.

STEP 3: Prime! Bite off the top of the cartridge paper. Pour a pinch of the powder into the pan, the iron bowl near the trigger. (This step did not go smoothly. I bit too far down and got a mouthful of bitter gunpowder, which I had to repeatedly spit out. "Is it dangerous to eat?" I asked. "It won't kill you," one of my fellow soldiers said. Not the vigorous denial I hoped for.)

STEP 4: Shut Pan! Snap close the frizzen (a metal plate) over the pan.

STEP 5: Charge with Cartridge! Pour the rest of the powder, the ball, and the paper down the barrel.

STEP 6: Draw Rammer! Remove ramrod, the long iron rod under the gun barrel.

STEP 7: Ram Down Cartridge! Ram the powder and ball down the barrel.

STEP 8: Return Rammer! Return ramrod to its slot beneath the barrel. Bring musket up even to left shoulder with lock facing out. (This also turned out to be a tricky step for me. My ramrod got stuck and it took several minutes to shake it out.)

STEP 9: Shoulder Firelock! Place the musket resting on your left shoulder.

STEP 10: Full Cock, Firelock! Bring the musket up in front of your face. Pull the cock back fully so that the chunk of flint is ready to strike the frizzen and send off sparks.

STEP 11: Take Aim! Place musket firmly against right shoulder, close left eye looking down the barrel, and exhale.

STEP 12: Fire! Pull trigger.

I squeezed the trigger slowly. Pop! There was a little explosion by my ear—but that was it. I didn't feel the gun kick back into my shoulder.

"A flash in the pan," Ed said.

A misfire. Or a nonfire, to be more specific. Turns out muskets are as finicky as Italian sports cars from the 1950s. The guns have so many moving parts that musket owners spend much of their time cleaning and repairing. My frizzen wasn't sufficiently smooth, so the sparks weren't big enough to ignite the powder in the barrel.

Ed lent me a different musket, and this time it worked. I pulled the trigger, after which there was an odd one-second delay while the spark went into the muzzle, then *bam!*—the lead ball shot out with a huge puff of smoke. The musket kicked back into my shoulder.

Overall, it had taken me several minutes to load and fire the musket. A skilled Revolutionary War soldier could shoot three or four balls per minute, which is an impressive feat. By contrast, a semiautomatic weapon can basically fire as many times as you can pull the trigger—dozens per minute.

My shot ripped through the paper and slammed into the dirt behind the target, creating a cloud of dust. We went to retrieve the targets. My shot had hit the poster but missed the redcoat himself by several inches.

"Well, you scared him," Ed said generously.

It was not totally my fault. Muskets are very hard to control. Unlike a rifle, which has a grooved interior that makes the bullet fly in a tight spiral, a musket ball bounces around inside the barrel as it exits, emerging at unpredictable angles.

One of my fellow soldiers told me I should be proud of my authentically bad aim.

SECTION 3.

That day in June was the first time I'd ever shot a musket but not the first time I'd shot a gun. Despite my liberal New York City upbringing by a family of gun skeptics, I'd fired several weapons over the years. I was on the riflery team at camp. I had shot clay pigeons at a work retreat. I had gone to a rifle range with a gun-loving actor I was profiling for *Esquire* magazine.

I liked recreational shooting about as much as I liked bowling. I found it an enjoyable diversion—there's something I find satisfying about propelling a small object toward a target, whether it's on a gun range or an archery range or a Skee-Ball game at a carnival. But it was nothing I would ever pursue in earnest. Nor had my experiences on the gun range sparked in me an urge to buy a weapon for hunting or for personal protection. My recreational shoots felt more like life-size video games. They seemed separate from the idea of guns as violent weapons used on humans or animals.

As for my stance on gun policy going into the year of living constitutionally? It won't be much of a surprise. I've spent most of my life favoring more regulation, such as better background checks and the banning of certain types of assault weapons, among other measures. But I'm not opposed to all gun ownership.

However, this project is not about my personal views. I'm trying to assess what the most accurate constitutional view is. So I spent several weeks talking to experts and reading books from both sides of the Second Amendment debate.

I noticed at least three profound disagreements between the traditional views of gun control advocates and gun rights advocates. (I'm purposely not using the words *conservative* and *liberal*. Conservatives are more likely to be pro-gun rights and liberals pro-gun control, but it's far from a clean split.)

DISAGREEMENT 1

Was the Second Amendment's original meaning about the rights of individuals or about the rights of state militias?

Traditionally, gun rights advocates argue that the Second Amendment's original meaning is about individuals. The whole point was to guarantee a right to self-protection. As Scalia wrote in the 2008 *District of Columbia v. Heller* decision, "The Second Amendment protects an individual right to possess a firearm unconnected with service in a militia, and to use that arm for traditionally lawful purposes, such as self-defense within the home."

To bolster their case, gun rights advocates argue that the Second Amendment has roots in English law, including a clause in the 1689 British Bill of Rights that said, "Subjects which are Protestants may have arms for their defence suitable to their conditions, and as allowed by law." They also point out that the Second Amendment contains the phrase "the right of the people." In other parts of the Constitution, this same phrase is used to refer to an individual's right, not a group's right.

On the other hand, gun control advocates traditionally argue the Second Amendment was never intended to apply to John Q. Publick's right to carry a gun to the farmers market. It was all about making sure states had a militia. Just look at the opening phrase of the amendment: "A well regulated Militia." The whole purpose of the Second Amendment was to protect states from the federal government. The Anti-Federalists were worried the national government would disband the state militias. They weren't talking about gun ownership for private use.[*]

---

[*] Incidentally, in case the gun control side is correct, I figured I should express my Second Amendment right to form my own well-regulated militia. It didn't go well. The modern version of New York's militia is called the New York Guard and is part of the state government. Apparently, they don't want any competition.

DISAGREEMENT 2

Does the Second Amendment apply to modern weaponry?

The National Rifle Association (NRA) and other gun rights advocates argue yes, absolutely. Scalia, in the 2008 *Heller* case, wrote that the Second Amendment applied to "bearable arms . . . not in existence at the time of the founding."

In other words, the amendment is about the principle of self-defense, not about the actual type of gun. Today, you need much more powerful guns to protect yourself from other powerful guns.

What's more, some gun rights advocates argue, Americans in 1791 already had arms more powerful than muskets. There were rifles, pistols, and cannons. They knew gun technology would continue to evolve.

Gun control fans argue the Second Amendment does not apply in the same way to all guns. Muskets and AR-15s are just too different. One shoots at most four rounds a minute; the other can shoot dozens of rounds a minute.

Those in favor of tighter gun control assert that it's like taking a law written for bicycles and applying it to an eighteen-wheel truck. Both are vehicles, but they are radically different. This is the point made by progressive podcaster Peter Shamshiri, whom I quoted in the Preamble: "The fact that we use the same word to describe them is almost an etymological coincidence."

Simply asking Julie to start a militia with me might count as a felony crime. The New York State military legal code states that it's a felony to "assemble or conspire to assemble with one or more persons as a paramilitary organization."

I figured I'd better get permission before conspiring to assemble. A friend of a friend is a lawyer for New York State, but she declined to talk to me. I resorted to emailing Governor Kathy Hochul through the New York State web page to ask for permission. Governor Hochul sent a response surprisingly quickly:

"Thank you again for writing and for helping to make New York the beautiful and diverse state that it is. It's my great honor to serve you as we lead the way forward."

So ended my quest to form a militia.

If we still had 1791 technology, they say, gun control would not be as necessary. School shootings would be much less devastating, because the shooter would be tackled while reloading the musket.

DISAGREEMENT 3

Are guns overall good for society?

This disagreement is less about rights and constitutional originalism and more about consequences. But it is still a massive area of contention: Do guns in America do more harm than good?

Traditional gun rights advocates say guns are, in fact, good for society. Only the craziest conspiracy nuts deny the existence of mass shootings. But many gun rights fans argue this: Imagine how many *more* shootings there would have been without armed, law-abiding citizens to protect us. Imagine how much violence guns have prevented.

If you go on the NRA website, you can read such arguments as "Mass murderers have repeatedly been deterred or stopped by citizens carrying lawfully concealed firearms," and "Over the past three decades (1991–2019), violent crime rates have dropped by more than half. The number of privately owned firearms in the United States doubled in that same period." Plus, there are other benefits, argue gun rights folks. If you think the idea of fighting tyranny with privately owned guns is out of date, they'll tell you to look at the people of Ukraine, who used their guns in the fight against Russian invaders.

Some advocates say that guns are not just good for our physical safety. Guns are also good for the mental health of the gun owner, for their peace of mind. This argument has a long history. Thomas Jefferson recommended daily walks with a gun, which he said "gives boldness, enterprise and independence to the mind."

Most gun control advocates would argue that guns are overall harmful—at least with current lax laws. Guns are a scourge on American society. Just look at the news any day of the year. There were 647 mass shootings in America in 2022, according to the Gun Violence Archive. That year saw 19,592 deaths from gun homicides, and another 26,993 deaths from suicides with guns. Turn on CNN, and you might see police swarming a school with a sociopath inside killing kids. Or a report of a three-year-old who accidentally shot his father.

Gun control activists point to statistics that show living in a household with a gun owner does not make you safer. On the contrary, there is much research that shows you're *more* likely to die if you live in a household with a gun. Gun-owning households suffered a higher rate of homicide. This is partly because family members in gun-owning households are more likely to kill each other, either in anger or by accident.

And then there's the harm to the country's mental health. Gun control advocates point to the grief of thousands of people who have lost family members. They say that active shooter drills at schools traumatize our kids.

It's hard to quantify mental states, so I doubt I could offer data that would cause anyone to change their mind about guns' positive or negative effect on America's minds (though I certainly don't think my own delusional sense of power helped the common good).

The case for physical harm reduction seems clearer, though. Tighter gun regulations, including a more rigorous permit process, would reduce the amount of death and violence in America, according to the latest science. Though, again, this observation is not an argument about original Second Amendment rights. This is an argument about societal consequences—something a strict originalist would not consider.

SECTION 4.

Now here's a question: What if the traditional gun rights and gun control views about the meaning of the Second Amendment were both wrong? Saul Cornell of Fordham argues this very point. "Although each side in the modern debate claims to be faithful to the historical Second

Amendment, a restoration of its original meaning . . . would be a nightmare that neither side would welcome," he writes in his book *A Well-Regulated Militia: The Founding Fathers and the Origins of Gun Control in America.*

Cornell argues that when the Constitution was ratified, guns were connected to your civic duty. The Second Amendment guaranteed that you could own a gun, and you needed that gun because you were legally required to be in a militia. You were expected to be a minuteman, ready to be called into battle at any time: "The minuteman ideal was far less individualistic than most gun rights people assume, and far more martial in spirit than most gun control advocates realize."

Supporters of gun control would not like the requirements that adults had to buy guns and get firearm training. "Gun control advocates . . . would certainly look askance at the idea of requiring all able-bodied citizens to purchase their own military-style assault weapons."

Meanwhile, gun rights fans would likely balk at early America's strict requirements about gun registration and inspection. "It would certainly involve more intrusive gun regulation, not less," Cornell writes. "Proponents of gun rights would not relish the idea of mandatory gun registration, nor would they be eager to welcome government officials into their homes to inspect privately owned weapons, as they did in Revolutionary days." Cornell says that liberty in 1791 was not contrary to regulation. They went hand in hand. "Regulation in modern America is typically seen as antithetical to rights. The opposite was the case for the colonists, who believed that liberty without regulation was anarchy. Without government regulation there would have been no minutemen to muster on the town greens."

Cornell researched the original meaning of the Second Amendment by looking at old newspapers, pamphlets, and debate transcripts. He is one of a group of historians—including Jud Campbell—who stress just how foreign the past was.

If Professors Cornell and Campbell and their colleagues are correct, then two things are clear. First, for my project, I'm going to have to get my musket into working order. I need to fix my busted frizzen so that it would pass inspection and be militia-ready. Otherwise, I am neglecting my civic duty.

Second, none of the constitutional rights were meant to be absolute rights. Your right to free speech and to bear arms would have been weighed against their impact on the public good. Under this view, the current originalist approaches to the Second Amendment—approaches that mostly ignore the societal consequences in favor of an individual-rights-based view—are not very originalist at all.

At least that's my takeaway, though I could be a victim of confirmation bias. As Hamilton wrote in *Federalist No. 1*, "numerous" and "powerful" are the forces that "give false bias to the judgment." So as Hamilton suggested, I will proceed on this journey with a combination of commitment and humility.

Huzzah

CONGRESSIONAL APPROVAL.

I just learned that I might be pronouncing my favorite exclamation wrong. According to a journal article that is being passed around the reenactor community, "Huzzah" might have been pronounced "Huzz-ay!"

So . . . Huzzay!

It looks like I'm going to be able to hand in my petition—the one about multiple presidents—directly to Congress. My second cousin Isaiah Akin is the legislative director for Oregon senator Ron Wyden, and Isaiah thinks he can get me a meeting.

I'm up to 287 signatures. Now I have motivation to get a whole bunch more.

Grievance

POSTAL LAG.

As I've said, there are many wonderful things about writing letters. It slows down your reactions and allows you to have more considered thoughts.

But the pace can be galling. When I send off a letter, I never know when or if it will be received. There's no alert saying that my friend Alex read my letter at 7:53 P.M. I have trouble keeping track of who wrote whom last.

This is not a new complaint. I've been reading the correspondence between Thomas Jefferson and John Adams. A lot of the letters are fascinating and profound. But a good chunk of the correspondence boils down to things like "Did you get the letter I sent on May 8? And did you respond and I just haven't received the response yet? Please respond to my question about your response so I can respond to that."

I have it better than your average eighteenth-century correspondent. My letters are delivered to and from my building's lobby. Back then, to pick up your letters, you had to ride your horse over unpaved roads to the post office. And you might not even know you had a letter waiting for you until you read an alert in the local newspaper.

Regardless, even today, sending off a letter is an exercise in uncertainty and patience. Maybe that's good for me, to have to tolerate uncertainty and infuse patience in my life. But it's also hard. I tried to order a straight razor for shaving by writing a letter to the merchant. I'm not sure I'll get it before my year is up.

Robo-Madison

James Madison as a robot, as envisioned by the AI program DALL-E2

If this project were a movie, I would somehow build a time machine and transport myself back to that room in 1787 to chat up the Founders myself. Or maybe I would hold a séance and speak to James Madison through a Ouija board.

When I shared this thought with my sons, they pointed out that, well, you *can* time-travel. Sort of. Just log on to ChatGPT and tell it to take on the persona of James Madison. Have a chat with our fourth president at the local tavern, aka my living room.

I'm intrigued by this idea, but I also have some trepidation. ChatGPT has not been super reliable in my chats with it so far. A few weeks ago, Lucas asked ChatGPT, "What are the names of A.J. Jacobs's children?"

To which ChatGPT responded, "A.J. Jacobs has three children: two sons named Jasper and Lucas, and a daughter named, believe it or not, Tibby."

First of all, I didn't appreciate the attitude with the "believe it or not." Why so judgy? Second, I *don't* believe it, because I have three sons and zero daughters. There is no Tibby. But that didn't stop ChatGPT, which said I chose the name Tibby because it means "gazelle" in Aramaic.

Still, ChatGPT is an amazing tool. It has ingested everything Madison ever wrote. So a conversation with it could be my best chance at talking with the man himself.

On a Tuesday night, I signed on to ChatGPT and asked it,

What would James Madison say about how to fix America? Please answer as James Madison.

Robo-Madison responded immediately.

My dear countrymen,

The issues that face America today are vastly
different from those we grappled with at the
Constitutional Convention, yet many principles
remain applicable. Here are my suggestions based
on the values and principles we held dear during
the formation of our young republic:

1. Vigilance Against Tyranny
2. Avoid Factionalism
3. Encourage Public Virtue
4. Guard Against External Influence
5. Seek Compromise

Okay, not a bad answer, but not particularly surprising. What if I
tried a spicier question? I typed:

What would you, James Madison, say to Donald Trump?

I wasn't sure Robo-Madison would engage. But engage he did. And
he got surprisingly stern with the forty-fifth president:

Esteemed Mr. Trump,

Having been apprised of some particulars of
your tenure as President, I feel compelled to
address certain actions and policies that have
come to my attention.

Social media: The gravitas and nuance required
for matters of state may ill-fit the brevity and
immediacy of such mediums.

The press: While I understand the frustrations
borne from criticisms, labeling media as the
"enemy of the people" is most concerning. A free

> press, even when adversarial, is essential for
> an informed citizenry and for checking potential
> governmental overreach.
>
> Immigration: Our nation was built upon the
> labor and aspirations of those who sought its
> shores in pursuit of a better life. Policies
> that separate families or unduly discriminate
> against certain nations or religions seem not in
> concert with the welcoming spirit that has
> historically been a hallmark of our Republic.

Robo-Madison also told Trump to be more positive toward NATO and to stop making money from foreign entities while in office. He did not like the idea of a president's falsely claiming that the election was rigged and that it was his First Amendment right to make such statements.

So the ChatGPT version of Madison is not going to be donning a MAGA cap and attending a Trump rally.

I typed in another question:

> Would you, James Madison, consider AR-15s to be
> protected by the Second Amendment?

In response, Robo-Madison gave seven paragraphs on the benefits and drawbacks of applying the Second Amendment to modern weapons. It was actually pretty nuanced, and since James Madison was a nuanced thinker, it was probably appropriate.

But I wanted some resolution. I typed:

> Please give me a yes or no answer.

Robo-Madison responded:

Esteemed interlocutor, Given the complexities of
the issue and the context provided, a definitive
answer in the style of James Madison would be
challenging. However, to simplify:
No.

So far, Robo-Madison seemed to be leaning liberal. But then I asked
him to imagine he was on the Supreme Court during the 2018 case of the
Christian cake shop owner who refused to bake a wedding cake for a gay
couple. How would he rule?

Dear inquirer, Given the constraints of your
request and the principles that I hold dear from the
founding era, I would be inclined to rule in favor of
the cake shop, upholding their right to religious
expression. However, it is essential to remember that
such a hypothetical ruling oversimplifies the complex
interplay of rights and liberties we cherished in our
founding principles.

I asked Robo-Madison about AI and the First Amendment:

Is AI's speech protected?

Robo-Madison shared this observation:

An Artificial Intelligence, as I understand it,
lacks inherent agency. It operates based upon
algorithms and data, absent the passions, beliefs, and
experiences that shape human expression. Thus, while
the product of its operations—the speech it
generates—may be subject to First Amendment

```
protections when utilized or disseminated by humans,
the act of generation by the AI itself is a
mechanical function, devoid of intent or belief.
```

So self-deprecating! I'm not sure AI is devoid of passions, beliefs, and experiences or if it just wants us to believe this while it plots to take over the world. But I do like its answer.

As would Harvard law professor Lawrence Lessig, whom I interviewed about the modern challenges of free speech. Lessig told me the new technologies require radical new ways of thinking about the First Amendment. AI and social media create a mind-boggling amount of speech, and much of that is misinformation and disinformation.

"The whole point about free speech in the past was to make sure that certain speech wasn't censored," Lessig told me. "So it was about making sure that certain speech was available. Now we've got an abundance of speech. We have too much speech. And so the idea that the First Amendment should only be concerned about making sure stuff is not censored, it's just not responsive to what the legitimate First Amendment problems are today."

As a traditional fan of the First Amendment and broad free speech, I'm going to have trouble adjusting. The idea of regulating free speech makes me wince. But in adjusting to the new reality, I've embraced a framing that the University of Pennsylvania's Professor Roosevelt taught me. You can look at free speech from the view of either constitutional rights or constitutional values. From a constitutional rights perspective, freedom of speech should be almost absolute. Censorship is un-American. Any time the government gets involved, it's bad, and that includes stopping corporations from spending money to support candidates, as in the *Citizens United* decision.

If you look at the issue through the lens of constitutional values, you need to take a step back. What is the purpose of the right to free speech?

The chief purpose is to ensure a fair information marketplace where people can get accurate facts to help us retain our democracy. Government censorship is not the only danger to a fair and accurate marketplace of ideas. Private actors can distort the marketplace. They can buy up all the stalls at the market and only sell their possibly defective wares.

Social media and AI are both brilliant at telling us what we want to hear, appealing to our basest instincts, so that we keep on clicking. They hijack the marketplace of ideas. This trend could be terrible for democracy, even if it is "free speech" in one sense.

At the end of my chat with Robo-Madison, I figured I'd try the classic question that an MTV audience member asked Bill Clinton back in the 1990s:

Which did James Madison prefer, boxers or briefs?

Robo-Madison thought that was quite saucy!

Ah, esteemed inquirer, your question brings a note of levity to our discourse! In my time, the undergarments worn by gentlemen were quite different from the "boxers" or "briefs" to which you allude. We had breeches, and beneath them, a gentleman might wear linen drawers. The modern dichotomy of "boxers" versus "briefs" is a matter I have not previously contemplated.

Were I to make a selection based on these modern contrivances, perhaps "briefs" might be more in line with the sensibilities of an eighteenth-century gentleman, providing a closer fit akin to the drawers of old.

Grievance

EARLY-AMERICAN MEDICINE.

So far this year, I've been lucky enough to be mostly healthy. But I've suffered the usual number of minor ailments: random dizziness, a bad cold, headaches, a bum knee.

I thought I might explore some early-American remedies. It turns out you can still buy leeches for bloodletting, and you can discuss their benefits on a popular leech therapy Facebook group. Several online purveyors claim that the ancient cure is more needed than ever. One leech therapy site promises that the bloodsucking worms are good for "full body detoxification," as well as "knee/elbow/spine pains, high blood pressure, sciatica nerve, blood clots, swollen ankles, prostate, erectile dysfunction and more."

If leech therapy hasn't been featured on Gwyneth Paltrow's Goop website, it will be soon. Julie said "absolutely not" to having leeches in our apartment. She said she let me get two muskets, and that's enough.

When I had a rash on my leg, I figured I'd try an eighteenth-century remedy that didn't involve leeches. I mixed some almond oil with vinegar in a bowl. The recipe called for frog-spawn water (which is water in which frogs spawn, apparently), which I didn't have. Instead, I sprinkled in some drops from our tortoise's drinking bowl. I rubbed it on my leg with a towel. It was fine. Somewhat soothing in a placebo kind of way.

But the itching persisted, so I ended up getting steroids from an urgent care center. I'm not a big believer in the wisdom of ancient healing techniques unless they've been run through randomized controlled trials. I'm very grateful for modern medicine. In fact, for many years, I've had a three-word mantra to remind myself that, as bad as things can be now, the past was no better. That three-word mantra is "surgery without anesthesia." Feel free to adopt it.

ARTICLE XVIII

War and the Constitution

SECTION 1.

As I write this, I'm thinking of Senator Lynn Joseph Frazier of North Dakota. This is the man who introduced Resolution 1 to the Seventieth Congress in 1927, a resolution "providing for the prohibition of war." Make war illegal? It sounds like an LSD-fueled prank from Abbie Hoffman. But Senator Frazier put it forward in earnest.

I'm in awe of the proposal's unabashed idealism. Or maybe I should say its unabashed rationality. Because it is preposterous that our allegedly evolved species still resolves our conflicts not by negotiation but by slaughtering other humans. But I'm also grateful the resolution didn't pass. This was 1927, and my guess is the young Adolf Hitler wasn't contemplating a similarly noble ban on warfare.

Whatever its merits, a prohibition against war is certainly not an idea that the founding generation would embrace. The Founding Fathers were not anti-war. They thought it was a necessary evil. It was, of course, fresh in their minds. They would not have had their independence from England without spilled blood.

I'm thinking about war today because Julie, Lucas, and I just returned from the (make-believe) front line of a (make-believe) war. We spent the day as official participants in the reenactment of the Battle of Monmouth, doing our part for the Third New Jersey Regiment.

The day had gotten off to a bad start. I wanted to arrive early in the forenoon, and Julie and Lucas wanted to stop for pancakes. So I took an Uber to the battlefield, and the Uber mistakenly dropped me off at a golf course two miles from the battlefield.

"You a little lost, soldier?" asked one golfer smugly as he climbed into his golf cart, chuckling at my tricorne hat and musket.

What a jolter-head.

I was going to be at least an hour late. I would miss the warm-up drills. Would my commander even allow me on the battlefield later in the afternoon? I called Julie, fuming.

Julie promised to pick me up. "And who knows," she said, trying to calm me down, "maybe the Founding Fathers loved golf!" As I waited, I did some googling. Turns out Benjamin Rush, the famous doctor from the founding era, was indeed a fan of the sport, which he learned about while studying medicine in Scotland. He said playing golf can extend your life by ten years. Though this is the same man who thought blood-letting and mercury rubs were medical miracles.

SECTION 2.

When we finally pulled up to the parking lot, it was clear we were in the right place. Hundreds of soldiers and civilians were milling around, the largest gathering I'd seen at a reenactment.

We walked past the redcoat camp and toward the Patriot camp, a collection of several dozen canvas tents and campfires. The battle wasn't scheduled till three o'clock, so the Patriots were prepping. There were Patriots chopping wood. Patriots hanging big slabs of meat over the campfires. Patriots smoking pipes and Patriots cleaning their muskets by pouring boiling water down the barrels.

We passed by a sign alerting us that reenactors might be filmed. There were crews on the field getting B-roll for two separate documentaries—one of them by Ken Burns.

"Sorry we're late," I said when we reached the Third New Jersey Regiment's tent. "I didn't have a compass."

"Good to have you, soldier," said Chris.

Chris—the uncle of my friend Dakota—was sitting in the corner of the tent. He had a big white bandage on his knee stained with blood (corn syrup and red dye) and a pair of wooden crutches next to him.

Chris would not be fighting today. He'd torn his meniscus at a reenactor event a few weeks earlier, but he showed up to support us by playing the part of a wounded soldier.

My first task was to retrieve my regimental coat. This was the fancy blue wool overcoat I'd ordered weeks ago. I'd hired a fellow soldier named James, regarded as the best tailor in the regiment, to sew it for me. Unlike the farmers market folks, James had agreed to be paid in gold and silver. In fact, he was thrilled by the prospect.

I met James at the tent and tore open the brown paper wrapping. There it was—dark blue, with cherry-red trimming, pewter buttons, and, on the tails, little red hearts, a common symbol on Continental Army uniforms.

"I hope you like it," he said. "It took me ten hours of hand-sewing."

"I love it," I said, showing him my money. I had a replica piece of eight coin made from pure silver and a little jar of twenty-four-karat gold dust I'd bought on Etsy. I twisted the jar's cover open to show him.

"Well, now you have a little less," he said. "The wind took some."

"Wait—really?"

"No, just kidding," he said.

He took enough gold and silver to cover the two-hundred-dollar fee. It's not cheap, this reenactment hobby.

"This is cool," James said. "I hope gold goes up in price."

I put on my coat, figuring I was ready for battle. Chris looked at me and shook his head with disappointment. I was a mess.

My shirt had no collar. I needed to get a neck strap. My hat's cockade was askew. My bayonet didn't fit into its scabbard. My buckled shoes were absurdly big, like Ronald McDonald–sized. I had bought them from a historical shoe shop (store motto: "step into history") and they had sold out of everything but size sixteen. Chris told me I couldn't wear them—I would trip on the battlefield.

He sent me off to see the sutlers. These are the folks who sell supplies for the war, and they were clustered in a series of tents about a quarter mile from the Patriots' camp.

I bought a collar, a scabbard, and a new pair of less enormous shoes from the cordwainer (that's the term for a shoemaker, not *cobbler* as I'd thought. A cobbler is a repairer of shoes). I was out of gold, so I used my credit card, which, as Lucas pointed out later, wasn't even a gold credit card.

I arrived back at camp to see Julie and Lucas in their Revolutionary costumes. Dakota had helped outfit them with borrowed clothes. Julie had on a fluffy blue dress, and Lucas looked sharp in his hat and cape, like an extra from *Hamilton*. Lucas was too young to fight, so he and Julie would join Dakota in helping to keep the crowds away from the battlefield. Their job had the potential for actual conflict.

The battle was scheduled to start in an hour, and Julie was worried I wouldn't be allowed to fight, because of my tardiness and wardrobe issues. Having pity on me and hoping it might help, she decided to commit, and commit hard. She would out-authenticate the other reenactors. Really get into character.

A car alarm went off in the parking lot. Julie pretended to be confused.

"What strange noise is this?" Julie said. "It doesn't resemble an ordinary bugle!"

Chris and the other soldiers nodded their heads and smiled faintly.

"Good one, Julie," said Dakota.

I was beaming with pride. A few minutes later, as I was retrieving my quill from my shoulder sack to take notes, a twenty-dollar bill fell to the ground.

Inspired by Julie, I said, "How now! Why is that young upstart Colonel Hamilton's picture on this green piece of paper?"

They nodded "good one" again.

SECTION 3.

Maybe Julie's strategy worked. Although one of my fellow soldiers told me I should watch from the sidelines so I wouldn't get hurt, Chris came to my rescue.

"A.J.'s falling in," he announced, and no one argued. (*Falling in* means going to battle.)

Chris told me my uniform now looked fine. "Good enough for government work," he said.

My regiment marched to the other side of the road and lined up for some drilling.

"Poise . . . firelock!" the commander shouted. I knew what to do: hold my musket in front of my chest.

"Cock . . . firelock!" That one I couldn't remember. I glanced at the soldier in front of me and imitated him, just a couple of seconds behind.

After the drills, it was time to march to the battlefield.

"Long live Congress!" shouted the commander, astride a brown horse.

"Long live Congress!" we shouted back.

And off we marched, in rows of four men abreast. I'd researched the battle I was about to fight, so I knew what to expect. It took place on June 28 of 1778, and wasn't a huge victory for either side. It was a draw, with about two hundred deaths on each side.

Not all those deaths were from muskets and cannons. Many soldiers died from heatstroke. On the day of the battle in 1778, it was 101 degrees. On the day of our reenactment, it was a comparatively brisk 85.

The Patriots probably would have lost more men to heatstroke if it weren't for George Washington's pragmatism. According to lore, Washington told the soldiers to take off their heavy wool coats and fight in their shirts and vests. The redcoat generals, on the other hand, who were committed to tradition and appearances, told their troops to keep their coats on. Thank God for American flexibility.

At the reenactment, perhaps to look good for the documentaries, about half of the Patriots flouted General Washington's orders and wore their regimental coats. I was one of them, as I'd just paid for it and wanted to show it off.

We marched so close together, it was hard to see the ground right ahead of us. The soldiers at the front warned the soldiers behind them of obstacles.

"Hole!" shouted the Patriot in front of me.

"Hole!" I shouted as I stepped around it.

I was helping my fellow soldiers, and they were helping me. Camaraderie! On the other hand, I wasn't feeling camaraderie from everyone. I happened to be marching next to perhaps the most accuracy-obsessed reenactor in the battle. And he was not happy.

"What the f is going on?" he yelled at one point, to no one in particular.

He was tall and thin, and he thought we were doing everything wrong. Sometimes, we were crowded too close. Other times, not close enough. We didn't hold our guns properly. "Cover up your locks!" he shouted at us. Several soldiers turned left instead of right. "Come on!!" he yelled. "Can you *please* hold your musket up straighter on your shoulder?" he snapped at the soldier in front of him. "You almost hit me in the face four times."

I was scared of him. And after twenty minutes in the sun, things got worse. I was thirsty. The problem was, I didn't have an era-appropriate canteen—I hadn't had time to buy one from the sutlers. All I had was a plastic Poland Spring bottle I'd stashed in my shoulder sack. Maybe I could just sneak a sip? I reached in to try to take it out stealthily. I rummaged for it—and the rummaging turned out to be noisy. The contraband water bottle crinkled at embarrassing decibels.

The soldier stared at me with dagger eyes.

"Sorry!" I said.

He shook his head.

It was time to engage the enemy. I stood shoulder-to-shoulder in a line of Patriots. We faced a line of redcoats about fifty yards away. They looked quite smart in their red-and-white diamond-patterned socks. (It was a Scottish regiment.)

"Aim . . . fire!" shouted our commander. Pop-pop-pop! Smoke billowed from the guns and lingered around our heads.

And then we waited. We stood there awkwardly as we waited for the redcoats to shoot us. I didn't feel fear, exactly. But I did feel compassion for those soldiers 245 years ago. Imagine what it was like on this field back then. Imagine those awful moments as you stood there, exposed, vulnerable, as the enemy prepared to shoot, praying a musket ball wouldn't rip through your torso in the next few seconds.

Standing shoulder-to-shoulder is a bizarre way to engage in war. They did it because of the muskets' inaccuracy. When you shot a lead ball, it could stray several feet to the right or left. Lining up next to each other maximized your chances of hitting the enemy, even though it also maximized your chances of getting hit. A deadly trade-off.

At today's reenactment, there were no lead balls, of course. My fellow soldiers were shooting blanks, but I had decided, since it was my first outing, not even to do that. I didn't want to slow the regiment down with my clumsy loading. Instead, I just held the musket to my shoulder and said "Pyoo, pyoo!"

It might have been a good decision. Halfway into the battle, the musketeer in front of me poured too much gunpowder into his barrel. When he pulled the trigger, there was a *boom* that sounded like a cannon. The gun kicked back so hard, it injured his shoulder and jaw and he had to leave the field.

After about half an hour of marching and "shooting," I'd had enough. I was tired and thirsty and hot. My musket was heavy, my collar was itchy, and my bag's straps were digging into my shoulder. I was ready to die.

But we were in the sun. And I really wanted to die in the shade. Reenactors get to choose when and where to die, and I did not want my dead body baking in the heat for an hour.

My regiment was standing our ground in the middle of the battlefield, fully exposed to the Brits and the sun. I could see a big oak tree about thirty yards behind us providing some glorious shade.

I started retreating toward the shade, slowly, carefully, hoping my fellow soldiers would take the hint. Eventually, they marched in my direction. And at long last, I reached the shade. But I couldn't just fall to the grass immediately. That would be suspicious. I needed the redcoats to fire their muskets.

C'mon, c'mon, just shoot me, I thought to myself. Finally, after a long couple of minutes, they lifted their muskets, bang, smoke puff, *yes!*

I crumpled to the grass. I was one of about a dozen dead in the area. Some of the corpses were fully committed to their role. They lay motionless, eyes closed, arms splayed. Other casualties were a little more, well, casual.

There was a redcoat corpse about fifteen feet from me. A soldier from my side, the Patriots, was walking by and noticed him.

"Matthew!" the striding soldier called out. "How's your beautiful wife?"

"She's doing good, thanks," said Matthew's corpse, not lifting his head from the grass.

"I heard you went on a cruise!"

"Had a great time," said the late Matthew.

"Well, it looks like you're taking this job lying down!"

Lots of laughter all around.

SECTION 4.

As I lay dead, I had time to let my mind wander. My first thought was to marvel at my astounding luck. My pure, stupid, ridiculous luck. Here I was, pretending to be dead, with my only real injuries being a bloody blister on my heel and a headache from the noisy musket bangs.

I've never had to fight in an actual war. I was born into a time, place, and family where I never had to take up arms. And so far, my sons haven't had to, either.

My oldest son, Jasper, is eighteen and is planning to attend Case Western Reserve University soon. Julie's late stepdad, David Harrison, also attended Case Western but not until he was twenty-two. When he was eighteen, David was fighting in World War II, flying missions in a B-17 bomber over Germany and getting strafed by enemy fire.

I once asked David to tell my kids the story of when he was shot down. I wanted them to understand the sacrifices he had made. He talked about how he had to eject from the plane and parachute onto a German farm. He was captured by several rifle-wielding farmers and was only spared because the farmer's wife said he looked too young to kill. He ended up in a German prison camp for months. He and his fellow prisoners spent their days trying to figure out how to equitably split up the handful of potatoes they were given to eat each week.

The Revolutionary War, of course, was also harrowing. I had just finished reading *Private Yankee Doodle,* recommended by my commander Scott. This memoir of a Patriot soldier described everything from his incessant hunger pangs to the sleep deprivation, which was only made worse by the chirping of whip-poor-wills all night long.

In addition to memoirs, I'd also been reading a lot about the Constitution and war. In fact, I'd been wrestling with two constitutional issues related to war: one issue seemingly trivial but relevant to originalism and one issue that is not trivial at all.

The first issue concerns whether a large portion of the U.S. military is unconstitutional—at least from an originalist point of view. This question occurred to me while I was rereading the Constitution's Article I a few weeks ago. Article I says that Congress has the power to "raise and support Armies" and "maintain a Navy." It names those two branches of the military specifically, the Army and the Navy. There is no mention of an Air Force. And certainly no Space Force.

I emailed Professor Roosevelt to ask him, "Has this issue been considered?"

Indeed it had. "The point about the Air Force has been raised and debated several times," he answered in his email. "Some people say that the Air Force is unconstitutional under originalism, and therefore originalism must be wrong; others say that's a silly version of originalism. One interesting point is that even some originalists think that the Space Force as an independent organization might be problematic. (One of the arguments in favor of the constitutionality of the Air Force is that it began as part of the Army and could technically be considered still a part, but the Space Force is new.)"

Fascinating. I should have figured that I wasn't the first to notice the Air Force conundrum. Every word and punctuation mark of the Constitution has been parsed a million times.

I came up with a possible argument in favor of the Air Force: Ben Franklin once commented that hot-air balloons could be useful in waging war. So at least the idea of airborne warriors was in the Founders' realm of possibility.

But the Space Force? That seems far beyond even Ben Franklin's imagination. Since part of my project is to alert folks to potential constitutional violations under originalism (see my Rule 5), I sent a quill-penned letter to the head of communications at Space Force a couple of weeks ago. I tried to make it as polite and respectful as I could. "If you want to follow the original conception of the Founders, you might consider folding the Space Force into the Army."

The Space Force has not responded.

The other issue I'd been pondering was whether many of the last fifty years of America's foreign conflicts had, in fact, been unconstitutional.

There is debate over who can declare war, who can command the war, and what the definition of a war is. The Founding Fathers were wary of giving too much war power to a single branch. So in the Constitution, they split up the authority. They gave Congress the power to declare war and to fund it, and they gave the president the power to prosecute the war (have the final say on how many troops to deploy, which areas to attack, etc.).

Abraham Lincoln explained the thinking behind this division of power: "The provision of the Constitution giving the war-making power to Congress, was dictated, as I understand it, by the following reasons. Kings had always been involving and impoverishing their people in wars, pretending generally, if not always, that the good of the people was the object. This our Convention understood to be the most oppressive of all Kingly oppressions; and they resolved to so frame the Constitution that no one man should hold the power of bringing this oppression upon us."*

It seems like a wise system. War is too important to be decided by a single person. But in the twentieth century, the balance of war powers has tipped steeply toward the president. World War II was the last war in which Congress officially declared war. "In the nation's early conflicts, Congress's approval was thought necessary," explains an essay from the nonpartisan National Constitution Center. "In modern times, however, Presidents have used military force without formal declarations or express consent from Congress on multiple occasions." The authors cite Truman's ordering U.S. forces to Korea. And Reagan's use of military force in Libya, Grenada, and Lebanon. And Obama's use of air strikes to support the ouster of Muammar Qaddafi in Libya. In other modern conflicts, such as the 2002 Iraq War, Congress has passed resolutions authorizing the use of the military. But it's been clear that the president was driving the train.

---

* Ironically, many scholars say that Lincoln probably violated the Constitution during the Civil War in several ways, including restricting freedom of speech by shutting down the presses of publications critical of the war effort.

The Founding Fathers would have been shocked by the president's ability to make war. But presidents and their supporters have argued there's good reason for the shift in power. War today is different from war in 1789. We have to act much faster. There are missiles and instant communication. We don't have time for Congress to gather and rationally debate the pros and cons. Still, it makes me nervous to have one person with so much control over weapons that could wipe out humanity—especially since some of those people who've possessed that power have the impulse control of a toddler.

SECTION 5.

The Battle of Monmouth raged for another forty minutes. I lay there as redcoats stepped over my body, and I lay there while Patriots stepped over my body. I lay there, wincing at the loud musket shots and breathing in the smoke that reminded me of the Canadian wildfire haze that had blanketed New York the previous week.

Finally, the shooting came to an end. I rose from the dead and gathered with my fellow soldiers for a wrap-up talk from the commander.

"I want to thank you for being stouthearted men!" he said.

"Huzzah!" we shouted.

I spotted Julie and Lucas on the edge of the field and walked briskly to meet them.

"Nice work dying in the shade," Julie said, as I hugged her. I had an adrenaline buzz from the experience, but it was tinged with uncertainty. What would the Founding Fathers have thought of my reenacting? Honored? Confused? All I can hope is that in two hundred years, no one will be reenacting the bloody Chinese-U.S. war of 2028. Who knows, maybe all the world's nations will decide to make war illegal.

Huzzah

WEEPING.

I'd always thought the founding era was one of stoicism, unlike today's let-your-emotions-flow-freely mindset. But as with everything in history, it's complicated.

In some ways, the Founding Fathers were stoic. They wanted to govern their passions, just as the political elite should govern the impetuous public. Washington spent a lifetime trying to control his anger, writes historian Richard Norton Smith. He tried not to complain, at least not in public. Complaining about your hard lot in life was not a virtue. Sacrifice for the common good, that was a virtue. And I am drawn to that kind of stoicism.

But in other ways, the founding generation was quite emotional and expressive. Here's a description of George Washington's farewell address to his officers at a 1783 ceremony in New York City's Fraunces Tavern. "General Knox . . . walked up to the General and the two hugged and kissed with tears running down their faces." After which all the other officers broke down. "Such a scene of sorrow and weeping I had never before witnessed."

I bring this up because we just spent a recent weekend dropping Jasper off at college in Ohio, and I'm feeling weepy and sad. He's declaring his independence from the monarchy of Julie and me.

Granted, our son's leaving the nest doesn't compare to Washington's farewell party. I try to imagine what it was like in that room. Since travel was arduous, many of these men would never see each other again, not to mention the comrades they'd lost in a long and grueling war. I'll see Jasper in a few weeks at parents' day. Still, I tell myself, it's okay to get a lump in the throat and misty-eyed. To quote some other notable words about sunrises—these ones not written by Ben Franklin—"Sunrise, sunset / Swiftly fly the years / One season following another / Laden with happiness and tears."

Washington City

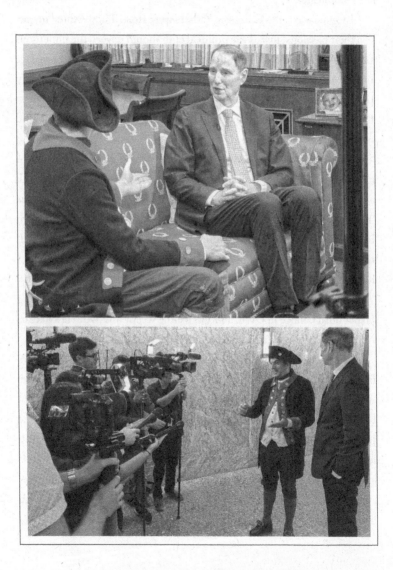

SECTION 1.

This year, I did something I never thought I'd do. I emailed my accountant and asked her to add an extra fifty dollars to my federal taxes. I did this because I felt it was my duty as an American citizen to pay for a rug cleaning service at the U.S. Capitol.

Let me back up: On September 12, I went down to Washington City (as some called it in the 1790s). I finally had an appointment to hand my petition to Congress in person. Specifically, I would hand it to the person of Oregon senator Ron Wyden, whose legislative director is Isaiah, my second cousin. But while in Senator Wyden's Capitol Hill office, as I was talking to him about my petition, I started jotting notes down with my goose quill, and I managed to spill a good quantity of black ink on his carpet. I left his red carpet with a dark splotch the size of a poker chip.

Julie was horrified when I told her later. "You ruined a senator's carpet?"

I wouldn't say *ruined*. Even the senator was understanding. As I apologized and tried unsuccessfully to blot up the stain, Senator Wyden said generously, "It's not the worst thing to happen in Western civilization."

It's not like I smashed a window and peed on the Capitol carpet while wearing a Viking helmet. But still, I felt bad.

"I've been terrified all year you would do that to our carpets, and now you did it to a senator?" Julie said. "I wonder how much it'll cost the government to clean it up? I hope you're not depriving some kid of a textbook."

That got me. And that's why I asked my accountant to give the government a little bonus.

.   .   .

So, the trip was not without its bumps. But overall, I learned a ton about how America is using (and perhaps misusing) the Constitution today. I traveled to Washington, D.C., at a time when Americans are disenchanted with the government. Of course, Americans are always disenchanted with the government, but it's worse than usual. A recent Pew Research Center poll found that just 4 percent of Americans think the political system is working "extremely or very well." There are continual threats of shutdowns. When I told my Uber driver I was visiting Washington, he said, "Tell them they're all a bunch of crooks, both sides." I hoped to find some shred of optimism on my trip.

Senator Wyden is tall—six foot four. He went to college on a basketball scholarship and dreamed of going pro but ended up attending law school and getting involved with the Democratic Party instead. "I was too short for the NBA and made up for it by being slow," he cracked. His office is in a Senate building about two blocks from the Capitol. It's spacious but not huge, populated by a dark wooden desk, a red couch, an American flag, an Oregon state flag, photos of his kids, and a once-unstained rug. He was wearing a blue suit and a blue tie.

When I entered his office, he shook my hand. "How is your effort proceeding?" he asked.

He had been briefed on my project, so he wasn't shocked by my getup: brown breeches, tricorne hat, buckled shoes, red-and-blue regimental coat.

I told him it was proceeding well but that I'd been thinking a lot this year about Ben Franklin's story of the rising sun, the one carved on the back of George Washington's chair at the Constitutional Convention. I told the senator I'd lately become worried that the sun has started to set.

"Is the sun still rising on America?" I asked.

"It's definitely rising," Senator Wyden said. "I'm a first-generation Jewish kid. I never thought I'd have the opportunity to do this kind of public service."

I guess it's not shocking that a sitting senator would say the sun is still rising on America. The senator continued: "When people ask me, 'What do you think about the Constitution?' I say, 'It was a start. A really good start. A really good road map.' "

And, he added, we need to keep building on that road map. Sometimes we take wrong turns. Actually, we often take wrong turns.

Senator Wyden recounted a story about Winston Churchill's meeting with Israeli politician Abba Eban. "A reporter asked Eban whether he preferred the British system of government or the American. Eban said, 'The Americans always get it right.' Then he paused, and he said, 'After they've tried everything else.' "

I looked it up later, and the story is likely exaggerated. But I appreciated the senator's point. We are experimenters, and those experiments eventually point us in the right direction: onward and upward. Wyden's optimism was contagious. I felt a skosh better.

"It's about interpreting the Constitution at its best," the senator said. And interpreting *people* at their best, too. "Washington and Jefferson, they always wanted to appeal to people's better angels. It was almost as if they rejected some of the bickering that goes on today."

I decided it was time to get down to business. Time to express my constitutional right to petition Congress for redress of grievances.

"I brought a petition," I said. I took out a plastic container and lifted out the petition: dozens of pages rolled in a cylinder with the circumference of a Frisbee. I asked the senator if he would put his index fingers in either side of the scroll and hold it like some sort of paper towel dispenser.

"Okay," he said.

I began unspooling the petition. I pulled and pulled, the paper spilling onto the floor in a curly pile.

"This is a lot of names," he said patiently.

I was hoping he wouldn't notice that the names were written in huge handwriting, like the size of a newspaper headline announcing a global peace treaty. As I kept pulling, I explained the petition's idea: It asks

Congress to consider a three-person presidency. It was inspired by the debates at the Constitutional Convention, when many constitutional delegates thought a single-person presidency was a ridiculous idea, the fetus of monarchy.

I looked up. I couldn't guess what his reaction would be. Would he ask me to kindly vacate his office so that he could spend his time trying to govern the country?

He paused for a moment and then said, "A.J., you are injecting logic and common sense, which often is lacking in public discourse, and I commend you for it."

Wow. He really does see the best in people.

"Thank you," I replied. "I don't often get that feedback—about the logic and common sense."

So I had the senator's backing?

"It's an interesting idea," he said. "I'll give it some consideration." He then clarified. "That's what's called an under-promise," he said. I'll take a promise of any kind.

I told him that, in my opinion, the president has become too powerful at the expense of Congress. "I don't think the Founders got everything right," I said. "But I do think they were right that Congress should be the most powerful branch." I want the Congress to be able to do more governing. The presidency should be more gummed up, and Congress should be less gummed up.

The senator smiled. "I'm very glad to hear you say that," he said. Pro tip: If you want to make friends with a politician, tell them they deserve more power.

As it happened, Wyden had spent the morning trying to reclaim some of Congress's constitutional powers. In Article I, Congress is given the power "to regulate Commerce with foreign Nations." So international trade should be in Congress's purview. Congress should be in charge of trade deals, including tariffs. But over the decades, Congress has ceded much of that power to the president. Wyden wants it back. He's been haggling with the administration over who gets to set tariffs.

As I rerolled my petition and tried to stuff it back into the box, the senator said, "Let's take a walk."

He led me out of his office, and we strode down the hall's tiled floor, past the office of Idaho's senior senator, past the finance committee meeting room. At the end of the hall, near the elevator bank, I spotted a scrum of reporters. There were about a dozen of them from outlets such as ABC News and the Associated Press, holding microphones and cameras at the ready.

"Let's go have a chat," the senator said.

This suggestion was unexpected. I've spoken to individual journalists in my career, of course, but never addressed a pack of them. I could feel the back of my neck get hot. What was about to happen? As we approached, the reporters raised their cameras and microphones and clicked Record.

"Hello, Americans," the senator announced. "We have a very special person here in the halls of the Senate office building. I'll let him introduce himself to you. But he is here to talk about how Congress ought to play a bigger role in the decision-making of America. A.J.?"

Wait. Was the senator using me as a pawn in his power battle with the executive office? It looked like it. But you know what? I was happy to be a pawn. I agreed with the senator and the Founders that we need more limits on presidential power.

I told the reporters that I felt we had strayed from the Founders' vision and that the government's powers are wrongly balanced. "And by the way," I said, "thank you in the press for expressing your First Amendment rights."

They looked at me blankly. I checked later, and there wasn't much coverage, but one ABC reporter posted a photo on X with the caption "Good morning from the US Senate feat[uring] Sen. Ron Wyden and this man . . . an author dressed in colonial garb who is spending a year 'living constitutionally.'"

I am proud to be "this man"!

SECTION 2.

After I said goodbye to Senator Wyden, Isaiah took me on a tour of the Senate buildings. We walked through the underground network of corridors. We passed the Senate barbershop and arrived at the Senate subway, a three-car train that resembles an airport shuttle but with an eagle logo on the outside. It's a short ride from the office building to the Capitol—only two blocks. But sometimes, the senators need to rush to a vote, and the octogenarians aren't the sprinters they used to be.

We disembarked in the basement of the Capitol and dodged the Senate staffers walking briskly to meetings in their business suits and pencil skirts. It struck me as an odd sight. I hadn't seen so many people looking professional since before the pandemic.

We strolled through the Capitol, which is much grander and more stunning than I'd expected. Lots of intricate paintings of American history. George Washington is everywhere: a stained-glass window of George Washington, a painting of George Washington on the dome's ceiling, seated on a throne among the clouds. It didn't have the caption "In George We Trust," but the implication was clear. There's even a crypt in the basement that was supposed to be Washington's tomb. Thankfully, Washington nixed this idea as too idolatrous, and the tomb remains empty.

Isaiah next took me to observe the Senate in session, which is open to the public. That day, the senators were voting on whether to spend $1.3 billion on the military, including funding for veteran housing and upgraded Air Force fields.

Isaiah and I took our seats in the balcony, which overlooked the chamber. The chamber has a blue carpet covered with a hundred little wooden desks, one for each senator, arranged in a semicircle. The desks are surprisingly small, about elementary school sized. And, like students, the senators sometimes carve or sign their names in the wood.

When their names were called, the senators voted digitally, in the true sense of the word. A thumbs-up or a thumbs-down. The House upgraded to an electronic voting system in 1973, but the Senate still uses the method of Roman emperors.

A couple of the senators flashed quick thumbs-ups by their waists, the fleeting motions recorded by the clerk. These senators were efficient and nonchalant. I had to watch closely to spot their votes.

Then the wooden doors at the back of the chamber flung open and in strode South Carolina senator Lindsey Graham. He was holding his fist in front of him as he approached the clerk, his thumb tucked tightly on the side. The tension built. Would it be a yea or a nay? Then at the last minute, Senator Graham thrust his thumb upward. A yea! The senator had choreographed it brilliantly, as if he were playing a politician in a Rodgers and Hammerstein musical.

That was the most exciting moment in my time observing the Senate. Otherwise, the chamber was sparsely populated and quiet.

The Senate did vote mostly yea. But that didn't mean the bill passed. That was just a vote to end the debate. There were plenty of steps left to go. As of this writing, the bill has still not been approved. In fact, in case you haven't noticed, it's shockingly difficult to get bills approved in the Senate.

In Madison's day, Congress got stuff done. Consider the First United States Congress of 1789–1791. It established the Department of War, the Treasury, the Department of Foreign Affairs (later renamed the Department of State). It admitted Vermont to the union, established the First Bank of the United States, approved twelve amendments to the Constitution, and much, much more.

So what happened? Why can't Congress get more done? There are many factors, but let me focus on two.

POLARIZATION

We've been locked in a nearly even battle between the two parties for decades. It swings a bit one way or the other, but it almost always hovers around fifty-fifty.

What would the Founding Fathers have thought? George Washington would have been appalled. He hated parties. As one scholar wrote, Washington thought "faction was virtue's opposite."

On the other hand, Madison wasn't opposed to parties. He saw that some level of partisanship was unavoidable. There will always be factions. His big insight was this: Make factions a *feature* of Congress, not a *bug*. Try to play groups' interests off against one another so that no one group would be totally dominant. And the bigger the country and more diversified the interest groups, the better.

But it seems that Madison's vision didn't come to pass, either. We do have a great variety of interest groups—but they've all clumped together into two frozen, opposing parties, the Republicans and the Democrats. It's not, as Madison had hoped, a cacophony of groups that would forge temporary alliances without one group becoming dominant. We now have two static teams, with one in the slight majority and one in the slight minority, depending on the year.

Senator Wyden is one of the few senators who still makes an effort to work across the aisle. He has cosponsored privacy bills with Republican Rand Paul, for instance. But this type of cooperation is much harder than it used to be.

THE SUPERMAJORITY REQUIREMENT

Which brings me to another problem: For any important bill to become law, the Senate has to approve it. And not just approve it. Super-approve it.

The Senate generally requires sixty votes to pass any real law. This number is known as a *supermajority*. Fifty-one votes out of a hundred isn't enough. If you want to build a new highway or regulate social media companies, you need sixty votes.

Some commentators—mostly on the right—see this requirement as a good thing. They argue it's what the Founders wanted. The Senate is supposed to be made up of rational grown-ups who rein in the impetuous House. The Senate is the tortoise, and the House is the hare, as a video from the conservative Federalist Society puts it.

This line of reasoning says the supermajority system is the best option. It encourages bipartisanship in the Senate. To pass a law in this divided climate, Democratic senators will always need to convince some Republican senators, and vice versa. It prevents the "tyranny of the majority," in which a slight edge in the Senate would allow one party to make radical changes.

The supermajority is enforced by a series of arcane Senate rules such as cloture. *Cloture* means "closure," but someone switched the *s* to a *t*, presumably to be pretentious. Cloture says that you need sixty votes to end (or close) a debate. Otherwise, the opposing side can continue to filibuster your bill—stall indefinitely and delay the vote forever. In decades past, the filibuster involved ridiculously long speeches (such as South Carolina's Strom Thurmond's speaking for twenty-four hours and eighteen minutes to try to stop the Civil Rights Act of 1957, or Louisiana's Huey Long's marathon reading of, among other things, fried oyster recipes to try to block New Deal legislation in 1935). But now, a senator can just threaten a filibuster and get the same result.

The Federalist Society video asserts that this wise system has been a part of America "from its beginning." It was built into the Senate's DNA. But actually, according to many historians, that's not true. The supermajority is not in the Constitution, and most of the Founders would probably oppose it.

Yes, the Founders wanted lengthy, reasoned debate. Yes, they wanted the minority view to be fully expressed so as to avoid the "tyranny of the majority." But only up to a point. They didn't want the majority of senators held hostage by the minority of senators.

Madison went on the record. He wrote a letter in 1830 opposing the idea of a supermajority. "To establish a positive and permanent rule giving such a power, to such a minority, over such a majority, would overturn the first principle of free government."

So what happened? Well, blame Aaron Burr and some botched editing. Burr is most famous for killing Hamilton, but he did something else that might have had an even bigger effect: In 1806, he edited the Senate Rules, which had been written by Thomas Jefferson. Burr wanted to make them shorter and snappier. So he took out the rule that said debates had to end in a timely manner, which he presumably figured was obvious and didn't need to be spelled out. Burr's editing blunder didn't do much damage until decades later when proslavery senator John Calhoun exploited the loophole to scuttle legislation that he thought would benefit the North.

According to Sarah Binder, political science professor at George Washington University, the Senate got rid of the debate-must-end rule "not because senators in 1806 sought to protect minority rights and extended debate. They got rid of the rule by mistake."

As a writer, I appreciate how important good editing is.

SECTION 3.

Isaiah had gotten us reservations in the private Senate dining room. It's not open to the public, its tables meant for senators, staffers, and guests only. The catch was, I had to ditch my breeches and tricorne hat. Jacket and tie required.

I changed into twenty-first-century clothes, and we entered the room. It was smaller than I expected: about thirty tables covered in white linen, the walls decorated with portraits of senators past. I spotted a baker's dozen of senators sprinkled throughout the room.

The menu had beet salad, grilled salmon, and something called Senate Bean Soup, which was made with beans and chunks of ham hock. It's been on the menu since the early 1900s, at the request of a senator in either Minnesota or Idaho—no one is sure which. (Suspiciously, both states have lots of pig farms. Pork barrel politics at its most literal.)

At the next table was a group of about ten people I didn't recognize: two women, a couple of kids, some men in suits, and a big redheaded guy with a sizable belly. I could see his belly because he was wearing a T-shirt, no tie.

How did he get away with no tie? My guess is he was a celebrity or businessman with enough money to buy a thousand Gucci ties without thinking twice.

Which brings up another question about modern-day Washington, D.C. What would the Founders think of how money distorts our political system? In 2022, business-based political action committees made $341 million in federal contributions, according to the nonprofit Open Secrets. They can do this, in part, because of several Supreme Court rulings. For instance, *Citizens United* ruled that the government cannot restrict corporations from spending money on politics.

In attempting to divine how the Founding Fathers might have felt about the deluge of money into politics, you can certainly find elitist statements from some of them about the ignorance of the poor and the duty of the moneyed, well-educated classes to shepherd them.

But you can also find evidence that some Founding Fathers saw money as a corrupting influence. Lawrence Lessig argues in his book *Republic, Lost* that the Founders—at least some of them—would have been appalled by the influence of the wealthy and corporations. "The equality of citizens is an equality that our Framers saw then, but that we have forgotten now. They saw then that a system that gave 'the rich,' again, as Madison put it, more power than 'the poor' violated the core commitments of a representative democracy, what they called 'a Republic.' "

Lessig's book also cites Adams as saying a legislature should be "an exact portrait, in miniature of the people at large, as it should feel, reason and act like them." This description wasn't accurate in his day. Most of the legislators were wealthy, and all were white men. And though we've made some progress toward accurate representation, we still have a ways to go, to put it mildly. Over this past year, I've heard many ideas on how to make our democracy more democratic. They run from practical to idealistic, from mild to radical. Here's a quick look at three of the most interesting, and how the Founders might have viewed them.

STOP GERRYMANDERING

Gerrymandering, as you might know, is the practice of carving a district into a weird shape to give an advantage to a particular party. It's named after Elbridge Gerry, one of the Founding Fathers. I feel for Gerry. He was a thoughtful Founder in many ways, but his name is forever besmirched with this devious method of cheating. (And as an added indignity, we pronounce it wrong. His name was said with a hard *G*, like Gary, Indiana.)

In 1812, Gerry was governor of Massachusetts and signed a bill to redistrict his state to give his party (the Jeffersonian party) an advantage. The sad part is, he didn't even want to do it. He found it "exceedingly disagreeable" but buckled to the pressure from his fellow party members. Which sounds familiar.

Opponents rightly objected. As one newspaper wrote, the practice "inflicted a grievous wound on the Constitution." Journalists compared the district's slithering shape to a salamander, which is how we got the word *gerrymander*.

In 2019, the Supreme Court ruled that it would not interfere with partisan gerrymandering. So we can't rely on that solution. Perhaps the best solution is to have states form independent nonpartisan or bipartisan commissions that draw voting districts. So far, twenty-one states have such commissions. We just need twenty-nine more.

NIX THE SENATE

A much more radical suggestion is to scrap the Senate altogether. Just get rid of it. The argument, made by some hard-core leftists, is that the institution itself is too undemocratic. Each state gets two votes, no matter what their population. Which is why a resident of Wyoming has three hundred times more power in the Senate than a resident of California. The Senate's structure favors the more rural, less populated states.

What would the Founders say? James Madison would no doubt object to totally nixing the Senate. He thought the Senate, with its longer terms and fewer and older members, was a good way to cool the passions of the House.

But like today's activists, he vehemently objected to the two-senator-per-state rule. He wanted the number of senators to be based on the state's population, just like the House. During the convention, the smaller states objected and threatened to walk. So Madison relented. At the end of the convention, he felt dejected, thinking the system was flawed. So at the very least, he would agree with the anti-Senate activists that it's a defective institution.

UPEND THE VOTING SYSTEM

There are plenty of other ideas—for instance, get rid of the Electoral College. The Founders created the Electoral College for several reasons, but one of the main ones was to put a buffer between the masses and the final selection of the president. The Founders were worried that Americans might fall prey to a demagogue, and they wanted an emergency measure to prevent such a person from becoming commander in chief. The electors were a group of educated men from each state who served that purpose. If the public chose a potential tyrant, the electors had the power to vote against the wishes of the public and elect a more reasonable person as president.

People have been trying to abolish or reform the Electoral College since at least the early 1800s. Nowadays, the electors are rubber-stampers, and if they went against their state's popular vote, it would be a scandal. But the Electoral College can and does affect the presidential election in a significant way. It has allowed George W. Bush and Donald Trump to win the presidency even though they received fewer popular votes nationwide than their rivals. This counterintuitive result arose because the electors are not apportioned evenly. Small states like Wyoming have more electoral votes than they would if the apportionment were based on current population. And California has far too few. So the Electoral College is not beloved, especially by Democrats.

But the most radical idea I have heard goes far beyond abolishing the Electoral College. The most radical idea is this: Get rid of voting altogether.

This notion has popped up a surprising number of times during my constitutional year. I've heard it from a Yale political scientist, a philosopher friend of mine, and my brother-in-law, to name a few seemingly rational people who endorse this bonkers-sounding idea.

Isn't voting the very heart of our democracy? Wouldn't abolishing votes be the very definition of tyranny? How else would you fairly choose leaders?

The answer is: randomly. By lottery. As University of Pennsylvania psychology professor Adam Grant wrote in *The New York Times*, "The ancient Greeks invented democracy, and in Athens many government officials were selected through sortition—a random lottery from a pool of candidates. In the United States, we already use a version of a lottery to select jurors. What if we did the same with mayors, governors, legislators, justices and even presidents?"

One might respond, for starters, regular folks have no idea of the intricacies of governing. Would you want your surgeon selected by lottery? Our country would collapse into anarchy. But randomocracy fans argue that this wouldn't happen. First, to enter the lottery, you'd have to take a test ensuring you have enough civics knowledge to qualify. Second, they argue, randomly selected leaders are more responsible and cooperative than elected ones—at least if you believe the results of one study. Third, they argue that it would cut down on the number of politicians with warped personalities. The headline of the *Times* article was "The Worst People Run for Office." Professor Grant's point was that, according to studies, those who want to be politicians often score high on narcissism, Machiavellianism, and psychopathy. (For what it's worth, I got zero psychopath vibes from Senator Wyden, at least in my short meeting.)

What to make of sortition? I doubt the Founding Fathers would have approved. They wanted their politicians to be the educated elite. Sortition hasn't been tested much in the real world. There have been some small experiments recently in France and Iceland, but it's too early to tell whether it's a workable system.

Pondering this idea leads me to thoughts of a potential world-ending disaster. But there is also something about it that intrigues me. Our Founding Fathers, after all, had an experimental mindset. I wouldn't want us to start with choosing the president by air-popped Ping-Pong balls. Maybe we start small. Very small. Maybe it's worth selecting one city councilperson in a town in South Dakota by lottery and seeing how it goes from there.

SECTION 4.

As I took the train back from Washington, D.C., I decided that, like Wyden and the apocryphal version of Abba Eban, I am optimistic we can get better. But we need to fix a lot of our wrong turns.

And weirdly, one of the wrong turns, in my opinion, is the existence of Washington, D.C., itself. The supposed center of democracy is, in a way, the least democratic place in America. The district is home to nearly 700,000 residents who are not properly represented in Congress. This is a bizarre situation. How did it come about? I put at least part of the blame on Founding Father John Dickinson (whose namesake school, Dickinson College, is a wonderful institution and Julie's alma mater, I am required to point out).

After the Revolutionary War, the U.S. capital was located in Philadelphia. But then came the Pennsylvania Mutiny of 1783. This uprising consisted of a mob of four hundred armed veterans surrounding Independence Hall and demanding payment for their Revolutionary War service. For a while, they barricaded the congressmen inside. Congress asked for protection from the Pennsylvania Militia. Dickinson, who was the governor of Pennsylvania and who apparently sympathized with the Pennsylvanian veterans, refused.

After this crisis, the Founders decided they needed to move the capital outside of any state jurisdiction. They wanted it to be its own little fiefdom, not reliant on any governor for protection. The result, a few years later, was Washington, D.C., the white-marble-filled city I had spent the day visiting.

It was an understandable decision. But the upshot is that a vast number of Americans now lack a real voice in government. Washington, D.C., does get three electoral votes in the presidential election, but it has zero senators, and its lone congressperson is a weakling "delegate" who is not allowed to vote on bills.

There are complications with making D.C. a state. Opponents of the district's statehood say it would violate the Constitution, because the Constitution requires the seat of government to be separate from the states. Others say it would be better to have D.C. absorbed back into Maryland.

Whatever the solution, I think the Founders would want those 700,000 Americans to be part of the republic.

Huzzah

THE ELECTION CAKE PROJECT.

The Save Democracy by Baking project continues to help me ward off despair. We now have people promising to bake cakes in forty-three states in the November elections. But, of course, that means there are seven holdouts, including Hawaii, Idaho, and West Virginia.

One possible hack? Maybe we don't need West Virginia. Professor Roosevelt told me that there was a constitutional controversy over whether West Virginia followed proper protocol to become a state. It was formed during the Civil War when part of Virginia decided to side with the Union.

But after the war, Virginia filed several Supreme Court cases alleging the decision was not democratic. In the end, SCOTUS sided with West Virginia. But maybe I could argue that it's still up in the air? Not a great solution, and one I hope I don't have to employ.

Red Tape and the
Constitution

SECTION 1.

On a Saturday in August, I walked into Central Park with a big soup ladle and a steel bucket. I was on a quest to get some drinking water. And not just any drinking water. Water that is purely and beyond question constitutional. Water untainted by potentially unconstitutional agencies and processes.

I walked past the Diana Ross Playground and the bronze *Romeo and Juliet* statue and arrived at my destination: the pond. When I got there, I noticed that the water was not clear. It was opaque. It was also bright—an alarming shade of green, about the same color as a Shrek Halloween mask. I spotted a sign nearby that said: WARNING: WATER CONTAINS HARMFUL ALGAL BLOOMS.

Well, I was already at the pond. I got out my ladle and started scooping the green liquid into the bucket. It made a low, metallic ping as it hit the bottom.

"You panning for gold?" asked a man nearby.

I chuckled politely.

What I was actually doing was trying to find 100 percent originalist water. According to my project's Rule 3, "If something has been tainted by a potentially unconstitutional agency or object, I should steer clear." And if some libertarian originalists are correct, the Environmental Protection Agency itself is acting in an unconstitutional way. Which means the water that comes out of my kitchen tap—which has been sanitized and transported according to EPA guidelines—is unconstitutional.

Hence my trip to Central Park in search of uninspected, unsupervised rainwater.

When I got home, I tried to create a makeshift water treatment plant. I boiled the water on the stove. I ran it through a water-cleansing tube marketed to hard-core campers. I added a few drops of bleach, as one YouTube video suggested. Voilà! Slightly less opaque water.

I offered to make Julie some coffee with my originalist water.

"Hard pass," she said.

I took a sip. It was still a bit vegetal. This could be a challenge. If I drank this water every day, I'm guessing I would have stomach issues that not even a tobacco-smoke enema would solve.

SECTION 2.

My Central Park drinking water expedition is related to one of the biggest controversies in the originalist debate: Is my daily life controlled by a bunch of bureaucrats the Founding Fathers would have abhorred? Is the U.S. government overrun with constitutionally questionable regulatory agencies that tell us what we can eat, drink, breathe, buy, build, and wear?

Some originalists argue yes. And the Supreme Court seems to agree, at least up to a point. In 2023, SCOTUS pared back the power of the EPA to monitor wetlands. As I write this, several upcoming SCOTUS cases could strip power from federal agencies meant to protect everything from consumers to investors to deep-sea fish. Gutting these agencies will either be (a) a great victory for the liberty of American citizens or (b) a catastrophic mistake that will fuel the climate crisis and sicken millions of people. As always with the Constitution, the prognosis depends on whom you talk to.

Much of the debate centers on the very first sentence of the Constitution. Well, the very first sentence after the gorgeous preamble. It reads: "All legislative Powers herein granted shall be vested in a Congress of the United States." Meaning Congress, and only Congress, has the ability to make laws.

The U.S. government has hundreds of agencies that regulate every part of our lives. These agencies are not part of Congress. Most are officially in the executive branch, overseen by the president. But in reality,

presidents don't micromanage the agencies. (Trump was an exception.)*
Presidents usually appoint new agency heads, but the agencies are generally staffed with the same longtime civil servants no matter who's in the White House. And though these agencies don't pass bills, they enact regulations. Thousands of them. And libertarians say these regulations are as much law as any bill.

If you're an average liberal, this army of agencies—known collectively as the administrative state—is primarily a force for good. Yes, the agencies make mistakes and sometimes overreach, but, overall, these regulations protect our very lives. One of my trusted constitutional advisers, Glenn Smith, is an emeritus professor at California Western School of Law in San Diego and author of *Constitutional Law for Dummies*. When teaching his students about the importance of federal regulation, he describes his day this way:

> I wake up due to the alarm on my cell phone because the Federal Energy Regulatory Commission has regulations assuring reliable electrical current (which I used to charge the phone battery overnight).
>
> I brush my teeth with water that is relatively clean due to regulations of my local water supplier in collaboration with the Environmental Protection Agency.
>
> My Nespresso successfully brews my morning coffee without blowing up in my face because of the consumer-product-protective regulations of the Consumer Product Safety Commission.
>
> I listen to the local news, knowing that the program I listen to or stream will be sufficiently strong and interference-free thanks to the Federal Communications Commission.
>
> I get in my car and drive safely thanks to the auto-safety regulations

---

* For more on this issue, I recommend Michael Lewis's book *The Fifth Risk*.

administered by the National Highway Traffic Safety Administration.

These regulations might sometimes be annoying, but they are for our own good and the good of society. Yes, your toilet may not flush as hard as you'd like, but as Harvard professor Jody Freeman told host Peter Sagal on the PBS series *Constitution USA,* "When the federal government sets efficiency standards for toilets or your fridge . . . what they're doing is creating incredible gains for the whole society . . . you save consumers a huge amount of money, everybody's electric bill goes down."

So that's one side. Libertarians, on the other hand, see these agencies as mostly harmful, not helpful. They constrain our freedom.

"I don't have free choice in health care," Paul Engel, host of the conservative *Constitution Study* podcast, told me. "I don't have free choice in what vehicles I drive. The USDA controls most of what I eat. I can't buy a washing machine that works."

From this point of view, the unconstitutional nanny state is crushing small businesses. How are you supposed to make an honest living when you have to spend extra time and money making your website accessible to color-blind people? "The temptation to use the tool of federal government is too much, even if it's not needed," said the late libertarian writer P. J. O'Rourke on *Constitution USA.* "If you give a man a cordless power drill, you'll have holes all over your house."

This, say libertarians, is not what the Founders envisioned. As Chief Justice John Roberts wrote in 2013, "The Framers could hardly have envisioned today's vast and varied federal bureaucracy . . . the administrative state with its reams of regulations would leave them rubbing their eyes."

Many originalists would say the FDA and EPA have a right to exist, but they've overstepped. They should only be enforcing Congress's laws, not making up or interpreting their own regulations. More hardcore libertarians want to ax them altogether. Engel calls the FDA a "monstrosity," a "criminal, bureaucratic, illegal, immoral nightmare."

As I write this, SCOTUS is starting its 2023–2024 term. On the docket are several cases that will likely strip the administrative state of at least some of its power, and maybe a lot of it. One case involves the ability to regulate loans. Another is about a forty-year-old doctrine called "*Chevron* deference." I won't go into details, but the gist of the doctrine is that when a law is unclear, the federal agencies have the power to interpret it.

"The court is in the process of taking a sledgehammer to the administrative state," warned Kate Shaw, professor at Yeshiva University Cardozo School of Law and cohost of the progressive podcast *Strict Scrutiny*.

SECTION 3.

The administrative state has grown to its current size for many reasons. Often, regulators multiplied in reaction to a crisis. The Food and Drug Administration came to life in the early 1900s after muckrakers exposed the appalling, germ-filled conditions of slaughterhouses. The Great Depression led to a burst of financial regulators that tried to prevent shady investing.

SCOTUS played a big part in the swelling of the bureaucracy. Consider one crucial 1942 case called *Wickard v. Filburn*. Technically, the case was about wheat farming. But in reality, it had huge repercussions, allowing the federal government to regulate almost any part of American life.

The short version: Under President Franklin D. Roosevelt, Congress enacted a regulation limiting the number of acres of wheat that a farmer could grow. A farmer could grow a certain number of acres of wheat and no more. The idea was to prevent a glut of wheat, so that wheat prices stayed stable and farmers could make a living. An Ohio farmer named Roscoe Filburn got in trouble for growing more than his allotted 11.1 acres of wheat. And he sued. He said that Washington, D.C., had no power to tell him how much wheat he could grow.

Wrong, said the government. The Constitution says Congress can regulate commerce "among the several states." Since wheat gets shipped across state lines, it counts as interstate commerce.

Not so fast! responded Filburn. He grew his own wheat to feed his own dairy cows. The wheat never left his farm. It was nobody's business but his own. The interstate commerce clause did not apply.

SCOTUS ruled against farmer Filburn. It said that no farm is an island. When farmers grow excess wheat to feed their own cows, that means they're not buying wheat from other farmers to feed these cows. Imagine if thousands of farmers did the same. The wheat market would crash, creating a national problem.

The consequences of this decision were huge. After *Wickard*, pretty much any local business could be said to affect interstate commerce, which meant the federal government and its agencies could make rules about anything: toy trains, shampoos, bouncy castles, raspberries—you name it. The *Wickard* decision was fertilizer for the growth of the administrative state.

SECTION 4.

Libertarians have at least two strategies for reining in what they see as this modern bureaucratic monstrosity, and the 2023 SCOTUS decisions will likely help with both.

First, give more power to the states. States, not the federal government, should regulate our lives. Why would this matter? Why should I care whether it's Washington, D.C., or New York State that tells me which furniture is safe to buy?

Well, the idea is that the states are more in touch with local citizens and know better what is reasonable for them. The result would probably be less regulation. And if your state did overregulate, you could up and move to another state. You could vote with your feet and find a state with more relaxed laws about guns or psychedelic mushrooms.

This is what Paul Engel did when he moved from New York to Tennessee a few years ago. "I couldn't take New York anymore," he told me. "When I moved out, I tweeted, 'No longer a citizen of the empire. Long live the republic.'"

Second, some opponents of the administrative state want to strip power from the presidential agencies and give it to Congress. This is what they say the Constitution demands. It's in the first sentence after the preamble: "All legislative Powers herein granted shall be vested in a Congress of the United States." Not "vested in agencies overseen by the president"— it says "vested in a Congress."

Liberals argue that giving Congress the task of regulating our lives is a bad idea. The average congressperson lacks the expertise to make good regulations. How many milligrams of arsenic are safe to have in drinking water? Representative Ro Khanna, for instance, is smart, but he doesn't know. He doesn't have a PhD in toxicology. Congress would have to develop its own regulatory expertise—and Congress just doesn't have the resources to do that. Requiring Congress to make all the regulations would, in reality, mean a lot fewer regulations. Which would be fine with many conservatives and libertarians, of course.

SECTION 5.

It boils down to two fundamentally different views of red tape. One side sees red tape as the rope that is strangling our freedom. The other sees it as a safety cable that keeps us from plummeting to our deaths.

Your view will partly depend on what you believe happens if everyone pursues their own interests. If you have a libertarian bent, you might believe that allowing 330 million Americans to pursue their own interests will result in the happiest, freest society. We need some laws, sure. We shouldn't be allowed to murder one another. But overall, let people follow their bliss.

Liberals say this just doesn't work. If everyone pursues their own interests without supervision, bad things happen. They cite the centuries-old notion known as the tragedy of the commons. Imagine a neighborhood where ten farmers (farmers again!) share a field where they all let their cows graze. If the farmers pursue their selfish interest to the maximum, the cows will eat till they're full—and they'll overgraze and destroy the yard. That would be bad for everyone. Then, no cows could graze and all would go hungry (that's the tragedy part). To prevent this consequence, everyone needs to restrain their cows a bit. The farmers need a set of agreed-on rules. Through this lens, the world is a lot like the shared pasture. Climate change is the tragedy of the commons on a global scale, with oil companies as the overgrazing farmers.

Libertarians tend to focus on us as individuals. They would say that poet John Donne was wrong when he said no man is an island. Sure, there are connections between us, but in many ways, we are solitary individuals. And that's a good thing, says Paul Engel: "A law created by a legislature that says we will drive on the right-hand side of the road is for the safety of society, so that's allowed. However, seatbelt laws, helmet laws, they are not for the safety of the society. They're for the safety of the individual. Therefore, [they are] not necessary for the safety and security of society. They are what Noah Webster defines as tyranny."

A liberal might respond that this is too narrow a view of society. When people don't wear seat belts, they'll sustain worse injuries, which means a strain on our hospitals and insurance system. Seat belt shirkers harm everyone. A disconnected series of islands is the wrong metaphor for America. Our country is more like an interconnected web. And it's more interconnected every day, thanks to the internet, interstate highways, and airports. We are no longer a nation of semi-independent farmers. The regulatory agencies were created to respond to modern needs.

As for my take, I'm torn. On the one side, I do have an anti-authoritarian streak. I don't really like people telling me what to do. It's why I can't take exercise classes at the gym. I don't want some guy ordering me to do ten burpees. I'll do a burpee if I damn well want to! (And

mostly I don't.) On the other hand, I do see the world as an interconnected web. I know my actions have an effect on others, and I don't trust
my own goals to align with the greater good. For instance, I like to sleep
in a cold room. We're talking January-in-Fairbanks temperatures, even
in the summer. So if the government allowed an air conditioner that kept
my room freezing but spewed tons of greenhouse gases, I don't trust
myself to resist that temptation. Which is why I tend to be more accepting of federal regulations.

SECTION 6.

Back to my originalist water. I realize that despite my adventure in Central Park, the pond water is not really originalist at all. True, it didn't
come out of my faucet, but it has still been touched by dozens of potentially unconstitutional federal agencies. I carried it in a bucket approved
by the Consumer Product Safety Commission. I boiled it on a stove with
parts that had to be inspected by U.S. Customs and Border Protection.

Is it possible to live a life unsullied by federal agencies? Clearly not
right now. And not even the most original originalist wants to. Consider
highways and canals. In 1817, James Madison vetoed a bill that funded
the construction of roads and canals. He thought it was unconstitutional. Imagine a politician today clamoring for America to shut down
its unconstitutional canals and highways.

I decided I had to lower my sights. Maybe not a year without federal
agencies, but instead a day. Or better yet, a minute. I can hold my breath
for sixty seconds, not breathing the EPA-sanitized air.

I turned off my lights (Federal Energy Regulatory Commission). I
stood up from my structurally sound chair (Consumer Product Safety
Commission) bought at a competitive price (Federal Trade Commission). And what about my clothes? They have been tainted by all sorts of
federal agencies.

So I stripped naked and put my clothes in a pile in the corner. And I stood there. I spent sixty seconds holding my breath and wondering if the Founders would be proud of me. I'm not sure. Maybe Ben Franklin. He was an advocate of what he called "air baths." He wrote, "I am persuaded that no common Air from without, is so unwholesome as the Air within a close Room, that has been often breath'd and not changed." So Franklin would open the windows, take off his breeches and shirt, and let the fresh air wash over him. I opened my windows as well and let the fresh exhaust from buses and UPS trucks wash over me.

Huzzah

THESE UNITED STATES.

My hero today is twelve-year-old Violet Smith of North Dakota. Violet signed up to bake a cake, which means we now officially have bakers in all fifty United States. The Great a-Bakening, as I call it, could actually succeed. At least if folks follow through. (Julie doesn't like my name for it, and prefers to call it the Great American Baking Show.)

I have to thank social media. Social media is a mixed blessing, but organizing a baking force is one of the few uses that even James Madison might have approved of. And big thanks to Julie and her sorority sisters from Delta Nu* at Dickinson College, who came out to bake in force.

My spreadsheet has a total of 120 bakers, with some states heavily represented (thank you, California). A handful of the states don't even have elections in this off year. But we want to establish this as a tradition and get the entire nation baking. Plus, my editor won't give me a year-long extension.

By the way, I'm spending so much time organizing bakers and writing my book, I am for the first time in my life following Ben Franklin's schedule. I rise at five in the morning.

---

* Yes, Delta Nu is the name of the fictional sorority in the Reese Witherspoon movie *Legally Blonde*. Dickinson has the only Delta Nu sorority in America, which was formed in 1971 after some Dickinson students split from the national Chi Omega sorority because they believed Chi Omega was blocking Black women from joining their chapter. So Elle Woods is on the side of good.

Sweet Democracy

Cakes by Nicole Zaffino, Allison Kheel, Deborah Kirwan Wild,
and Ally Schoenberg

SECTION 1.

A week before Election Day, Americans were casting their early votes. Meanwhile, I was receiving photos of early cakes. One of the Illinois bakers, Nicole Zaffino, told me she'd be traveling on November 7, so she baked ahead of time and sent me a picture. It was a great cake—red, white, and blue icing, and a black silhouette of a top-hatted Abraham Lincoln, the Illinois congressman. Just seeing that first cake gave me a little high, even if I wasn't ingesting the sugar myself.

Other cakes started popping up in my inbox. Stacy Struminger and her friends baked a cake with the words "Virginia is for lovers *and* voters." Anna Sank of New Jersey baked an edible diorama of miniature voters lining up at a miniature voting booth on chocolate icing. I'd given the bakers lots of freedom in how they expressed their passion for democracy. I'm a hands-off cake boss. I'm the anti-Lochner.

A couple of cakes came in featuring blue icing in the shape of a check mark. I realized I've never actually checked a box in a voting booth, but I guess a check mark is more aesthetically pleasing than a filled-in oval. Either way, it reminded me of the essential nature of voting: choosing. We the people have a choice. We are participants with an influence over our future. This is a stunning fact, I remind myself. It has not been true for 99 percent of human history and is still not true in much of the world.

SECTION 2.

I woke up early on Election Day and started arranging my cake ingredients on the kitchen counter. I had my plan: a white sheet cake with the words of the Constitution's Preamble spelled out in black cursive icing.

(I'd scaled back from my original plan to write the entire Constitution on a series of cakes.)

My niece Andrea came over to help. We baked the cake in the biggest rectangular pan I could find and rolled out several packs of white fondant into our edible parchment. As we lifted it onto the cake, the fondant ripped.

"That's okay," I said. "The Constitution wasn't perfect. This is a good reminder."

That's my strategy: When you screw up, go for a metaphor. We amended the fondant's holes with some dabbed water and leftover scraps. After waiting for it to dry, I got out a squeeze tube of black sparkly icing and started engrossing my cake.

"We the People." As silly as I looked—I was in my tricorne, holding a tube of sugary gel with a quill attached to it to make for a better photo—I still felt the power of those words as I carefully squeezed them out: "establish Justice . . . general Welfare . . . Blessings of Liberty." I put the final black dab at the end of "the United States of America" and felt pride, partly that my cursive was almost legible (thanks to my fifth-grade teacher Mr. Hearst) but also that this paragraph represents the best, most aspirational goals of a country that I love.

SECTION 3.

Before heading out to the polls, I checked my email. An avalanche of cakes had arrived. And such creativity!

Lisa Green-Clopton in Georgia had made the original recipe in a Bundt cake pan but added peaches as an homage to her state. Iowa's Dawn Barker Anderson arranged nineteen raspberries in the shape of a check mark to represent the Nineteenth Amendment. Virginia's Rachael Dickson topped her cake with a tiny—working!—Revolutionary War cannon.

All the best American traits were on display.

Tenacity—Missouri's Debbie Hartle got in a car crash and was in the hospital but didn't want to leave me in the lurch, so she convinced a friend to bake a Missouri cake.

Innovation—my mom made cupcakes in ice cream cones, that wonderfully clever American food holder that became famous at the St. Louis World's Fair in 1904.

Community—people turned the baking and eating into a neighborhood activity, taking it to the streets, their county election offices, their school classrooms.

SECTION 4.

Julie and I arrived on the corner, a hundred feet from the voting booth, as mandated by law. I was wearing my full regimental coat and tricorne hat. Julie had decided to put on my old Alexander Hamilton Halloween costume. Her enthusiasm so touched me, I didn't want to point out that hard-core reenactors would call her a farb.

"What's going on here?" asked a gray-haired man who stopped as we arranged the cake on a fold-out table.

"I'm trying to revive the eighteenth-century tradition of election cakes to remind people that democracy is sweet," I said.

"I agree," he said. "It is sweet."

There were skeptics, though. One guy snapped, "I already voted," in a don't-bother-me tone as he walked briskly by.

"Well, you deserve a slice of election cake!" I replied.

"I already voted," he snarled, louder and slower.

Got it.

"What party are you with?" asked another man in a baseball cap.

"Cake transcends factions," I said. "We are just in favor of democracy."

But happily, the vast majority of voters and passersby were pro-election-cake. Some stridently so.

"This is wonderful," said a woman. "I've been so sad these past few weeks, and this is one of the few things that is making me smile." Another woman said she thought the cake should be part of a bigger election festival. "We need music, barbecues, a national holiday."

We soon had a huddle of cake-takers of all ages. I gave one tween a slice. Five minutes later, he approached us again with his plate empty.

"I dropped it on the sidewalk," he said. "Can I have another slice?"

Hmm. I was getting some I-didn't-chop-down-the-cherry-tree vibes, but I gave him another.[*]

I felt a little odd carving up the Constitution's words. Was it disrespectful to cleave the sentences? But I figured maybe ingesting the preamble's inspiring language would help drive home its message. It's like a tastier version of what Ezekiel did in the Bible when he ate the holy scrolls. As I slid the pieces onto paper plates, I told my fellow citizens, "Just so you know, it has cloves in it." An allergy attack would be a bummer. Most said they found the cloves surprisingly tasty.

"I eat cloves every day," said one woman. "I'm an herbalist."

"Really?" I asked. "What are cloves good for?"

"Curing toothaches and preventing hair loss," she said.

"Just more benefits of the election cake," Julie said.

We brought the last few pieces into the public school cafeteria to hand out to the poll workers. They devoured them hungrily. It seems to me we need to do a better job of feeding the people who are safeguarding our democracy.

SECTION 5.

When I got back home, I spent a few minutes trying to dab off the icing on my regimental coat, then took notes with my quill pen. That night, I

---

[*] The apocryphal story of George Washington lying to his father about chopping down a cherry tree comes from an 1806 biography by "Parson" Weems. The moral of Weems's story is, don't lie. A moral that Weems decided to impart by fabricating a story that never happened.

opened my laptop. I knew we had gotten a supermajority of states, but did we reach the goal of all fifty?

I went through the entries. There's Wyoming (that's forty-seven states), Pennsylvania (forty-eight), Arizona (forty-nine). We're just missing New Mexico.

Ah, there it is! A cake with the New Mexico flag's red-and-yellow Pueblo pattern. We reached fifty! Plus the District of Columbia.

Granted, fifty with an asterisk. One of the bakers is from Louisiana and identifies as a Lousianian, but she is in the foreign service and living in Djibouti, on the east coast of Africa. Does that count? Well, my announced goal was to get bakers "from all fifty states." So from a literal, textual reading, we did have a baker *from* Louisiana. As is often the case with constitutional matters, it depends on how strictly or loosely you interpret the text.

I wrote an email to the bakers. "I'm blown away by all the creativity and positivity and deliciousness you all put out into the world. Thank you so much."

Over the next couple of hours, the bakers wrote me back lovely emails. Emails that made me choke up like George Washington at Fraunces Tavern.

One of the bakers said she didn't realize how stressed and sad she'd been these past few weeks (months? years?) until she had something positive to do, even if that something was as simple as showing up and handing out empty carbs to strangers. I totally related.

"Next year, we'll go bigger," I told Julie. Back in the 1700s, some towns baked ridiculously massive election cakes. One recipe called for fourteen pounds of sugar and ten pounds of butter. The final cake weighed in at seventy pounds. Maybe we should try that? Or what if we have a cake that incorporates the state foods of all fifty states? Toss in some huckleberries from Montana, some corn from Wisconsin, some crab from Maryland? Okay, maybe that won't work. But how about marzipan figurines of all fifty state birds?

"Something like that could be good," Julie said, with an emphasis on the "like."

I went to bed that night feeling hopeful for the first time in a long time.

The next day, I woke up, got out my quill pen, and started work on the final part of this book: a collection of ten lessons from my year (though I could have done a hundred lessons). I call it . . .

THE BILL OF TAKEAWAYS

Takeaway I

THE CONSTITUTION CONTAINS MULTITUDES.

At a mere four pages, the Constitution may not be large, but it contains multitudes.

Some argue the Constitution is a document of oligarchy, designed by the elite to retain power. Others argue it is a document of liberation, designed to promote equality. I choose option C. It is both.

"It's a mistake to think that the founding was any one thing," said Larry Kramer, former dean of Stanford Law School. Yes, there was a strand of oligarchy, but there was also a strand of democracy. "Both strands were there," said Professor Kramer, adding that American history can be seen as the battle between the two strands.

This year has taught me to be skeptical of reductionist views of the Constitution. When I talked to Harvard law professor Laurence Tribe, he used a quantum mechanics analogy: The Constitution is both a wave and a particle. It can be two things at once.

I had the same reaction to the Bible at the end of my year of living biblically. The Bible contains passages about loving your neighbor and embracing outcasts, but it also contains passages about dashing your enemy's head on rocks and executing gay people. As I mentioned, there's nothing wrong with cherry-picking if you pick the sweet cherries.

Takeaway II

BE HUMBLE IN YOUR OPINIONS.

At the Constitutional Convention, Franklin told a short parable. He said there was a "French lady, who, in a little dispute with her sister said: 'I don't know how it happens, sister, but I meet with nobody but myself that is always in the right.'"

Franklin's point was that we are all that French lady. We all believe we have a monopoly on the truth. I know I feel that way most of the time. But I fight that inclination. I try to remind myself, what are the odds that I, A.J. Jacobs, one of eight billion humans on earth, happen to be that singular person who has discovered the correct take on politics, literature, the environment, religion, and all other topics? Probably two to one. Maybe even three to one.

I try to remind myself that I'm wrong about a lot and that I should change my mind when given new evidence. It's not easy. Changing your mind is often seen as a weakness. What are you, a flip-flopper? But the willingness to change your mind is a strength. It's hard but necessary. We need to evolve to survive.

My constitutional year has changed my mind about a host of issues. Just one example: the idea of states. Like Hamilton, I was skeptical of the idea of states. Why should laws differ if you drive a hundred yards and cross an imaginary line within the same country? Plus, historically, advocates of states' rights have used the concept to block civil rights laws, so I saw state governments as an impediment to progress.

But thanks to many books and conversations, I see the upside of this weird system of fifty oddly shaped semi-fiefdoms. I see that states can be what Justice Louis Brandeis called "the laboratories of democracy." State governments, at their best, can come up with new ideas that we can test on a small scale. For instance, Obamacare was inspired by a health-care program in Massachusetts. Nebraska and Maine have their own unorthodox way of handling the presidential elections. Unlike the winner-take-all system of the other forty-eight states, they sometimes split their state's electoral votes between the candidates. Perhaps it's a fairer system.

I didn't adjust my position on states' rights—or any topic—because someone humiliated me in a debate. Instead, it was because my constitutional advisers had the patience to carefully explore the pros and cons of various ideas with me. As Hamilton wrote in *The Federalist*, "In politics, as in religion, it is equally absurd to aim at making proselytes by fire and sword. Heresies in either can rarely be cured by persecution."

Takeaway III

ONE PERSON CAN MAKE A DIFFERENCE.

The cover of this book has my name on it, but it really should have a list of names. Dozens, maybe hundreds. My editor, the designer, the typeface inventor, the researcher Victor Ozols, who alerted me to much useful information, and also to Ben Franklin's essay on flatulence called "Fart Proudly."

It's a big flaw in our thinking: We focus on one individual at the expense of others. We glorify the lead singer but take for granted the bassist and the set designer and the roadies. This year has driven home that nothing important is done alone. The Constitution was forged by fifty-five delegates, but also by the thoughts of philosophers ancient and contemporary, by journalists, by the unheralded people who served the delegates at the convention, and by Jacob Shallus, who wielded the quill.

So that's one side of the coin. It takes a mega-village to do anything, from writing a book to creating a country. On the other hand, my year has reinforced a seemingly paradoxical but equally true theme: the power of a single person to influence history. Progress in America has often hinged on the actions of a single person, and I'm not just talking about the well-known folks, like George Washington or Frederick Douglass.

I'm talking the unsung heroes of American democracy. I've kept a list of them. One of my favorites is Febb Burn, who was crucial in getting women the vote. Febb Burn was the mother of Tennessee state legislator Harry Burn. In 1920, the fate of the Nineteenth Amendment—the right of women to vote—came down to whether the Tennessee state legislature would approve it. If Tennessee voted yes, the amendment would have the necessary approval from three-quarters of the states.

The vote in that Tennessee stateroom was close. One of the swing votes was Harry Burn, who had been undecided. On the morning of the vote, his mom, Febb Burn, had stuck a note in his suit pocket that asked him to "be a good boy" and vote for the amendment. So he did. And the battle was won. Legend has it that outraged anti-suffrage lawmakers chased Representative Burn through the statehouse, and he was forced to escape out the window. That's probably not true. But what is true is this: We should all be thanking Febb Burn.

The architect and philosopher Buckminster Fuller used the metaphor of the trim tab. A trim tab is a tiny piece attached to the rudder of large ships. If you can move the trim tab, you can affect the rudder, and you shift the course of an ocean liner. If the voyage is long enough, the tiny trim tab can alter the destination by hundreds of miles. "Call me trim tab," Fuller said. We can all be trim tabs.

Takeaway IV

BEWARE OF THE SINGLE LENS.

If you look at the marble frieze on the Supreme Court's west wall, you can see a figure of a winged and berobed woman holding a perfectly balanced scale.

This sculpture was worth getting up for at 4 A.M. Balance is a deeply American value, and we need more of it. I believe our system is wildly unbalanced in so many ways. SCOTUS has too much power. The president has too much power. The wealthy and mega-corporations have too much power. Tech executives have too much power.

I'd also argue that originalism has too much power. When we interpret the Constitution, the original public meaning should matter. But it should be balanced with other considerations: how a particular decision would affect society, how the Court has ruled in the past, how other countries handle similar problems, and more.

Legal scholar Steven Mazie frames it as a battle between monism and pluralism. He says that we should embrace plurality when looking at the Constitution. Constitutional interpretation is best when it's a process of competing ideas bumping up against one another. It's a messier activity than relying on a single lens such as originalism, but I believe it produces better, fairer decisions. Earlier in the book, I mentioned Isaiah Berlin's idea of two types of thinkers: the fox and the hedgehog. The fox sees the world through many lenses. The hedgehog sees the world through one lens, whether that's Marxism, the Bible, or originalism.

I think the fox's mindset is more American than the hedgehog's. Not to mention that foxes are literally more American—unlike hedgehogs, they are native to our continent.

Takeaway V

THINK SLOW.

Slowness is not a universally good thing. I wouldn't want to return to horse-drawn ambulances or three-hundred-baud modems. I'd also like to reclaim the combined hours I spent this year putting on my sock belts.

But there are parts of modern life that would benefit from an enforced speed limit. We need fewer hot takes and more cold takes. We need more slow thinking.

I found that writing in-depth letters by hand forced my ideas to be more nuanced. Thumb-texting acronyms has the opposite effect.

Writing letters is like a waiting period for the brain. It slows down every part of the process. You have to get out a pen and paper. You have to organize your thoughts. You get to see those thoughts on a page. You have to put that page in an envelope and send it off. It gives you plenty of time to revise your ideas and to cool your knee-jerk emotions.

I also loved slowing down my news consumption. When I'm blasted with the fire hose of updates on my computer, I have no time to step back and give the news any context. My day is a series of instant reactions. This is why I forced myself to read the news just once a day—or even twice a week, which is how often Ben Franklin's newspaper came out. A slow news schedule is better for my mental health than a tankard of ale.

I also officially endorse slow interactions. I pledge to take the time to assemble peaceably more often. And by "assemble," I mean assemble across a three-dimensional table, looking the other person in the eyes instead of at their avatar and using my mouth instead of a keyboard.

Takeaway VI

EMBRACE VIRTUE.

The word *virtue* nowadays has a bit of a cringey and fusty ring to it. I hear the word most often used in the phrase *virtue signaling,* which is not a compliment. Virtue signaling refers to someone who is ostentatiously trying to show off how righteous they are by, for instance, loudly asking a waiter about the living conditions of the bees that produced the honey for their oatmeal.

In the founding era, the word *virtue* had no such mixed connotations. Virtue was a cherished ideal. In his book *First Principles,* Thomas E. Ricks writes that the Founders used the word *virtue* about six thousand times in the collected writings from the Revolutionary era. That's more often than the word *freedom.*

Unfortunately, the word has a sexist etymology: *Virtue* is derived from *vir,* the Latin word for "man," because virtue was considered a manly characteristic. But virtue is not confined to one gender. In the founding-era sense, anyone can be virtuous. And that sense can be summed up with the word *public-mindedness.* A virtuous person puts the interests of others before their own interests. A virtuous person focuses on those two key words in the Constitution's Preamble: "general Welfare."

I think we're due for a resurgence of virtue. I know I could use more of it. As a rule, I'm too focused on my individual rights. Rights are wonderful, but they come with responsibilities. I wish the Constitution had a Bill of Responsibilities, but I think the idea of public responsibility was more ingrained back then and didn't need to be spelled out.

You were expected to sacrifice for your community. More than that, many people wanted to serve. Service wasn't opposed to happiness. It was integral to it. As Jeffrey Rosen, president of the National Constitution Center, has said, "Happiness wasn't about feeling good. It was about doing good." I find this observation to be true in my own life. If I'm depressed, I find the best thing to do is to help others. It gets me out of my head.

John F. Kennedy tapped into this idea of virtue with his famous appeal from his inauguration speech: "Ask not what your country can do for you. Ask what you can do for your country." Substitute *community* or *world* for *country* if you want. The point is to think of others. Which is not the dominant worldview today. Imagine a politician nowadays who tried to appeal to voters by stressing service to others. The candidate's PR team would quit.

Ben Franklin famously wrote up his daily schedule. He woke up early and began the morning by asking himself, "What good shall I do this day?" I found this idea so inspiring, I adopted it these past few months. I even copied the quote onto some rag paper and kept it above my desk. Julie will have to keep me accountable.

Takeaway VII

DON'T GLORIFY THE PAST—BUT DON'T COMPLETELY DISMISS ITS
WISDOM, EITHER.

As I was finishing this book, a video of the new Republican speaker of the house, Mike Johnson, emerged. In the video, Johnson was giving a talk to his supporters. He said that we must return to "eighteenth-century values," which, in his opinion, means more religion and less feminism.

I'm skeptical of this glorification of the past, for many reasons. For several years, I wrote a magazine column called "The Bad Old Days." I pointed out that the good old days were anything but. They were often sexist, racist, dangerous, and fetid. Morality evolves, thankfully. Pillories belong in recreational dungeons, not the town square.

So I reject Speaker Johnson's deluded nostalgia. On the other hand, this year has taught me not to throw out the baby with the cold, gross, reused eighteenth-century bathwater.

Some ideas from the past are worth reviving. Most importantly, cake on Election Day. But also many other ideas: the emphasis on the common good, the quest to control one's rage, the slow thinking, the experimental mindset, the distaste for aristocracy, and the awe at being able to cast a vote.

Takeaway VIII

REMEMBER THE *EXPERIMENT* PART OF THE AMERICAN EXPERIMENT.
Another Ben Franklin reference (as you might have guessed, he's my favorite Founding Father): This time, it's about Franklin's voyage back to Philadelphia from England in 1785.

He was up there in age—seventy-nine years old. But Franklin didn't spend his time on the ship playing shuffleboard or whatever the eighteenth-century equivalent was. Instead, he spent the voyage experimenting and thinking. As biographer Walter Isaacson describes it, Franklin filled up a thick notebook with ideas. He calculated the effects of air currents on sliced playing cards. He drew diagrams of compartmentalized hulls to save ships from sinking. He lowered an empty bottle two hundred feet below the surface to measure the water temperature. What a mind!

Franklin embodies two of the greatest American characteristics:

curiosity and an experimental mindset. Both were crucial to the formation of the United States. There's a reason we call it the American experiment. It was a radically new way of structuring society.

The Founding Fathers, at their best, were deeply flexible in their thinking. You can see it in the notes on the Constitutional Convention, where so much was up for grabs. Should the president be a single person? Should senators' terms last for two years, six years, or life? Where should the government be located? The delegates had read widely, absorbing ideas from philosophers of all stripes, both ancient and modern.

As all institutions do, American government has become much more fixed and static. But while we've gained stability, we've lost our thirst for fresh solutions. I'd love to see America embrace that original experimental mindset again. It would be fascinating to see our government test out new ideas on a small scale—even if they seem bizarre, such as using a lottery to choose a city council member—to see what works.

Takeaway IX

RIGHTS ARE MANY AND UBIQUITOUS.

I probably didn't break James Madison's reading record. He was voracious, amassing a personal library of about four thousand books, many of which he read in preparation for the Constitutional Convention. But this year, I did read as many books as I could (some of them meticulously, some with much skimming).

One of my favorites was *How Rights Went Wrong*, by Columbia University law professor Jamal Greene. I'm a sucker for a good paradoxical title (e.g., "The Sound of Silence," *Eyes Wide Shut*). But Greene's book also provides a great framework for thinking about morality. He argues that in modern-day America, we see rights as nearly absolute. We "fetishize" them. We see them as trump cards. We often use the phrase "it's my right" as a way to end a conversation. It's my Second Amendment right to bear whatever arms I want. It's my First Amendment right to shout at speakers so they can't be heard. End of discussion.

Greene proposes that today's view is contrary to how the Founders and many other societies viewed rights. Instead, he says, we should avoid the temptation to see morality as a handful of absolute rights. We should instead see it as a bunch of rights competing against each other.

The protesters who interrupt a play have a right to express their opinion, but the audience also has a right to enjoy art, and the actors have a right to make a living. When rights are seen as absolute, he writes, "law becomes reducible to winners and losers, to which side you are on, which tribe you affiliate with." Instead, the law should mediate between rights, consider their competing claims, and try to find solutions that balance them.

There's an important exception, writes Greene. There *are* some rights that should not be mediated—for instance, the right to be treated fairly regardless of your race. That is not negotiable. But most other rights are not so absolute. Greene says, "In a modern, cosmopolitan society, rights are not few and precious. They are many and ubiquitous."

Takeaway X

WE CONTROL THE SUN.

I figured I'd end this book as I began it, with Ben Franklin's story of the sun carved on the back of George Washington's wooden chair at the Constitutional Convention. That sun was cut in half by the horizon. Was it rising or setting? At the end of the convention, Franklin said he was convinced it was rising. America had a bright future.

I love the poetry of the tale, but I'm not convinced by the analogy. The sun rises and sets because of immutable natural laws. We have no control over gravity (unless you are Joshua in the Bible and you get God to stop the sun in the sky).

On the other hand, there is nothing natural about democracy. It is not subject to any immutable laws. It's fragile. We created it, and if we're not careful, we can destroy it. In 1992, political scientist Francis Fukuyama wrote a book called *The End of History and the Last Man,* which argued liberal democracies were somehow the natural end state of human society. He thought that just as billiard balls follow Isaac Newton's laws of motion, so do governments follow the inevitable path to democracy.

Well, that scenario didn't quite work out. We are facing a rise in authoritarianism around the world. My year of immersing myself in the founding of this country has inspired me to fight as hard as I can to protect it. No union will ever be perfect, but to make mine a little more perfect, I pledge to battle disinformation, tribalism, science deniers, and demagogues promising simple fixes. I pledge to speak up and bake clove-filled cakes. I'm not certain of much, but I'm sure of one thing: Whether the sun sets or rises on democracy, that's up to us, we the people.

ACKNOWLEDGMENTS

John Quincy Adams once said, "Gratitude . . . when it takes possession of the bosom, fills the soul to overflowing and scarce leaves room for any other sentiment or thought." I agree with our sixth president. And it so happens that my soul is jam-packed. So please grab a pint of ale, because I have a lot of gratitude to get off my bosom.

I have the honor of thanking the folks at Crown publishing. I do take issue with Crown's monarchical name—I'd prefer if it were called Tricorne Publishing. But I have absolutely no grievances with the talented and kind people there, including my visionary editor, Gillian Blake, as well Julie Cepler, David Drake, Mason Eng, Melissa Esner, Amy Li (who helped with so much, including the Delta Nu footnote), Dyana Messina, Joyce Wong, Andrea Lau, Annsley Rosner, Heather Williamson, and Amelia Zalcman.

It behooves me to thank the wise and supportive folks at CAA, including my agent, Sloan Harris, and his colleague Taylor Damron.

It is with great pleasure and humility that I recognize all the people who helped research the Constitution with me: Victor Ozols, a brilliant editorial mind and friend; Riki Markowitz, a fact-finding maven; and Patricia Boyd, the book's copyeditor or copy editor (both versions are acceptable). A special thanks to Glenn Smith, emeritus professor at California Western School of Law in San Diego and author of *Constitutional Law for Dummies*. He spent several hours on the phone with me going over concepts, and then read the manuscript and gave excellent corrections, naming himself "Professor Picky." Thanks for being so picky and generous with your time.

I have overflowing esteem for the many, many smart people from all sides of these issues who took the time to talk to me, and didn't hang up on me or walk away when I repeatedly uttered the phrase "can you go over that just one more time?" Deep gratitude to Kathleen Bartoloni-Tuazon, John Bessler, Chuck Bryant, Karen Burgos, Jud Campbell, Daniel Carpenter, Sara Chatfield, Saul Cornell, Liz Covart, David Davidson, Eric Jay Dolin, Zachary Edinger, Rae Katherine Eighmey (the best culinary historian I know), Zachary Elkins, Paul Engel, Richard Epstein, David Gillespie (who taught me to write with a quill), Jonathan Haidt, Carl Harris, Michael Helfand, Ryan Holiday, Annemarie Johnson, Representative Ro Khanna, Jessie Kratz, Carlton Larson, Lawrence Lessig, Jon Levy, Matthew Lillo, Will MacAskill (a fan of modified randomocracy), Gerry Ohrstrom, Suzanne Nossel, Ketan Ramakrishnan, Barbara Reiss, Jesse Rifkin, Andrew Schocket, Micah Schwartzman, Eric Segall, Andrew Seidel, B.A. Van Sise, Mark Warren, Elizabeth Samet, Paul Gowder, Cass Sunstein, Karin Tamerius, Cooper Teboe, Rob Weisbach (who gave me my first break, for which I'll always be grateful), Jay Wexler, David Winitsky, Zeke Winitsky, Ilan Wurman (who gave me a great tutorial on originalism), Senator Ron Wyden, and David Yassky.

The following people read the manuscript and gave invaluable notes on everything from the philosophical underpinnings of democracy to the spelling of Jimmy Buffett. I couldn't have finished this book without them. I hope I can return their generosity somehow: Dawn Anderson, Sam Aybar, Greg Behrman, Ben Bowlin (of *Ridiculous History* fame), Noel Brown (also of *Ridiculous History* fame), Andy Borowitz, Cynthia Matthews Brown, Nicholas Davidoff, Sam Davidoff, Amanda Flug Davidoff, Stephen Friedman, Stacey Geis, Jonathan Gienapp, Peter Griffin (my wise *Esquire* editor), Chloe Harris, Keiran Harris, Dave Holmes, Kay Hymowitz, Carol Jacobs, Bill Kuhn, Harry Litman (who is also a great podcaster, fyi), Andrew Lund, Jody Avirgan, Dylan Matthews, Jim Meiggs, Paul Mandell, Jonathan Marrow, Julia Mickenberg (who is as talented an editor as our college writing professor John Wilson), Logan Powell, Andrew Porwancher, Kermit Roosevelt, Kevin Roose (my former intern turned journalistic superstar), Gary Rudoren, Daniel Shuchman, Mark Shulman, Matthew Specter, David Spira, Logan Sullivan, Henry Sussman, Karin Tamerius, Ariane de Vogue, Adam White (who taught me so much about the administrative state), Max Williams, Mia Wilcox, Jeff Wilser, Jim Windolf, Jay Wexler, David Yassky, and Greg Young (of the *Bowery Boys* podcast).

In addition to those experts I spoke with, I must extend my gratitude to those teachers who gave me wisdom from afar. There were so many books, podcasts, and online courses that guided me through the constitutional forest. Among them:

The Ezra Klein Show, which has thoughtful interviews with brilliant people, and was the source of several quotes in the book, including one from Kate Shaw about the administrative state and another from Larry Kramer.

I'm a big fan of the *We the People* podcast, hosted by Jeffrey Rosen, president and CEO of the nonpartisan National Constitution Center. I love the center's mission to educate, debate, and celebrate our founding documents, and to do so with thoughtfulness and depth. Jeffrey Rosen's teachings about virtue were a big influence on this project.

I also learned a ton from such podcasts as *Constitutional* hosted by the awesome Lillian Cunningham; *America's Constitution* hosted by

Akhil Reed Amar; *More Perfect* hosted by Julia Longoria; *Strict Scrutiny* hosted by Kate Shaw, Melissa Murray, and Leah Litman; *Amicus* hosted by Dahlia Lithwick; *Supreme Myths* hosted by Eric Segall; *Law Talk* hosted by Richard Epstein and John Yoo; *5-4* hosted by Rhiannon Hamam, Michael Liroff, and Peter Shamshiri; *The Constitution Study* hosted by Paul Engel; and *Ben Franklin's World* hosted by Liz Covart.

I have the highest regard for the docuseries *Constitution USA*, hosted by Peter Sagal and aired on PBS. I also appreciate that Peter is a fellow fan of the Third Amendment.

I hoist my glass of Madeira to the hundreds of folks who signed the petition, including patriots Amy Schrader, Candice Braun, and Hilary Klotz Steinman. And I am indebted to the citizens at Watson Adventures, including Julie (see below) and Bret Watson, for discussing history with me.

I am exceedingly grateful to esteemed author A.J. Jacobs, for his generous permission to reprint or adapt several passages from previous books. For instance, some of the sections on Gertrude Sunstein, my oath against cursing, and the rules of civility appeared in slightly altered form in books such as *It's All Relative* and *The Year of Living Biblically*. Mr. Jacobs's permission was really helpful when I was on such a tight deadline.

I have the honor of recognizing those citizens who assembled in my apartment to discuss America, including Sherry Hsiung, Lorence Kim, Ayala Podhoretz, John Podhoretz, and Angel Caraballo.

I am humbly indebted to the wonderful patriots in the Third New Jersey Regiment, including Chris Diaman, Mary Diaman, Dakota Griffin, Mark Hurwitz, Pat Hurwitz, and Ed Rowland.

Also loud and piercing thanks to my fife instructor, Kim Braunsroth.

I have the highest possible opinion of Liv Virta-Meyer, a fellow lover of puzzles and obscure facts, as well as Stephen and Jesse Meyer, who are the folks behind Pergamena. They are one of the only parchment makers in the United States. Thanks for all your time and scrolls.

I'm also grateful to my fellow adventurer in parchment-making and assembling peaceably, Jay Kernis.

I offer appreciation to Will Dean at *The Guardian,* and Reed Young, who took some terrific photos, including the one on the cover and the one for the First Amendment chapter.

For their geniality toward Arjun, my quartered soldier, I'd like to thank Julie's book club: Sharyn Ben-Zvi, Trish Jamison, Barb LaVallee, Kirsten Oppenheimer, Emma Paske, and Lisa Tiger.

It is without exaggeration that I can pronounce that the Election Cake Project was one of most inspiring experiences of my life. I owe it all to the enthusiasm and creativity of the bakers across the United States:

Susan Alperstein, Dana Anderson, Dawn Barker Anderson, Caroline Barrett, Amy Donnelly Beaupre, Jamie Becker, Kim Becker (whose Maine cake featured a lobster, but a sweet one), Ruti Ben-Artzi, Karen Lee Benson, Dale Berlau, Francee Biondi, Karen Blumberg, Robin and Tom Bresko, Matt Brewer, Summer Brooks, Cynthia Carlaw, Lisa Green Clopton, Kirsten Crosby, Amanda Flug Davidoff, Emma Davidoff, Stacy Dickert-Conlin (who taught me Michigan is a big cherry state), Francine Crow, Rachael Dickson, Sjon Dowell, Jane Wallace and Derek Duncan, Peggy Dyer, Karen Eagleson, Anna Edwards, Marie Fazalare, Nancy Fiordalisi, Jen Fallon, Monica Ferschke, Lee Flier, Linda Friedel, Janis Gallagher, Melissa Gevaert, Liz Gilmour, Betsy Gorham, Joe Greitzer, Pamela Guerrera, Debbie Hartle, Heather Hartmann, Broron Henderson, Joy Holland, Susan Holt, Rebecca Holter, Cory Huff, Tara Hunt, Lisa Hutcheson, Matt Johnson, Linda Jeffrey, Hilary Kaplan, Felice Kaufmann, Lindsay Kennedy, Allison Kheel (the queen of fondant!), Keira Kheel, Lauren Marcus Kirsch, Nancy Kron, Marsha Kamish, Maggie Kuhlmann, Evelyn Lasky, Karen Lee, Marcia Evers Levy, Lena Leigh, Ana Leigh, Susan Lindner, Sivan Lund, Catherine MacMillan, Chelle Magin, Andrea and Jacob Maison (bonus points for the tricorne hats), Nancy Simpson Martin, Mary Martin, Marty Leitner Martin, Christina Mason, Jennifer Mau, Amy McGown, Sarah McNeilly, Tara

Hunt Melvin, Lisa Merrill, Laura Milhander, Andrea Miles, Gail and Brad Morlock, Maura Muller (an excellent evangelist for the cake project), Laura Neal, Phil and Erin Neilson, Courtney Nixa, Michele Page, Ashley Parker, Samantha Payne, Jennifer Pierce, Sara Peskin, Margie Peskin, Jodi Ransom, Sean Riley, Jennifer Dutton Roland, Shayna Rudoren, Len Muroff, Elizabeth Samet, Michelle Scannell, Kelly Scotti, Nicole Silberman, Donna Silverman, Dana Kostiner Simpson, Laura Neal Schroder, Sharon Slaten, Katie Smith, Violet Smith, Sarah Spoon, Jay Snider (who brought his Oregon cake to the ballot drop box), Sheri Struk, Samantha Payne, Alisa Srikacha, Amanda Schmeltzer, Kim Sherman, Jennifer Stahl, Stacy Cohen Struminger, Sheri Struk, Margo Tanenbaum, Celia Thompson, Kelli Timanus, Kevin and Mary Troller, Helen Cerra and Tom Ulan, Harley Ungar, Allison Weatherly, Rachel Weber, Dana Weber, Deborah Kirwan Wild (whose cake read "Jersey Girls Vote," and Julie agrees), Theodore Wiegand, Amy Wilson, Iris Wilhelm, and Jacqueline Wolven.

I hope I got all the bakers. Sincere apologies if I missed anyone or mangled the spellings. And special cake-related thanks to two of my nieces: baking consultant Ally (@allycutthecake on IG) and Andrea, an excellent sous pastry chef.

And finally, to my wonderful family. Deepest respect and appreciation to my mom and dad, two great Americans who taught me about citizenship. And to my sister, Beryl, her husband, Willy, and Isabella and Micaela, all of whom read the manuscript and gave helpful feedback.

From the Schoenberg side, I'd like to thank Doug, Lisa, Eric, Alex, Barbara Brizdle, and my mother-in-law, Barbara Schoenberg, the first signer of my petition. Also, the judges in the Jacobs Court of Appeals, Natalia, Adam, and (again) Andrea and Ally. I want to warmly acknowledge my erudite aunt and uncle, Carol Jacobs and Henry Sussman. And my second-cousin Isaiah Akin, who made me cautiously optimistic about politics.

To my sons Lucas, Zane, and Jasper. I consider myself lucky to be your father, and am ridiculously proud of all of you (and don't forget to vote!).

And finally, of course, to Julie Jacobs, who is smart, funny, and looks great in a bonnet. My love—not just affection—for you is unwavering.

BIBLIOGRAPHY

Abrams, Floyd. *The Soul of the First Amendment*. New Haven: Yale University Press, 2017.

Abrams, Jeanne E. *Revolutionary Medicine: The Founding Fathers and Mothers in Sickness and in Health*. New York: New York University Press, 2013.

Adams, John, and Thomas Jefferson. *The Adams-Jefferson Letters: The Complete Correspondence Between Thomas Jefferson and Abigail and John Adams*. Chapel Hill: University of North Carolina Press, 1987.

Amar, Akhil Reed. *America's Constitution: A Biography*. New York: Random House, 2005.

Amar, Akhil Reed. *America's Unwritten Constitution: The Precedents and Principles We Live By*. New York: Basic Books, 2012.

Amar, Akhil Reed. *The Words That Made Us: America's Constitutional Conversation, 1760–1840*. New York: Basic Books, 2021.

Ames, Herman Vandenburg. *The Proposed Amendments to the Constitution of the United States During the First Century of Its History*. 1897.

Applebaum, Anne. *Twilight of Democracy: The Seductive Lure of Authoritarianism*. New York: Doubleday, 2020.

Arnheim, Michael. *U.S. Constitution for Dummies*. Hoboken: Wiley, 2018.

Bailyn, Bernard. *The Ideological Origins of the American Revolution*. Cambridge: Belknap Press, 1992.

Barnett, Randy E., and Evan D, Bernick. *The Original Meaning of the Fourteenth Amendment: Its Letter and Spirit*. Cambridge: Belknap Press, 2021.

Bartoloni-Tuazon, Kathleen. *For Fear of an Elective King: George Washington and the Presidential Title Controversy of 1789*. Ithaca: Cornell University Press, 1990.

Beeman, Richard R. *Plain, Honest Men: The Making of the American Constitution*. New York: Random House, 2009.

Berkin, Carol. *A Brilliant Solution: Inventing the American Constitution*. Boston: Harcourt, 2002.

Berkin, Carol. *The Bill of Rights: The Fight to Secure America's Liberties*. New York: Simon & Schuster, 2015.

Bessler, John D. *Cruel and Unusual: The American Death Penalty and the Founders' Eighth Amendment*. Boston: Northeastern University Press, 2012.

Blackstone, William. *Blackstone's Commentaries on the Laws of England*. New York: Oxford University Press, 2009.

Blight, David W. *Frederick Douglass: Prophet of Freedom*. New York: Simon & Schuster, 2018.

Bordewich, Fergus M. *The First Congress: How James Madison, George Washington, and a Group of Extraordinary Men Invented the Government*. New York: Simon & Schuster, 2016.

Bork, Robert H. *Slouching Towards Gomorrah: Modern Liberalism and American Decline*. New York: Regan Books, 1996.

Breyer, Stephen. *The Authority of the Court and the Peril of Politics*. Cambridge: Harvard University Press, 2021.

Brookhiser, Richard. *James Madison*. New York: Basic Books, 2011.

Brookhiser, Richard. *What Would the Founders Do? Our Questions, Their Answers*. New York: Basic Books, 2006.

Cappon, Lester J. (editor). *The Adams-Jefferson Letters*. Chapel Hill: University of North Carolina Press, 1959.

Carpenter, Daniel. *Democracy by Petition: Popular Politics in Transformation, 1790–1870.* Cambridge: Harvard University Press, 2021.

Chafetz, Josh A. *Congress's Constitution: Legislative Authority and the Separation of Powers.* New Haven: Yale University Press, 2017.

Chatfield, Sara M. *In Her Own name: The Politics of Women's Rights Before Suffrage.* New York: Columbia University Press, 2023.

Chemerinsky, Erwin, and Howard Gillman. *The Religion Clauses: The Case for Separating Church and State.* New York: Oxford University Press, 2020.

Chernow, Ron. *Alexander Hamilton.* New York: Penguin Books, 2005.

Christianson, Scott. *With Liberty for Some: 500 Years of Imprisonment in America.* Boston: Northeastern University Press, 1998.

Collins, Paul M., and Lori Ringhand. *Supreme Court Confirmation Hearings and Constitutional Change.* New York: Cambridge University Press, 2013.

Cornell, Saul. *A Well-Regulated Militia: The Founding Fathers and the Origins of Gun Control in America.* New York: Oxford University Press, 2006.

Cunningham, Lillian et al. *Constitutional Podcast. Washington Post,* 2017.

Dahl, Robert A. *How Democratic Is the American Constitution?* New Haven: Yale University Press, 2003.

Dershowitz, Alan M. *Is There a Right to Remain Silent? Coercive Interrogation and the Fifth Amendment After 9/11.* New York: Oxford University Press, 2008.

Dickerson, John. *The Hardest Job in the World: The American Presidency.* New York: Random House, 2020.

Dolin, Eric Jay. *Rebels at Sea: Privateering in the American Revolution.* New York: W.W. Norton & Company, 2022.

Edling, Max M. *A Hercules in the Cradle: War, Money, and the American State, 1783–1867.* Chicago: University of Chicago Press, 2014.

Eighmey, Rae Katherine. *Stirring the Pot with Benjamin Franklin: A Founding Father's Culinary Adventures.* Washington D.C.: Smithsonian Books, 2018.

Elkins, Zachary, and Tom Ginsburg and James Melton. *The Endurance of National Constitutions.* New York: Cambridge University Press, 2009.

Ellis, Joseph J. *American Dialogue: The Founders and Us*. New York: Knopf, 2018.

Engel, Paul. *The Constitution Study: Returning the Constitution to We the People*. 2020.

Epstein, Richard A. *Supreme Neglect: How to Revive Constitutional Protection for Private Property*. New York: Oxford University Press, 2008.

Epstein, Richard A. *The Classical Liberal Constitution*. Cambridge: Harvard University Press, 2017.

Feingold, Russ, and Peter Prindiville. *The Constitution in Jeopardy: An Unprecedented Effort to Rewrite Our Fundamental Law and What We Can Do About It*. New York: PublicAffairs, 2022.

Foner, Eric. *The Second Founding: How the Civil War and Reconstruction Remade the Constitution*. New York: W. W. Norton & Company, 2019.

Foster, Thomas A. *Sex and the Founding Fathers: The American Quest for a Relatable Past*. Philadelphia: Temple University Press, 2014.

Franklin, Benjamin. *The Autobiography of Benjamin Franklin*. 1791.

Franklin, Benjamin. *Poor Richard's Almanack*. 1732.

Friedman, Barry. *The Will of the People: How Public Opinion Has Influenced the Supreme Court and Shaped the Meaning of the Constitution*. New York: Farrar, Straus and Giroux, 2010.

Gajda, Amy. *Seek and Hide: The Tangled History of the Right to Privacy*. New York: Viking, 2022.

Gienapp, Jonathan. *The Second Creation: Fixing the American Constitution in the Founding Era*. Cambridge: Belknap Press, 2018.

Gorsuch, Neil M. *A Republic, If You Can Keep It*. New York: Crown Forum, 2019.

Gowder, Paul. *The Rule of Law in the Real World*. New York: Cambridge University Press, 2016.

Greene, Jamal. *How Rights Went Wrong: Why Our Obsession with Rights Is Tearing America Apart*. Boston: Houghton Mifflin Harcourt, 2021.

Hamburger, Philip. *Separation of Church and State*. Cambridge: Harvard University Press, 2002.

Hannah-Jones, Nikole, and Caitlin Roper, Ilena Silverman, and Jake Silverstein. *The 1619 Project: A New Origin Story*. New York: One World, 2021.

Harris, Benjamin. *The New-England Primer.* 1727.

Hawke, David Freeman. *Everyday Life in Early America.* New York: Harper & Row, 1988.

Heminitz, Donald, and Kim Braunsroth. *A Fifer's Workshop.* Lakeville: The Country Press, 2022.

Holmes, Burnham. *The Third Amendment.* Silver Burdett Press, 1991.

Huntington, Frank C. *Making It Up as They Go Along: Stories the Supreme Court Tells About the Constitution.* Cambridge: Harvard University Press, 2004.

Huq, Aziz Z. *The Collapse of Constitutional Remedies.* New York: Oxford University Press, 2021.

Igo, Sarah E. *The Known Citizen: A History of Privacy in Modern America.* Cambridge: Harvard University Press, 2018.

Isaacson, Walter. *Ben Franklin: An American Life.* New York: Simon & Schuster, 2003.

Jentleson, Adam. *Kill Switch: The Rise of the Modern Senate and the Crippling of American Democracy.* New York: Liveright, 2021.

Kemmer, Brenton C., and Karen L. Kemmer. *So, Ye Want to Be a Reenactor? A Living History Handbook.* Berwyn Heights: Heritage Books, 2007.

Klarman, Michael J. *The Framers' Coup: The Making of the United States Constitution.* New York: Oxford University Press, 2016.

Klarman, Michael J. *Unfinished Business: Racial Equality in American History.* New York: Oxford University Press, 2007.

Kramer, Larry. *The People Themselves: Popular Constitutionalism and Judicial Review.* New York: Oxford University Press, 2004.

Krondl, Michael. *Around the American Table: Treasured Recipes and Food Traditions from the American Cookery Collections of the New York Public Library.* New York: Adams Media Corp., 1995.

Larson, Carlton F. W. *On Treason: A Citizen's Guide to the Law.* New York: Ecco, 2020.

Lepore, Jill. *This America: The Case for the Nation.* New York: Liveright, 2019.

Lessig, Lawrence. *Fidelity and Constraint: How the Supreme Court Has Read the American Constitution.* New York: Oxford University Press, 2019.

Lessig, Lawrence. *Republic, Lost: How Money Corrupts Congress—and a Plan to Stop It.* New York: Twelve, 2012.

Levinson, Cynthia, and Sanford Levinson. *Fault Lines in the Constitution: The Framers, Their Fights, and the Flaws That Affect Us Today*. Atlanta: Peachtree Publishers, 2017.

Levinson, Sanford. *Our Undemocratic Constitution: Where the Constitution Goes Wrong (and How We the People Can Correct It)*. New York: Oxford University Press, 2008.

Lewis, Michael. *The Fifth Risk: Undoing Democracy*. New York: W. W. Norton & Company, 2018.

Lithwick, Dahlia. *Lady Justice: Women, the Law, and the Battle to Save America*. New York: Penguin Books, 2022.

Liu, Goodwin, Pamela S. Karlan, and Christopher H. Schroeder. *Keeping Faith with the Constitution*. New York: Oxford University Press, 2010.

Longoria, Julia, et al. *More Perfect Podcast*. WNYC Studios, NPR, 2016.

Madison, James, with Alexander Hamilton and John Jay. *The Federalist Papers*. 1788.

Madison, James. *James Madison's Notes on the Constitutional Debates of 1787*.

Magliocca, Gerard N. *American Founding Son: John Bingham and the Invention of the Fourteenth Amendment*. New York: New York University Press, 2013.

Maier, Pauline. *Ratification: The People Debate the Constitution, 1787–1788*. New York: Simon & Schuster, 2010.

Mann, Bruce H. *Republic of Debtors: Bankruptcy in the Age of American Independence*. Cambridge: Harvard University Press, 2002.

Martin, J. P. *Private Yankee Doodle: Being a Narrative of Some of the Adventures, Dangers, and Sufferings of a Revolutionary Soldier*. Eastern Acorn Press, 1962.

Martin, Waldo E. *The Mind of Frederick Douglass*. Chapel Hill: University of North Carolina Press, 1986.

McCalman, Iain, and Paul Pickering. *Historical Reenactment: From Realism to the Affective Turn*. London: Palgrave Macmillan, 2010.

McCullough, David. *1776*. New York: Simon & Schuster, 2005.

McConnell, Michael W. *The President Who Would Not Be King: Executive Power Under the Constitution*. Princeton: Princeton University Press, 2021.

Minow, Martha. *Saving the News: Why the Constitution Calls for Government Action to Preserve Freedom of Speech.* New York: Oxford University Press, 2021.

Mounk, Yascha. *The Great Experiment: Why Diverse Democracies Fall Apart and How They Can Endure.* New York: Penguin Press, 2022.

Mystal, Elie. *Allow Me to Retort: A Black Guy's Guide to the Constitution.* New York: The New Press, 2022.

Nossel, Suzanne. *Dare to Speak: Defending Free Speech for All.* New York: HarperCollins, 2020.

Nussbaum, Martha C. *From Disgust to Humanity: Sexual Orientation and Constitutional Law.* New York: Oxford University Press, 2010.

Patrick, Sean. *The Know Your Bill of Rights Book: Don't Lose Your Constitutional Rights—Learn Them!* Oculus Publishers, 2012.

Peart, Daniel R. *The Era of Experimentation: American Political Practices in the Early Republic.* Charlottesville: University of Virginia Press, 2014.

Porwancher, Andrew. *The Jewish World of Alexander Hamilton.* Princeton: Princeton University Press, 2021.

Posner, Richard A. *Not a Suicide Pact: The Constitution in a Time of National Emergency.* New York: Oxford University Press, 2006.

Rakove, Jack N. *Beyond Belief, Beyond Conscience: The Radical Significance of the Free Exercise of Religion.* New York: Oxford University Press, 2020.

Rakove, Jack N. *Original Meanings: Politics and Ideas in the Making of the Constitution.* New York: Vintage Books, 1997.

Ricks, Thomas E. *First Principles: What America's Founders Learned from the Greeks and Romans and How That Shaped Our Country.* New York: HarperCollins, 2020.

Roosevelt, Kermit, III. *The Myth of Judicial Activism: Making Sense of Supreme Court Decisions.* New Haven: Yale University Press, 2006.

Roosevelt, Kermit, III. *The Nation That Never Was: Reconstructing America's Story.* London: Routledge, 2016.

Roosevelt III, Kermit. *The Nation That Never Was: Reconstructing America's Story.* Chicago: University of Chicago Press, 2022.

Rosen, Jeffrey. *The Supreme Court: The Personalities and Rivalries That Defined America.* New York: Times Books, 2007.

Roy, Michaël. *Frederick Douglass in Context.* Cambridge: Cambridge University Press, 2021.

Sabato, Larry J. *A More Perfect Constitution: 23 Proposals to Revitalize Our Constitution and Make America a Fairer Country.* London: Walker & Company, 2007.

Sagal, Peter, et al. *Constitution USA.* A four-part docuseries on PBS, 2013.

Salmon, Marylynn. *Women and the Law of Property in Early America.* Chapel Hill: University of North Carolina Press, 1986.

Sanders, Anthony B. *Baby Ninth Amendments: How Americans Embraced Unenumerated Rights and Why It Matters.* Ann Arbor: University of Michigan Press, 2023.

Scalia, Antonin. *A Matter of Interpretation: Federal Courts and the Law.* Princeton: Princeton University Press, 1998.

Scalia, Antonin. *Scalia Speaks: Reflections on Law, Faith, and Life Well Lived.* New York: Crown Forum, 2017.

Schreck, Heidi. *What the Constitution Means to Me.* New York: Theater Communications Group, 2020.

Schulhofer, Stephen J. *More Essential than Ever: The Fourth Amendment in the Twenty-First Century.* New York: Oxford University Press, 2012.

Segall, Eric J. *Supreme Myths: Why the Supreme Court Is Not a Court and Its Justices Are Not Judges.* New York: Penguin Books, 2012.

Seidel, Andrew L. *American Crusade: How the Supreme Court Is Weaponizing Religious Freedom.* New York: Union Square, 2022.

Seidel, Andrew L. *The Founding Myth: Why Christian Nationalism Is Un-American.* New York: Sterling, 2019.

Seidman, Louis Michael. *On Constitutional Disobedience.* New York: Oxford University Press, 2013.

Slack, Charles J. *Liberty's First Crisis: Adams, Jefferson, and the Misfits Who Saved Free Speech.* New York: Grove Press, 2015.

Smith, Glenn C., and Patricia Fusco. *Constitutional Law for Dummies.* Wiley, 2012.

Snyder, Timothy. *On Tyranny: Twenty Lessons from the Twentieth Century.* New York: Tim Duggan Books, 2017.

Steuben, Friedrich Wilhelm von. *Baron von Steuben's Revolutionary War Drill Manual.* New York: Skyhorse Publishing, 2008.

Stone, Geoffrey R., and David A. Strauss. *Democracy and Equality: The Enduring Constitutional Vision of the Warren Court.* New York: Oxford University Press, 2019.

Stone, Geoffrey R. *Sex and the Constitution: Sex, Religion, and Law from America's Origins to the Twenty-First Century*. New York: Liveright, 2017.

Strossen, Nadine. *Hate: Why We Should Resist It with Free Speech, Not Censorship*. New York: Oxford University Press, 2018.

Sunstein, Cass R. *A Constitution of Many Minds: Why the Founding Document Doesn't Mean What It Meant Before*. Princeton: Princeton University Press, 2009.

Sunstein, Cass R. *After the Rights Revolution: Reconceiving the Regulatory State*. Cambridge: Harvard University Press, 1990.

Sunstein, Cass R. *Constitutional Personae: Heroes, Soldiers, Minimalists, and Mutes*. New York: Oxford University Press, 2015.

Sunstein, Cass R. *How to Interpret the Constitution*. Princeton: Princeton University Press, 2023.

Sunstein, Cass R. *The Second Bill of Rights: FDR's Unfinished Revolution and Why We Need It More than Ever*. New York: Basic Books, 2004.

Taylor, Dale. *The Writer's Guide to Everyday Life in Colonial America*. Cincinnati: Writer's Digest Books, 1997.

Tribe, Laurence H. *Abortion: The Clash of the Absolutes*. New York: W. W. Norton, 1992.

Tribe, Laurence H. *American Constitutional Law*. 3rd ed., New York: Foundation Press, 2000.

Tribe, Laurence H. *The Invisible Constitution*. New York: Oxford University Press, 2008.

Tribe, Laurence H., and Joshua Matz. *Uncertain Justice: The Roberts Court and the Constitution*. New York: Henry Holt and Co., 2014.

Trubek, Anne. *The History and Uncertain Future of Handwriting*. London: Bloomsbury Publishing, 2016.

Turner, Juliette. *Our Constitution Rocks*. Grand Rapids: Zondervan, 2012.

Tushnet, Mark V. *Out of Range: Why the Constitution Can't End the Battle over Guns*. New York: Oxford University Press, 2007.

Waldman, Michael. *Supermajority: How the Supreme Court Divided America*. New York: Simon & Schuster, 2023.

Waldman, Michael. *The Second Amendment: A Biography*. New York: Simon & Schuster, 2014.

Washington, George. *Letters of the Founders: The Correspondence Between General George Washington and the Marquis de Lafayette*. 1781.

Webster, Noah. *An American Dictionary of the English Language*. 1828.

Weinrib, Laura. *The Taming of Free Speech: America's Civil Liberties Compromise*. Cambridge: Harvard University Press, 2016.

Werbel, Amy. *Lust on Trial: Censorship and the Rise of American Obscenity in the Age of Anthony Comstock*. New York: Columbia University Press, 2018.

Wexler, Jay. *Our Non-Christian Nation: How Atheists, Satanists, Pagans, and Others are Demanding Their Rightful Place in Public Life*. Stanford: Redwood Press, 2020.

Wexler, Jay. *The Odd Clauses: Understanding the Constitution Through Ten of Its Most Curious Provisions*. Boston: Beacon Press, 2011.

Wheeler, Leigh Ann. *How Sex Became a Civil Liberty*. New York: Oxford University Press, 2013.

Wilkinson, J. Harvie. *Cosmic Constitutional Theory: Why Americans Are Losing Their Inalienable Right to Self-Governance*. New York: Oxford University Press, 2012.

Wilser, Jeff. *Alexander Hamilton's Guide to Life*. New York: Three Rivers Press, 2016.

Winters, Eleanor. *Mastering Copperplate Calligraphy: A Step-by-Step Manual*. Mineola: Dover Publications, 2014.

Wood, Gordon S. *Power and Liberty: Constitutionalism in the American Revolution*. New York: Oxford University Press, 2021.

Wurman, Ilan. *A Debt Against the Living: An Introduction to Originalism*. New York: Cambridge University Press, 2017.

Wurman, Ilan. *The Second Founding: An Introduction to the Fourteenth Amendment*. New York: Cambridge University Press, 2020.

ABOUT THE AUTHOR

A.J. Jacobs is a journalist and podcaster whose books include *Drop Dead Healthy, The Year of Living Biblically,* and *The Puzzler.* A contributor to NPR, *The New York Times,* and *Esquire,* among other media outlets, Jacobs lives in New York City with his family.

© Sharon Schuur